The International Film Industry:
Western Europe and America
Since 1945

Indiana University International Studies

The
International Film
Industry

WESTERN EUROPE AND AMERICA SINCE 1945

Thomas H. Guback

BLOOMINGTON

INDIANA UNIVERSITY PRESS

LONDON

Published in Canada by Fitzhenry & Whiteside Limited,
Don Mills, Ontario

Library of Congress catalog card number: 69–15998

Manufactured in the United States of America

Contents

ACKNOWLEDGMENTS viii

NOTE ON SOURCES x

INTRODUCTION 3

1 *Film Distribution: Export* 7

2 *Protection of European Film Industries* 16

3 *American Films in the European Market* 37

4 *European Films in the American Market* 68

5 *The Foreign Policy of the American Film Industry: Monopoly and Free Trade* 91

6 *The Foreign Policy of the American Film Industry: Representation and Revenue* 108

7 *The American Film Industry and the American Government in Postwar Germany* 124

8 *Financial Assistance to European Film Production* 142

9 *Trends in the European Film Industry: American Investment in European Film Production* 164

10 *Trends in the European Film Industry: Coproduction* 181

11 *Conclusions* 198

APPENDIX A *Royal Decree for the Aid of the Belgian Film Industry* 204

APPENDIX B *French-Italian Film Agreement of August 1, 1966* 209

APPENDIX C *Currency Exchange Rates* 214

NOTES 216

SELECTED BIBLIOGRAPHY 233

INDEX 239

Tables

Table

Chapter 2

1 Baremo-authorized American Distribution   31
2 Feature Film Production in Selected Countries   35

Chapter 3

1 Italy: Nationality of Feature Films Imported   39
2 Netherlands: Nationality of Feature Films Imported   40
3 Switzerland: Nationality of Feature Films Imported   40
4 Denmark: Nationality of Feature Films Imported   41
5 Ireland: Nationality of Feature Films Imported   42
6 Spain: Nationality of Feature Films Imported   43
7 United Kingdom: Nationality of Films Registered for
     Distribution   44
8 Italy: Nationality of "Italian Version" Films Released   46
9 West Germany: Nationality of Films Released   47
10 Austria (Vienna): Nationality of Feature Films Released   48
11 Sweden: Nationality of Feature Films Released   49
12 Norway: Nationality of Feature Films Released   50
13 Finland: Nationality of Feature Films Released   51
14 Italy: Division of Gross Box Office Receipts   53
15 France: Division of Gross Box Office Receipts   55
16 United Kingdom: Rentals, British and Foreign Films   56
17 West Germany: Distributors' Share of Receipts   57
18 Denmark: Distributors' Share of Receipts   58
19 Netherlands: Division of Box Office Receipts   59
20 France: Distribution and Share of Market   60
21 Norway: American Companies Distributing Film   61
22 United Kingdom: Films Registered for Distribution by
     Selected Companies   63
23 West Germany: Production Year of Films Released in 1964   64

Table

24 France: Nationality of Films in Circulation   65
25 France: Year of First Release of Films Circulating in 1966   66

Chapter 4

1 Foreign Film Circulation in U. S.–Canadian Market   85
2 Nationality of Sharers of Box Office Receipts in
   U. S.–Canadian Market   86
3 Comparison of Rentals, U. S.–Canadian vs. Foreign   87
4 American Share of Foreign Imports and Earnings   88

Chapter 10

1 Feature Film Production and Coproduction (Foreign)   183
2 French Use of Color and Scope   184
3 French Coproductions Compared in Cost with National
   Films   185
4 Production Budgets of French Coproduction and National
   Films   186
5 Cost Index, French Coproduction and National Films   187
6 Ratio of French Investment in Coproduction and National
   Films   187
7 French Investment in Coproduction and National Films   188
8 Coproduction Partners of Italy, France and West Germany   189
9 Italian Coproductions, 1950–1956   191

Figure

Chapter 9

1 International Production Possibilities of Magnus Films
   Corporation   177

ACKNOWLEDGEMENTS

I offer special thanks to Professor Dallas W. Smythe, University of Saskatchewan, Regina, for the encouragement and stimulation he provided during the early years of this study.

An expression of gratitude also is due the Research Board of the University of Illinois. Through its two grants, I was able to spend more than a year in western Europe gathering material which made this study possible. I am indebted also to the University of Illinois Institute of Communications Research and its director, Howard S. Maclay, as well as to the Department of Journalism and its head, Jay W. Jensen, for the support, moral and otherwise, given during the last two years.

Dr. Gertrude Robinson read the manuscript and made many helpful suggestions. Albert Kreiling, Kiyoshi Nagata, and Sidney Robinovitch, as research assistants over the years, were invaluable for tracking down elusive bits of information and for verifying statistics and sources. Patricia Johnson turned heavily marked copy into readable form.

Finally, I want to express a large measure of appreciation to my wife, Denise, because her consideration and patience truly have been boundless. As if these qualities are not enough, she also translated materials from Dutch and German and reviewed my own translations of French.

Claire helped too.

T. H. G.

Urbana, Illinois

ABBREVIATIONS

AMPEC–Africa American Motion Picture Export Company (Africa)
ANICA   Associazione Nazionale Industrie Cinematografiche ed Affini
BFPA   British Film Producers Association
EEC   European Economic Community
FBFM   Federation of British Film Makers
FTC   Federal Trade Commission
IFE   Italian Film Export
IMG   Informational Media Guaranty
IMPDAA Independent Motion Picture Distributors Association of America
ITU   International Telecommunications Union
KRS   Kinematograph Renters Society
MPAA   Motion Picture Association of America
MPEA   Motion Picture Export Association of America
NFFC   National Film Finance Corporation
RFDA   Rank Film Distributors of America
SIMPP   Society of Independent Motion Picture Producers
SPIO   Spitzenorganisation der Filmwirtschaft
UFI   Universum Filmindustrie
UPU   Universal Postal Union

NOTE ON SOURCES

Material for this study of European-American film industry relations has come predominantly from interviews, supported by printed sources and correspondence. Collection of data began on a major scale in 1961, although some preliminary research was done before then to test the feasibility of the project. The author was fortunate to spend the 1962–63 academic year in Europe expanding the research which had been carried on in the United States. He returned to Europe for short periods in 1965, 1967, and 1968. During the European phase of investigation, the author talked extensively with key people in business, government, official international bodies, academic circles, labor groups, and other professional areas allied to the film industry. The time spent in Europe proved useful for acquiring considerable amounts of documentation, original material, and statistical data not available in the United States, as well as for viewing films and for firsthand examination of the various countries. Research was conducted in the United Kingdom, Ireland, France, Belgium, the Netherlands, Norway, Denmark, West Germany, Switzerland, Italy, and Spain.

As the task began of interviewing people in the United States and Europe, it soon became apparent that the only way of obtaining any amount of information was to conduct the interviews on a "no attribution" basis. In a great number of instances, an interview was granted solely upon the condition that the interviewee would not be quoted by name in the text. Some statistical data, trade agreements, and related information were obtained on the same condition. In taking these requests into account, the author decided to follow a consistent policy of not attributing to a particular individual, company, or association any statement made during an interview.

It is appropriate, however, to recognize and thank a number of people, companies, and associations who were especially helpful. By necessity, this list is abbreviated and the author pleads guilty to the sin of omission. Claude Degand, Centre National de la Cinématographie, Paris; Jean-Claude Batz, l'Université Libre de Bruxelles; National Film Finance Corporation; British Film Producers Association; Federation of British Film Makers; Kinematograph Renters Society; Association of Cinematograph, Television and Allied Technicians; Dirección General de Cinematografia y Teatro, Madrid; Associazione Nazionale Industrie Cinematografiche ed Affini, Rome; Nederlandsche Bioscoop-Bond; Spitzenorganisation der Filmwirtschaft, Wiesbaden; Press and Information Service of the European Communities, Brussels; Chambre Syndicale Belge de la Cinématographie, Brussels; Nordisk Films Kompagni, Copenhagen; Kommunale Kinematografers Landsforbund, Oslo; Norske Filmbyraers Sammenslutning, Oslo; Television Program Export Association; Motion Picture Export Association; Metro-Goldwyn-Mayer; Twentieth Century-Fox; Paramount; and Columbia.

A wide range of printed materials was used in this study. Documents and information from governmental and international bodies have been very important. They include reports, laws, legislative debates and hearings, and statistical analyses. Trade publications, as noted in the bibliography, also have contributed in some measure to the storehouse of information. One of these is *Variety* which has been important for cuing investigation to time periods and events during the last twenty years.

Motion picture companies and trade associations in the United States and Europe also have been useful sources of information. Annual reports, publications, and speeches by key personnel have yielded material for this survey. Scholarly and professional writing on European and American film relations have provided structured and thoughtful examinations which other sources of information frequently lacked. The scarcity of these writings, however, is certainly a reason for this study.

Correspondence with key agencies and people has been helpful for throwing light on specific problems and for clearing up questions which have arisen.

To the greatest extent possible, material has been checked to assure accuracy of detail. Published information has been matched with material collected from other sources for verification. Interviews provided the chance for corroborating details and for seeing matters from different points of view. In a few instances, trade associations and some individuals declined cooperation—complete or partial—with the study.

The International Film Industry:
Western Europe and America
Since 1945

INTRODUCTION

> "There's not a two million dollar gross in the country now," said Brady. . . . "Probably not," agreed Stahr. He paused as if to make sure that all were listening. "I think we can count on a million and a quarter from the road-show. Perhaps a million and a half altogether. And a quarter of a million abroad."

So concluded Monroe Stahr in F. Scott Fitzgerald's *The Last Tycoon*, a penetrating study of Hollywood in the 1930's. Stahr's calculations were, for that time, keenly accurate. Some thirty years ago, the American motion picture industry was essentially a domestically based and oriented industry. Practically all of its revenues came from the United States. To be sure, American films were sold abroad but the resulting revenue hardly compared to what the domestic market yielded. Foreign revenue was simply an additional increment, extra profit upon which American film companies did not depend. The foreign market did not warrant enough attention to force Hollywood to modify significantly the content of its films to suit tastes abroad, nor to induce the film companies to maintain elaborate overseas organizations. Fitzgerald's Stahr, for example, felt that his picture could count on approximately 15 percent of its gross revenue coming from abroad.

Today, the situation is markedly different; the American film industry now derives at least half of its theatre revenue from foreign markets. Of course, some companies and some films exist on revenue derived predominantly from the United States. But for the industry as a whole, the foreign market has become highly important. Eric Johnston, the late president of the Motion Picture Association of America, referring possibly to member companies, stated publicly that "no other major United States industry is perhaps so heavily dependent upon exports for its economic health and well-being." He went on to declare:

> It's a little known fact that 9 out of 10 United States films cannot pay their way in the domestic market alone. It is only because of

revenue from abroad that Hollywood is able to turn out pictures of high artistry and technical excellence.[1]

While that might have been a slight exaggeration, it is true that just four countries in western Europe—the United Kingdom, Italy, France, and West Germany—can yield almost half of the domestic (i.e., United States) gross for a film. Beyond a doubt, western Europe as a whole constitutes today the most important overseas market for American pictures.

The object of this study is to uncover and analyze relationships between the American and European film industries, keeping in mind the financial stake American companies have in Europe. Penetration of the European market by the American industry has generated changes in policy and structure on both sides of the Atlantic— changes which have important implications for film production, film content, and film marketing. The economic base of the American industry has expanded and the related drive to secure Europe as a market has provoked clearly detectable reactions within the European cinema. In the same way, the need of European countries to protect and expand their own markets has been manifest in modifications of American organizations and in their plans for action.

Film is not only a business commodity but a vehicle of communication. It presents an image of the world, life, events, and thoughts. It tells what has happened, is happening, and will happen, in terms of the perspectives of those who make the film. Producers select the materials to be dealt with, and handle them in a way which they consider meaningful and which they believe will be acceptable to audiences. They choose from the total universe of real and unreal things certain elements, and then fashion these elements into productions which are to be viewed by people throughout the world. The content of a film, whether reality or fantasy, depends on the producer, and the way it is perceived depends upon the images it presents and the perspectives of the people who view it. Those elements selected for presentation command the audience's attention at the expense of other elements which are omitted. Film is important not only for what it says but for what it does not say. The boundaries of human experience can expand or contract on the basis of what people have presented to them. In this study we will suggest that economic imperatives have in part determined what elements will be embodied in film.

Three broad areas of investigation will be scrutinized in this study. First, we must describe the interaction between film industries in the United States and Europe. Second, we must analyze those structures and policies which have been developed to control, facilitate, or stabilize interaction. Finally, we must delve into the production of films to understand how response to interaction and economic imperatives bear on what is made available to world audiences.

The investigation begins with a discussion of the economic and technological nature of film, which differs from most other commodities in that it tends to be infinitely exportable. And we shall see that the need to export is not confined to the American industry, for European producers have been active in trying to expand their own markets.

The second chapter surveys the various schemes developed by European nations to protect their domestic markets from being flooded by American films. We will evaluate the effectiveness of screen quotas and import quotas in controlling the number of American films on the market and suggest why quotas have been generally reduced and eliminated during the 1960's.

In the following two chapters, we will discuss the transatlantic flow of films. First, we will examine the American film in Europe since the end of World War II. We shall study data on the number of American films available for exhibition in various markets, and survey their share of box office revenue. Then we will reverse our perspective and study the foreign film in the United States. We will examine certain forces which once worked to keep foreign pictures out of the American market but which have largely disintegrated in the last ten years. Our analysis will cover determined efforts on the part of foreign producers to penetrate the American market, and the means they used. Finally, we will review data on the number of foreign films in the United States, and the revenues accruing to them.

In chapters five, six, and seven, attention is directed to the foreign policy of the American film industry as it seeks both to expand and to defend its position overseas. Our investigation will cover the Motion Picture Export Association, which was founded in 1945 under the Webb-Pomerene Act to operate as a legal cartel representing the American industry overseas. We shall see this monopolistic organization demanding, in its overseas operations, free competition, open access to markets, and unhindered trade. The American industry has helped to determine the policies of foreign industries through membership in overseas film industry trade groups. On the other hand, American membership in these associations is often one way by which foreign industries or governments can control the activities of American companies. Thus membership can be both to the advantage and to the disadvantage of American interests.

The propaganda quality of film has also played a part in the American industry's policy in foreign operations. We will examine the extent and nature of cooperation between the American film industry and the American government, with particular reference to West Germany. The original purpose for having American films in West Germany—to educate the nation away from Nazi ideology—was abruptly changed to one of indoctrinating West Germany for its place in the Cold War. Hollywood's overriding concern for profit tended to work against the programs of our Military Government, and it was not until the film industry was, in effect, subsidized by Washington that it actively began distributing pictures in the West German market.

In the chapters following, we will concentrate on film production in Europe, beginning with a survey of the types of financial assistance made available to film production by European governments. Our major concern will be the subsidy which provides an increment of revenue to producers over and above normal box office receipts. We will refer to the rationale justifying governmental support of production, and to the reasons film must be considered a vehicle for expression as well as a commodity. In relation to subsidization, we will note how films are declared eligible for payment, and the connection between this and the definition of a national film. The impact the European Economic Community is having on film legislation, production, and trade will also be reviewed.

The American presence in Europe is not confined merely to American distribution companies and American films. American subsidiaries abroad, and foreign companies in which there is an American financial interest, have been making films which, meeting criteria for being declared "national" by European governments, thereby have access to subsidy funds. The analysis will reveal that rather than being regarded askance as American penetration, the practice is often encouraged by foreign governments. European-American cooperation in production also will be discussed in terms of its influence on film content. We will suggest that a new style of film is developing which cuts across domestic cultural characteristics.

The tenth chapter deals with the coproduction trend in Europe. The imperatives of coproduction will be examined relative to the bilateral treaties which govern this form of film making. The chapter also discusses American investment in films of the Common Market countries.

The final chapter draws together important points and offers a statement on European-American interaction in film making.

1: Film Distribution: Export

The motion picture is not only a means of communication and an art form. In a capitalist-oriented economy, film making is a business—well organized, heavily capitalized, and powerful. A film is often conceived, produced, and marketed in much the same way as many other commodities. One could point to factors which seemingly separate film from other products, but on closer examination many differences would prove illusory. The months, and occasionally years, of work involved in planning a film are analogous to time devoted to styling of autos and to research on development of electronic apparatus. Payments to key stars resemble remuneration to inventors in certain industries, while the copyright on a film is comparable to a copyright on printed matter and to a patent on a device or process. The communality runs even deeper because, like other commodities, the film must be sold.

Film does have a quality, however, which sets it apart from many other marketable items. This is the distinction between the overhead costs incurred in production and the incremental costs which are incurred when film is distributed. Virtually the entire cost of a film occurs in making the first copy. Securing a story, casting it, constructing sets, hiring artistic and technical workers, the weeks (or years) of shooting, editing scenes, preparing background music—the expenses for all of these are incurred in making the first copy. These are considered as overhead costs. The cost of a second copy of the same film, or the nth copy, is negligible compared to that of the first. The cost of an extra copy is the price of the raw stock, duplicating, and processing—the incremental costs. In these terms, a motion picture is a commodity one can duplicate indefinitely without substantially adding to the cost of the first unit produced. This is true whether the film is a multi-million dollar spectacular or a cheap grade B filler for the second half of a double feature. Moreover, no two *productions* are identical. Each is unique even if treating the same theme or story. The 1962 American remake of the German classic *The Cabinet of Dr. Caligari,* for instance, has slight similarity, except in name, to the original.

The economic and technological nature of a film compels the manufacturer and his agent, the distributor, to try to achieve the widest possible circulation for it. Extra prints represent little further investment, and it is in their interest to make many, distribute them widely, and attempt to recoup their total costs as quickly as possible. Although additional effort is involved in selling the product overseas, a print sent abroad does not deprive the domestic market of anything. In these terms, a given film tends to be an infinitely exportable commodity; prints exported do not affect domestic supplies nor the revenue resulting from domestic exhibition. We can have our film and foreigners can have it too.

These points are important to the producer and the distributor for they mean that serving an additional market does not involve much more investment than is already in a film. The decision to move into another market, however, does involve other factors. The example of the American industry illustrates what these have been and how they have influenced film expansion.

The beginning of the film industry in the United States was characterized by many small producers turning out one-reelers which were sold outright to exhibitors. Production expenses were recouped and profits were made within the domestic market. Film production in Europe flourished in the first decade of the century on quite the same scale, but the transatlantic trade in films was hardly important. The First World War threw Europe into turmoil, seriously disrupting the structure of existing industries. The picture trade in Europe was curtailed to a great extent during the war as economic pressures forced many producers out of business. The American industry did not suffer this fate. Hollywood continued to produce, and giants emerged to dominate it. The return of peace brought with it a numerical film vacuum in Europe and an opportunity for the American industry to fill it.

The Americans lost little time in turning out the additional prints needed. By 1925, American films had captured 95 percent of the British market and 70 percent of the French market.[1] In Italy during this same period, American films accounted for 68 percent of screen time,[2] a condition aggravated by dumping and underselling domestic producers.[3] In the smaller countries, the situation was quite the same.

While American pictures did penetrate the European market, the resulting revenue still did not compare with that from the home market. The American film continued to be made with the domestic market in mind, and the industry continued to be domestically oriented. Nevertheless, this grasp on the European market was solidified with the coming of sound, an innovation requiring substantial investment. While the silent film continued for a time to hold its position, it was clear that money could be made with pictures that talked. The advent of sound increased both production cost and the need for amortizing investment by selling the product as widely as possible. Whereas the World War had created the vacuum into which American films flowed, higher production costs provided the rationale for entrenchment in the European market. For the European producers, sound was a competitive factor which had to be recognized. Though the larger countries possibly constituted sufficient markets for their own wares, the smaller countries found themselves in difficulty. Their studios, too, had to be equipped for sound, and their films were also subjected to the same dubbing costs as films from larger countries. Their problem is exemplified:

> When films were silent and the Scandinavian producers could sell their films—as they did—all over the world, their achievement was remarkable in that they were competing successfully with stronger units in larger countries. When sound reached the cinema . . . the mere survival of [their] film-making became remarkable.[4]

Thus, two factors—the vacuum in Europe and the introduction of sound—accounted for the American industry's initial expansion into Europe. Other events, however, also worked to sustain Hollywood's penetration.

More recently, the contraction of the domestic United States market has provided important impetus. Average weekly theatre attendance today is but slightly more than half the 1941 figure, while population growth in the intervening years has stretched the imbalance. True, ticket prices are higher and revenue is greater, but the fact is that admissions have lost in volume. Without a doubt, television's free entertainment has lured audiences from theatres. Other living habits have undergone profound changes in the last quarter century as people motor more than ever before, do-it-themselves more, bowl more—to mention a few leisure pursuits.

While entertainment dollars were being reallocated, the American film industry was being forced to restructure itself. The Paramount case climaxed a long attempt to break the vertically integrated companies. Exhibition was spun off from production-distribution, and dissolution of monopolies of theatres was forced. It outlawed block booking and generated a more competitive approach to film making and film selling. The "sure outlet" Hollywood producers had depended upon for decades vanished almost overnight and distributors became more concerned with markets and marketing.

The cost of production, always an important factor, began to assume an even more significant role during this postwar period. Declines in attendance were followed by declines in production which further aggravated the cycle—there were fewer films to be seen by people who wanted to go to theatres. Hollywood's economic interest, once it was cut loose from predominant investment in theatres by the antitrust decrees, lay in maximizing *its* profits rather than exhibition profits. Producers concentrated more on the superspectacular style of film, hoping to lure back the missing millions. With few of the big stars still under contract to studios, the price for their appearance was bid up to fantastic size. Stars' salaries, location shooting, more elaborate production and filming techniques, these and other costs have generated budgets of such magnitude that $1,000,000 for a film is considered an extremely modest outlay. *The Longest Day* was finished at a cost of about $10,000,000 while *Mutiny on the Bounty*, originally budgeted at $8,500,000, was completed for $18,500,000. *Cleopatra,* probably the most expensive film in history, cost more than $30,000,000 to make.

In theory, the United States market could support this more costly style of production if admission prices were increased drastically and if competitive leisure activities did not exist.[5] But this is not the actual situation nor is it likely ever to be. The American industry, therefore, has been forced to spread its production costs over more and more markets. The reliance upon foreign markets has reached the point where now the industry receives slightly more than half of its theatrical revenue from foreign exhibition. While the American film has been present in Europe for half a century, only within the last two decades has this monetary dependence prevailed. As Eric Johnston once declared: "The domestic market today simply does not support a large volume of production in Hollywood."[6]

This point is as true in 1969 as it was in the early 1950's. Data presented to a United States Senate committee revealed that in 1950, 1951, and 1953, Paramount released seventy pictures of which fifty-one failed to recoup their negative costs in the United States *and Canada.*[7] (Some companies consider Canada a domestic market.) The vice president of Paramount told the committee that "if the Hollywood producers . . . had to depend upon revenue from the United States and Canadian markets, neither Paramount nor other companies could possibly remain in business."[8] A representative of United Artists informed the same committee that without foreign earnings "the industry would soon face insolvency and bankruptcy, or would have to change its method of production in such a way that the type and nature of its films would radically change."[9]

The implication this has for the content of American films was noted by a vice president of Columbia Pictures. He stated that because few films earn even their negative cost in the American market "it has become necessary to produce pictures palatable to tastes in England, Italy and Japan as well as here at home."[10] The extent to which a producer will go to shape content was revealed by another film executive. "If in making an American story," he said, "we could insert some incident that might take place in Paris, we would be glad to do it, because it would add flavor for the foreign market. We do a lot of this. . . ."[11]

The specific mechanics of shaping film content were explained by Eric Johnston when he was questioned by the Senate Committee on Foreign Relations:

> A man by the name of Addison Durland in my office handles that in our production code administration in Hollywood. It is his job, every time a script comes for approval by the production code, to read the script, determine if there is anything harmful to the country, or any country in which that picture is likely to be shown. If, in his estimation, there is anything harmful to the country involved, . . . or some particular situation which might be harmful to that area or to us, he notes it, discusses it with the producer of the picture, and requests that that scene be eliminated or modified. . . . [Durland] has specialized advice and in addition . . . he operates with a man in each one of the studios whose job it is also to do that. . . .[12]

What takes place in the producing companies has been disclosed by a representative of Paramount:

> We have in Hollywood a representative of my department. . . . His name is Luigi Luraschi . . . and [he] understands very thoroughly the problems that we encounter around the world.

We understand that the time to tackle these problems . . . is before we make our large negative expenditures in the pictures. Therefore Mr. Luraschi screens every script before it goes on the set, and he battles with the directors and the script writers with regard to scenes that he thinks will either offend a foreign nation or be offensive from the standpoint of placing America in a wrong light. . . .

I believe if Addison Durland was to tell our man, from his viewpoint and certainly after consultation with the State Department, that a scene was dangerous, and our man does not agree with him, he would not make a unilateral decision.

This would be taken up with our studio head, with myself, and perhaps with the president of the entire company. We regard it as being that important.[13]

The role of the State Department should be recognized. Since a later chapter explores the link between the American film industry and the American government, it is sufficient to observe here that the shaping of content is prompted not only by monetary but by propaganda considerations as well.

If films are being made with foreign countries in mind, a logical question is whether films are being made with America in mind. A representative of the Allied States Association of Motion Picture Exhibitors once told a Senate committee that "American producers now rarely make pictures especially adapted to American audiences." He added that this policy

has virtually eliminated the American family-type pictures and those featuring familiar American sports and customs. Recently I heard an exhibitor bemoan the fact that for more than four years he has not been offered a football picture, although the American people are football conscious for about four months each year. That is quite obviously due to the fact that football, as we know it, is as unfamiliar to foreign audiences as soccer is to most Americans.[14]

While this is not conclusive evidence, it does point to a trend in content prompted in great degree by the American industry's dependence upon foreign markets for revenue and dictated by the many coventures involving American and European producers.

The drive to exploit foreign markets has not been confined only to the American film industry. The motion picture is a business and any country's industry will try to expand if it feels it can create a market for its products elsewhere. The Italian industry has sought consistently to penetrate the United States. Because of the many American films exhibited in Italy and the revenue they have drawn from the box office, Italian producers have wanted reciprocity and an opportunity to exploit the American market. Their demands were met, in a fashion, when, following lengthy negotiations in 1951, an agreement was reached between an American cartel, the Motion Picture Export Association (MPEA), and the central trade association for the Italian industry, ANICA. The agreement created Italian Film Export (IFE) for the purpose of promoting and distributing Italian pictures in the United States.

According to the MPEA-ANICA pact, a small share of American earnings in Italy over a three year period was to be advanced by American distributors operating in Italy to Italian producers for support of IFE. An influential official in the Italian government has written that IFE's "special task has been and is to get a footing on the [American] market which, for obvious reasons, is the most difficult for us to enter. It has been up-hill work. . . ."[15] For reasons to be explored in a later chapter, IFE was never successful in the American market and the organization was dissolved. The French film industry tried to secure somewhat the same terms from the MPEA but was unsuccessful. The American companies had always felt uneasy about their agreement with ANICA and firmly resisted any extension of the policy.

The British film industry requires special attention and, indeed, several important studies have been written on its economics and art. One analysis of the industry in 1952 found that the "great hindrance to overseas distribution [is] the predominant position of the United States."[16] The study said that because American films occupied 70 percent of British screen time and had a virtual monopoly of their own home market, it was hardly surprising that America's success largely explained Britain's failure to achieve wide foreign distribution. If domestic British revenues were insufficient to support a film industry, the report said, then "viability will depend on overseas earnings."[17] As if answering this, an annual report of the British Film Producers Association commented during this period:

> The picture of our overseas film trade is a mixture of great endeavours, frustrations and achievements and if the volume of foreign earnings coming back to this country is not large in comparison with the earnings of American films there is no doubt that a sound overseas business is being built up the hard way. Provided the right pictures are produced and properly exploited, the value of these

overseas markets must prove to be a sound investment for the future.[18]

The British government has recognized the British film industry's need for foreign markets. In its official journal, the Board of Trade has summarized a speech of its former president, Harold Wilson:

> "Export or die" was a maxim which applied as much to the film industry as to the nation. No film industry in the world, and the British film industry least of all, could afford to organize itself on a basis of producing films solely for the home market. The industry must be so organized and financed that its first aim must be the production of an adequate number of first quality films, many of which would cost more than could be expected from home market revenues.[19]

More recently, distribution of British films overseas has been seen from a different perspective, although recognition of the need to export is still keen. While the attitude twenty years ago was one of trying to buck Hollywood, current British feeling reflects the success British films distributed by American companies have had in world markets. One study notes: "Without the American companies many British films would not be distributed abroad—or even made."[20] In the same way, the Federation of British Film Makers was prompted to declare in a recent annual report that "British films have been outstandingly successful throughout the world. . . ." It went on, stressing the export imperative, to declare that without this success in foreign markets "production in Britain would have collapsed."[21]

Certainly the American industry is not the only one interested in foreign markets. The need for additional markets is widespread and the major industries have actively sought to penetrate foreign areas. Furthermore, the rationale for these expansive drives is surprisingly similar. One should recognize, however, that while all industries hope to expand their economic bases, the organization, financial position, and distribution channels of the American industry have been such that its act of expansion had great impact upon foreign industries.

This suggests the following questions: If all industries are trying to export film, what occurs within markets? When domestic revenues are hardly sufficient to support domestic production, what happens when the necessity exists of sharing domestic revenues with imported films?

These matters are particularly pressing for European industries with domestic markets only a fraction of the size of the United States.

The answers are complex, for economic solvency, national prestige, and culture are involved. Siegfried Kracauer has pointed out that "films of a nation reflect its mentality in a more direct way than other artistic media. . . ."[22] The protection and preservation of national film industries as vehicles for local expression is a subject of great relevance. Because American films by their sheer number have constituted the single largest pool available in the European market, these nations have had to develop systems to protect their home markets and to make them reasonably secure and lucrative for local film production. An examination of these protective plans is the subject of the following chapter.

2: Protection of European Film Industries

Schemes for the protection of European-made films were, of course, the direct result of the invasion of American films in the 1920's. This exportation threatened industries abroad to such an extent that one study, for example, states: "by 1927 the British film industry was well on the way to extinction."[1] After the initial shock of penetration, European countries gradually raised barriers to the circulation of American films. Germany, in 1925, was the first to do so. Great Britain and France followed quickly.

But World War II destroyed to a great extent the protective measures developed during the 1920's and 1930's, and most European countries had to begin again to guard their industries. These barriers confronted the American film trade at a time when it could least afford hindrance to its foreign operations. Production costs were mounting, the domestic audience was diminishing, the backlog of films never shown abroad was large, and Europe represented a lucrative market. It was inevitable that American companies would try to sell their products abroad. As Eric Johnston told a Senate committee:

> Immediately after the cessation of the Second World War, there was a tremendous backlog of pictures that had not been shown in most foreign countries, and these pictures flooded in, *even more than the countries could absorb*. This is a perfectly natural commercial phenomenon. You can't blame the companies for doing that.[2] (Italics mine)

The effects of this "natural commercial phenomenon" were evaluated in a report prepared for UNESCO. Its authors wrote:

The large number of cheap American films available (initially increased, except in the United Kingdom, by the films which could not be shown during the war) apart from adding to the dollar deficit, is only one of the factors prejudicing the development of national film production industries. These industries, unable to recover their outlay on the films which they produce, are stunted in growth and become unable to meet the demands of the national market. The exhibitors, therefore, are driven to depend for their existence upon foreign, largely American, films.[3]

When a domestic industry which is a vehicle for national culture is severely threatened by foreign competition, a significant problem is posed. The sentiments of Europeans are convincingly summed-up in a question once raised by a British government official. "Should we be content," he asked, "if we depended upon foreign literature or upon a foreign Press in this country?"[4] When persuasion fails as a tool, a more powerful method must be used to resist unbalanced competition. That way is through protective measures which control the foreign industry's access to the local market.

Through such a policy, it is hoped that a portion of the market will remain for exploitation by domestic films and that national production will be able to survive and thrive. There is another rationale for the policy of restricting the circulation of foreign (chiefly American) films in a country. It was mentioned in the UNESCO report, and while not bearing solely on film, it has worked as a barrier to film trade. This is the balance of payments problem which weighed heavily in Europe after World War II. These two concerns have been the moving ideas behind restrictive measures.

Regarding the balance of payments issue: after the second war, European nations, in debt and with little or no dollar reserves, could not afford the questionable luxury of importing American pictures when their peoples and businesses demanded more essential commodities; these nations believed that dollars not spent on American films could be used to alleviate more pressing needs.

There were essentially two alternative means of restriction. First, they could reduce importation of American films, assuming that fewer American pictures on the market would result in fewer dollars exported. Superficially reasonable, the argument fails to recognize that there is no one-to-one correlation between films and earnings. However, in the long run and when applied to American films, this policy could be expected to conserve critical supplies of currency.

Belgium exemplifies this expectancy. With a small population and two official national languages, the country produces few feature films. Nevertheless, the Belgian government negotiated with the Motion Picture Export Association of America to limit imports of American films. The agreement decreed that MPEA companies could bring into Belgium only about 240 films annually. Since 1960, this restriction is no longer in force and Belgium is a free market. A shortage of dollars, not protection of local film production, was sufficient reason for the nation to restrict entry of American pictures.

The second alternative relates to the earnings of American films and has two variations. The first is a tax or duty on the value of each imported film—"value" meaning the expected earnings of a film. This step was taken by Great Britain. By 1947, American film companies were taking more than $60,000,000 annually out of the country. During the summer of that year, the balance of payments problem became so severe that the British government was forced to cut imports from hard currency areas. While films accounted for only about 4 percent of British dollar expenditures to the United States, they could hardly be overlooked in the general retrenchment. On August 6, 1947, the British treasury announced a customs duty of 75 percent on the value of each imported film, regardless of nationality. Because American films, by and large, were the only ones imported, the duty fell mainly on them. On August 9, the MPEA retaliated by announcing an indefinite suspension on all further shipments of films to Britain. This boycott, which lasted seven months, represented an important plank in the American industry's foreign policy platform. The reasons prompting the 75 percent duty were stated by the Financial Secretary to the Treasury, Glenvil Hall:

> I want to make it clear that neither is [the duty] intended to obtain additional revenue nor is it an aggressive act against Hollywood in the interests of our own British film industry. The step has been taken simply and solely because the country cannot afford to allocate the dollars necessary to pay for the exhibition of American films in this country at the present time.[5]

The duty, which resulted in the MPEA's withdrawal from the British market, gave virtually full protection to British film production and offered it its first really important opportunity to get a hold on the home market. By contrast, the blow to exhibition was great as theatres found their chief supply of films cut off. (Interestingly, when in 1964 the British government levied a 15 percent surcharge on imports, motion pictures and some other goods were exempt.)

The second variation regarding American earnings becomes apparent if we follow in detail events in the United Kingdom. During the boycott the MPEA and the British Board of Trade began negotiating for an agreement which would bring American films back to Britain without being subject to the 75 percent duty. The result of these negotiations was revealed in March, 1948, with the announcement that an Anglo-American Film Agreement had been concluded. The pact covered many points, some pertinent to our present interests. The duty was to be removed (and it was, on May 3). Concerning the earnings of American films in Britain, the pact stipulated that for two years beginning June 14, 1948, American companies could withdraw only $17,000,000 annually from the country. All other American earnings were blocked or "frozen" and could not be taken out. Aside from reducing the serious drain on dollars, this feature encouraged American companies to spend their blocked earnings in Britain. The pact permitted them to be used for producing films, for acquisition of rights to films and stories, for payment for costumes, props, equipment, printing and advertising, and for the purchase of real estate and studios, but not film theatres.[6] The pact permitted the free importation of American films but limited the amount of money the American companies could withdraw from the market.

France's policy on dollar spending was similar to that developed by Britain. The Franco-American Film Agreement of September, 1948, restricted the number of imported films and permitted limited remittance of American earnings up to $3,625,000 annually, leaving about $10,000,000 blocked each year. The pact listed several ways in which these frozen funds could be spent: joint production of films with French companies, construction of new studios, acquisition of distribution rights to French films, acquisition of story rights in France, etc.[7] Thus, the agreement regulated the number of American films entering France and partially restricted remittances.

Other restrictions and protections have their roots specifically in film industry economic policy. It was mentioned earlier that protection *per se* aims to prevent unbalanced competition from destroying or seriously injuring a domestic film industry. This idea can be developed and qualified by relating it to the size of the potential market available to a domestic industry.

The smaller nations of Europe—Switzerland, Belgium, the Netherlands, Ireland, and the Scandinavian countries—have no restrictions on film importation which can be linked with the need to preserve their national film production. None of these nations has an extensive industry, at least in quantitative terms. With limitations on available capital, and with inherent restrictions on supplies of talent because of small populations, these nations have not had to face the problem of preserving their native films. Even if protective barriers were erected, it is questionable whether local production could expand to fill the vacuum. In the situation actually prevailing, some film production has managed to survive, often based on the *rarity value* of local films, the portrayal of predominantly local humor or traits, and the fact that, for instance, "people will pay to hear Danish spoken from the screen." Moreover, there seems to be prestige value for a country of a few million people in having a film running at a theatre where it can compete successfully with one from the United States. While the production might not be as slick, and the editing might be a bit rough, to the local audiences it is "our" film.

The need for protection, then, is likely to exist in the larger nations which have the potential capital, talent, and audiences to form a base for a greater volume of film making. While some production might continue without protection, the aim is to provide the atmosphere in which something more substantial than minimal production predominates. Protection also seeks to safeguard local investments in production facilities and to serve as an outlet for the creative talents within the country. This would be important to the United Kingdom, France, Italy, West Germany, and perhaps Spain. Of these West Germany alone did not have a formal scheme of protection. Although the need for it was recognized, exterior forces worked with such vigor there that plans were never realized.

Two types of protective schemes, based on different assumptions, have worked successfully in the larger European markets. The first is a screen quota which reserves a portion of each theatre's screen time for domestic films. The quota may declare that a given percentage of a theatre's films, measured over a year, must be local in origin or that a certain number of weeks out of each quarter must be devoted to the exhibition of national films. In either case, the object is to free a share of screen time so that domestic producers will have the opportunity to fill it. The screen quota is not concerned with the number of foreign films brought into a country and made available for exhibition. In practice, any amount may be imported but they must find their own place in the unreserved portion of screen time.

The second restrictive plan places a quota on the number of films imported. It is a positive step in that it limits the quantity of competitive films brought in and made available to exhibitors. As a long range policy, the import quota is also effective because it limits the rapid buildup of a pool of old foreign films. In a country with only a screen quota, an exhibitor who fulfilled his obligation to show domestic films could turn to this rerun reservoir which could be offered at prices below those for any excess new local films not shown in the reserved portion of screen time. The import quota alone, however, does not provide assurance that local productions will be able to find their way to the screens. If imports prove to be very popular with audiences and warrant long runs in theatres, then domestic films, even if numerically greater, could still have difficulty in achieving exhibition.

Neither restriction by itself offers sufficient multilevel protection for a domestic industry. The import quota is somewhat more effective than the screen quota, a point substantiated by the MPEA when a spokesman declared the screen quota to be "the least undesirable method of affording protection to domestic film industries. . . ."[8] Nonetheless, the key to protection exists in applying both. Specific development and use of protective measures, and their relation to the American industry, can be illuminated by examining and contrasting them in France, Italy, Spain, and the United Kingdom.

Before World War II, France produced about 120 films annually. During 1946, even though studio equipment was judged inadequate for large scale production, the industry completed ninety-six films. It seemed that in spite of great difficulties, the French industry was making a comeback and that with reequipped facilities, production could be brought to prewar levels. This miniature boom, however, was due to end.

In May, 1946, an agreement was reached in Washington on the importation of American films into France. The pact was signed by Léon Blum, representing the French government, and by James Byrnes, the American Secretary of State. The agreement, going into effect in July of that year, annulled the prewar import quota which had limited imports of American films to 120 per year.[9] France became a free market as far as the American industry was concerned and there was nothing in the agreement to restrict dumping of old films. In place of the import quota, the pact initiated a screen quota which reserved four weeks during each quarter year for the exhibition of French films. In contrast to the British screen quota, which had been fixed generally above its industry's production capacity, the French quota "was retrogressive and fixed far below the actual possibilities of home production."[10] The quota was approximately 31 percent of each theatre's screen time, while the actual French share before the war had been running at 50 percent.

A crisis within the French film industry was the immediate reaction to the Blum-Byrnes Agreement. In 1947, with production falling to only seventy-four films, discontent was so widespread that committees for the Defense of the French Film were organized, and brought the case to public attention. By the end of the year, more than half of the French studios were said to have suspended operation, and unemployment reportedly rose to more than 75 percent in some branches of the industry. These conditions were called to the attention of the Assembly in early 1948. Negotiations with the United States were resumed in an effort to modify the Blum-Byrnes Agreement and to alleviate the serious downward spiral in which the French industry found itself. The talks were concluded with the signing in September, 1948, of a five-year agreement.

This accord was more favorable to the French industry in that it resurrected the import quota and raised the portion of screen time reserved for French films. According to the agreement, of 186 dubbed films to be imported annually, 121 could be American. Eleven import licenses were to be given to each of the following American companies: Columbia, Loew's (M.G.M.), Monogram, Paramount, R.K.O., Republic, Twentieth Century-Fox, United Artists, Universal, and Warner Brothers. Independent American producers were to receive the remaining licenses. The screen quota was raised from four to five weeks per quarter, an effective increase from 31 to 38 percent of screen time.

The terms of the import quota were such that while 121 American films could be brought in, the rest of the world's producing countries were limited to a total of only 65 imports. When this small amount was divided among nations, it was evident that the restriction on them was severe. Producers in Great Britain, for example, protested the small number of films they were permitted to send to France. The British Film Producers Association tried vigorously to obtain more licenses for its pictures. As its annual report for 1948–49 declared:

> In spite of all efforts by the [British] Government and by the Association's representatives, only 18 licenses were allocated to this country for [the year beginning July 1, 1948]. The Association accepted this meager allocation under protest and renewed its plea to the Government to secure a better allocation for the year

1949–50. A minimum of 20 was all that could be obtained [from French authorities].

Such experiences are not encouraging and reflect to some extent the poor bargaining power of sterling against dollars and *the powerful effect of Marshall Aid upon the economy of so many countries.*[11] (Italics mine)

We can note the relation of Marshall Plan aid to the exportation of American films. It has been contended that the aid was used as a lever to open and maintain markets for American films in the critical years after the second war. While the aid was supposed to strengthen faltering economies against risings from the left, American films were seen as propaganda vehicles for strengthening western European minds against pleas from the left. The argument to foreign governments was: If you take our dollars, you can take our films. Considered in these terms, it is not surprising that American films received advantageous terms in many western European markets at the expense of competitors.

Pacts similar to the one initiated in 1948 guided the film trade between the United States and France for more than a decade. The French, however, remained adamant in allocating to MPEA companies only 110 import licenses for dubbed films each year. Certain bonus plans were operative but these did not materially change the flow of American films to France. The French market until 1960 limited importation from America in an effort to prevent unbalanced competition from seriously injuring French film production.

Events in 1959 and 1960 helped to modify this policy. Included in a broad program to liberalize trade in general was a more generous allocation of import licenses for American pictures. The film pact between the French government and the MPEA, signed in June, 1960, may be viewed as an indication of this change in commercial policy. One American trade newspaper commented:

Recently concluded film agreement between France and the U. S. is a milestone, not only because it liberalizes film trade with France, but because it marks a drastic change in French policy that will have beneficial effect on the policies of other countries which, like France, have long been guided by restrictive principles. . . .

New French pact is a reflection of the French government's recognition that the country needs a new approach to business, especially [a] recognition that the French film business now seeks foreign market expansion [and therefore must offer reciprocity at home].[12]

The 1960 pact, retroactive to July, 1959, and in force for three and a half years from that date, allocated 446 licenses for the importation of dubbed American films, increasing the number each year during the period. Another feature eliminated barriers to the free remittance of American earnings in France. The accord represented a revision of former policy and on the surface permitted more American films to enter France. Subsequent agreements between the MPEA and the French government allocated 140 import licenses annually. However, even by 1960 American film production had fallen considerably and fewer new American films were available for export. As the danger from the quantity of American films declined, the number of pictures permitted to enter France increased.

The postwar development in Italy of a screen quota and an import quota is slightly different from that in France. While the need for both types of quotas was recognized early, restrictions on imports were initiated later in Italy than in France but were coupled with a scheme to support domestic film production.

The closing of the Italian market to the American industry during the second war caused a great backlog of pictures to be built up which entered at an unprecedented volume when the war ended. In 1946, for example, six hundred American feature films were exported to Italy. There was nothing to hinder this because Italy had neither an import quota nor a screen quota. Other film producing nations, also searching for markets, exported to Italy and this aggravated the situation. During the three postwar years, imports averaged close to eight hundred films annually. The magnitude of importation prompted an Italian government official to declare that Italian films "had to fight their way" on a home market which was "literally swamped." He blamed this saturation chiefly on the "output of America."[13]

An early step to check the indiscriminate importation of films was the law of July 26, 1949, the Andreotti Act, which inaugurated a novel system of taxing imports to support local production.[14] For each dubbed film imported, the distributor had to deposit 2,500,000 Lire (about $4,000) with the government's semi-official banking agent, the Banca Nazionale del Lavoro. Later, the sum was increased to 5,500,000 Lire (about $8,800). The money from the dubbing certificate, as it was called, went into a fund from which Italian producers could borrow capital at low interest rates for film production. The law further provided that a distributor could have his deposit returned, but without interest, after ten years upon presentation of the certificate to the Banca or its representative. In essence, the Andreotti Act devised a scheme of compulsory interest-free deposits to form a pool of capital for local producers. The law did not technically restrict importation of films, as a distributor could import as many as he wanted provided he acquired a dubbing certificate for each one.

One might think that such a law would bring retaliation against Italian films abroad. This was not the case, however. The Italian government offered exemptions from the dubbing fee in return for more import licenses for Italian films. Thus it would grant an exemption for one French film when France issued an import license for an Italian picture. As the United States had no formal restrictions on film importation, the American industry was unable to take advantage of this reciprocity.

The screen quota had a modest beginning in Italy. It went into effect in December, 1949, and required that eighty days be set aside each year for the compulsory exhibition of Italian films. (This was increased to one hundred days in 1956.) These eighty days amounted to only 22 percent of screen time, a figure lower than the first postwar screen quota in France. To qualify as a film which could be counted toward quota fulfillment, a picture had to be of Italian nationality, at least two thousand meters long (approximately sixty-five hundred feet), and of sufficient technical standards to be approved by a quota council. This last feature attempted to discourage the making of "quota quickies"—those films of little artistic merit produced solely for the purpose of filling the reserved portion of a theatre's screen time. There is evidence to suggest that this did not altogether bar such films from being counted toward quota. A UNESCO report published at the time noted that "there appears to be a departure from the spirit of the law, for it seems to be a widely held opinion that . . . many films are of very poor quality."[15]

By 1950, Italy had been able to establish a token screen quota and had taken moderate steps toward controlling excessive importation of films. While these measures did reduce American importation to about four hundred films in 1950, Italian authorities felt that even this amount was still too great for the market to bear. To resolve the problem, negotiations were opened between the MPEA and ANICA, the central organization representing the Italian industry. ANICA proposed cutting imports from the United States by at least a fourth. The MPEA, of course, rejected the idea, for to accept a reduction at this time without a fight meant an acknowledgment of Italy's position. Moreover, to draw negotiations out over months gave the American companies more opportunity to dispose of their films on the Italian market before restrictions could be imposed. The state of the market can be judged from an interview with Giulio Andreotti as reported by a trade journalist.

> Extent to which the Italian market has been "glutted" by foreign imports, Andreotti said, is indicated by the fact that 580 films were available for domestic distribution last year when "only from 300 to 400 pictures could be absorbed." Of the total, he declared, 400 features came from the U. S., 80 more from various other countries, while Italian production amounted to 100 films.[16]

The importation problem was not resolved until May, 1951. The MPEA signed an agreement whereby eight American companies agreed to limit to 225 each year the number of their films brought into Italy to be dubbed. The pact, valid for two years, applied only to M.G.M., Twentieth Century-Fox, Paramount, Columbia, R.K.O., Universal, United Artists, and Republic. An additional sixty American films could be imported into Italy by Italian distributors, making a maximum of 285 dubbed American pictures annually. Although this may appear to be more than the one fourth reduction the Italians had hoped to achieve, the pact did not significantly hinder exportation to Italy. For the most part, the stock of American films unshown in that country had declined, and from 1951 production in Hollywood began to decrease. The MPEA's agreement to limit exports can be viewed as an attempt on its part to bring stable operating conditions to the Italian market and to relieve uncertainty. As *Variety* commented in discussing the features of the 1951 pact: "From the American viewpoint, it was necessary to come to a conclusive agreement 'to protect American pictures in Italy,' according to the document."[17] The quota was tied to other features, chiefly details on the remittance of American earnings in Italy, and, without a doubt, this prompted the MPEA to accept some limitations rather than be faced with harsher terms.

The 1951 agreement later was renewed for an additional period and was terminated on August 31, 1954. The new 1954 pact provided for a further cut in the number of dubbed American films imported into Italy. The MPEA companies were limited to only 190 pictures each year and an additional fifty-five permits were allocated to independent companies.

Periodic film agreements continued to be negotiated until the early 1960's. The 1956 pact set annual imports from MPEA companies at 192 with an additional contingent for independent producers. This agreement was replaced in 1959 by one authorizing only 185 imports annually from MPEA members; independents also received a limited number of licenses. The import quota was abolished in 1962 and at that time Italy again became a free market for American films. The elimination of the quota undoubtedly was influenced by the decline in Hollywood's production.

In Spain, protection is exemplified by the baremo, a way of allocating import licenses to distribution companies. The scheme judges each company on a number of scales, and awards points according to this measurement. The number of points earned by a company determines the number of licenses granted to it. The conflict which gave birth to this unique system can be outlined in these terms: the Spanish film industry was anxious to penetrate the American market, and the American industry was anxious to solidify its own position in the Spanish market.

Events leading to the baremo began with the expiration of the 1954 film agreement between the MPEA and the Spanish government. Negotiations in early 1955 gave little encouragement that a solution to problems could be reached. As the basis for a new agreement, Spain proposed a reduction from one hundred to about eighty in the number of films American companies in Spain could import annually. Of these sixty-eight could be dubbed and the remainder could be shown with subtitles. In addition, an increase was proposed in the tax on imported dubbed film, especially for special process films such as those in CinemaScope. These demands were not very different from those made in other countries where the MPEA was doing business. The proposal which caused concern to the MPEA was a demand for reciprocity—the Spanish industry wanted MPEA members to distribute a number of Spanish films in the United States. The MPEA's reaction to this suggested rule was concisely stated in *Variety*.

> American [executives] were surprised at the reciprocity demand put forward by the Spaniards. It called for the American companies with offices in Spain to handle between them eight Spanish features in the U. S. and Canada. Furthermore, the U. S. [distributing companies] in Spain would have to agree to handle one Spanish [motion picture] locally for each five imports. Neither of these demands is acceptable—either in principle or practically—to the MPEA.[18]

These terms are reminiscent of the 1951 agreement between the MPEA and the Italian industry. Through it, the MPEA, in effect, subsidized the limited importation and distribution of Italian films in the United States. The MPEA, unhappy about that arrangement and concerned about the precedent it established, later thwarted similar requests from France. Now the Spanish industry was asking for reciprocity and the MPEA had no desire to retreat from the position it had taken in dealing with the French. Because the Spaniards would not modify their demands and the American companies had no intention of accepting them, the MPEA initiated a boycott of the Spanish market.

With MPEA companies refusing to distribute their own pictures, Spanish distributors found themselves with little competition from either American films or American companies. This general condition existed from the summer of 1955 to March, 1958, when the MPEA lifted the boycott and decided to resume shipping films to Spain. During this grace period, Spanish distributors reorganized themselves, acquired a substantial share of the market, and bought out a few American distributing companies operating in Spain. When the boycott ended, the MPEA found itself in the unenviable position of trying to relocate itself in a market which had undergone structural and policy changes. Because some American companies had closed their offices and had franchised Spanish distributors to handle their films, the MPEA ranks were reduced to Paramount, Twentieth Century-Fox, Warner Brothers, M.G.M., and Columbia.

The terms under which the American industry resumed doing business in Spain were more stringent than those proposed by the Spanish authorities before the boycott. Although the demand for reciprocity was dropped, the Spaniards remained adamant on the import quota for dubbed films and continued to adhere to their policy of requiring a local distributor to handle a Spanish picture for every four foreign films imported. Moreover, the baremo was inaugurated. An American journalist resident for many years in Spain and active in film affairs has written:

> To many film observers, the Baremo was conceived as a fool-proof device to protect expanded gains of these Spanish [distributors] developed during the . . . MPEA embargo years. Thus Baremo is, in a sense, a penalty brought on the Americans by their own previous "strike."
>
> Spanish government film authorities accepted the premise that new Spanish firms formed when American companies pulled out of the local scene and companies that mushroomed from regional to full national status during the same period merited the protective element the Baremo affords.[19]

The concept of the baremo went one step beyond being a mere import quota, for American imports as well as the business of American distributors were limited. Around the world, the MPEA had traditionally claimed the right to receive one lump sum of import licenses which it would divide and allocate to member companies. The baremo struck at the roots of this policy because under it division and allocation were removed from American hands and became a function of the Spanish government.

The baremo, to amplify the description, is a system of calculation by which distribution companies are awarded points according to certain standards, the points becoming the basis upon which the government allocates import and dubbing permits. The more points a company has, the more foreign films it is permitted to import and distribute. Each company is measured on a series of scales which have included the number and type of Spanish films it has distributed, the age of the company, the amount of capital, the annual turnover, the number of employees, and the number of branch offices it maintains in Spain. The most important factor, yielding the greatest number of points, is the number and type of Spanish films distributed. On this scale, the baremo obviously favors companies which have aggressively sought and distributed domestic pictures. However, the catch is that Spanish films, on the whole, have not been great money earners in Spain. American films are the important box office attractions. As a case in point, although American pictures represented only about one-third of the films on the market in 1962, they accounted for almost two-thirds of the total box office receipts. While Spanish films are generally equal in number to the American films, their share of the market earnings can be no greater than one-third. In actuality, Spanish films represent one-fourth or one-fifth of total box office receipts. Clearly, a distribution company would be more anxious to handle American than Spanish films, but it can receive authorization to import the former only after it has actively distributed the less popular and less rewarding Spanish films.

To the businessman, the baremo works in a circle. If he does not receive many import licenses, he will not need, nor can he probably afford, a large staff with many branch offices. Thus, when his points are computed on the basis of his small business, he will not receive many import licenses and his business is likely to remain small. To escape from the circle he must distribute many Spanish films and be willing to sustain a probable decrease in business revenue, or a possible deficit, for a time. By handling a large volume of Spanish releases, the distributor can obtain more import licenses, particularly for the more popular American films. When this level is reached, the revenues from American pictures can be used to support the distribution of Spanish films.

American distributors have not fared too well under the baremo. As we have said, only five American companies maintain regular offices in Spain; the others have either franchised local distributors to handle their films or keep only token representative staffs.[20] Even if a company has a regular office, there is no guarantee that it will be able to distribute all the American films it may have at its disposal. As an example, the manager of one American company stated that during a certain year his company had Spanish distribution rights to twenty-two American films. Under the baremo, however, the company was permitted to distribute only two of these pictures and the remaining twenty had to be handled by Spanish distributors if they were to be shown at all in Spain.

The competitive position in which the American companies find themselves in Spain is indicated in Table 1, which presents data for the first five years of the baremo's operation. From 1958 through 1962, quotas restricted the total importation of dubbed foreign films to 901. Of these, film agreements between Spain and the MPEA permitted only 394 American films to enter Spain. And of these 394, the baremo allocated only sixty-six, or 17 percent, to American companies with regular offices in Spain. Considering American and other foreign films as a whole, American companies were authorized to distribute only 114 out of 901, about 13 percent. Excluding American films from the importation figures, 507 non-American pictures were imported, but American companies were permitted to distribute only forty-eight of these, about nine percent. The balance of the distribution business fell to Spanish companies. It is clear that while the import quota works to limit the number of American films imported, the baremo functions to channel the greatest number of American (and non-American) films away from American distributors. The baremo continues to achieve this objective because in the 1964–1965 season 104 licenses were allocated to American films. Of these, Metro received four, Fox three, Warner Brothers two, and Paramount only one. The remainder went to Spanish distributors. Columbia Pictures, at that time, was not doing business in Spain due to government restriction.

The baremo, retaliation for the MPEA boycott of the Spanish market, has severely hindered American operations in Spain and has

TABLE 1

Authorizations Granted Under the Baremo to American Companies with Full-scale Offices in Spain for the Importation and Distribution of Dubbed Foreign Feature Films

	1958		1959		1960		1961		1962		Total		Grand Total
	Amer.	Non-Amer.	Amer.	Non-Amer.	Amer.	Non-Amer.	Amer.	Non-Amer.	Amer.	Non-Amer.	Amer.	Non-Amer.	
Columbia	2	2	3	1	2	4	2	3	2	3	11	13	24
Fox	2	3	3	–	4	1	3	3	3	4	15	11	26
M.G.M.	3	–	3	–	4	3	3	3	4	4	17	10	27
Paramount	3	1	3	–	2	1	1	2	2	2	11	6	17
Warners	3	2	3	–	2	2	2	2	2	2	12	8	20
Total	13	8	15	1	14	11	11	13	13	15	66	48	114
TOTAL IMPORTS	66	100	64	90	88	97	88	105	88	115	394	507	901

Source: Grupo Sindical de Distribucion Cinematografica

cost American companies a conservatively estimated $10,000,000 in business. This condition was brought on, according to one observer, by company presidents in New York who "completely misinterpreted" the Spaniards. The accomplishment of the baremo is that it treats equally all distributors of equal size regardless of nationality. As the president of the Spanish Distributors Association has written:

> Charges have been levelled at Spanish authorities and against Spanish distributors for pursuing a nationalist policy. The truth of the matter is that the Spanish government, without opposition from Spanish distributors, has been giving the same consideration to MPEA companies as it has to all Spanish companies. This cannot be termed a nationalist policy.
>
> MPEA has always claimed extra privileges for its member companies via special agreements that gave more [import] licenses to them than to Spanish companies equally important in size, influence and marketing organization. This position is neither just nor reasonable.[21]

In contrast to Spain, the United Kingdom imposes only the more conservative screen quota as a protective device. This measure has its roots in the Films Act of 1927 which authorized an exhibitor's quota beginning in October, 1928. It was extended by the Films Act of 1938 which was in force for ten years. Between 1928 and 1948, the acts provided for a gradually increasing quota. Beginning in 1928 exhibitors were obliged to reserve a minimum of 5 percent of screen time for British films, but by 1938 exhibitors had to reserve 20 percent. When the Films Act of 1938 became effective, there was an initial drop in quota to 12.5 percent, but by 1947 the quota for long feature films was to be 25 percent.

The drop from 20 to 12.5 percent requires a short explanation. The 1938 Act, in part, aimed to reduce production of "quota quickies." The Act initiated a cost test which determined whether a given film could be counted as part of the "quota" for theatres. When the law was written, it was felt that the new legal minimum cost level would result in an initial drop in total film production. The reduction in compulsory screen time took this expected decline into account.

World War II nullified the intentions embodied in the 1938 Act. Due to wartime restrictions on film production in Great Britain there had to be departures from the law, and from October, 1942, until October, 1947, the screen quota, as stated in the Act, was abandoned. In practice then, the quota was in effect for only five years during the ten year life span of the 1938 Act.

The Films Act of 1948 modified the established screen quota. Under the previous acts, the quota had been set in advance for ten year periods. The new law specified that the quota was to be set annually and only after consultation between the government and the film industry. A government spokesman declared at the time that there was a need to have the annual quota correspond to the number of films likely to be available. This was a clear reference to the 1942–1947 period when there were not enough films produced to fill the quota established in 1938. The writers of the 1938 Act, of course, could not have foreseen this difficulty brought on by the war.

In the first year of the 1948 Act the quota was set at 45 percent for first feature films and 25 percent for the supporting program. The 45 percent quota, effective in October, 1948, and running until the end of September, 1949, was a sharp increase over the previous year's figure of only 20 percent for first features. The new quota cut dramatically into the market for American pictures, as in the years preceding the 1948 Act, American films had managed to acquire from 75 to 85 percent of screen time.

The MPEA protested the 45 percent quota and issued a statement which, in part, declared:

> The Board of Directors of the Motion Picture Association of America . . . asked Eric Johnston . . . to request the State Department to make a vigorous protest to the British Government against the new British 45 percent film quota. . . .
>
> "This screen quota is excessive and unnecessary," said Mr. Johnston. "Its requirement obviously cannot be fulfilled by British producers. We can therefore only consider it as a gratuitous affront to the American Motion Picture Industry. We shall immediately ask the State Department to protest on the highest level in Great Britain. . . ."
>
> At the same time the State Department will be asked to protest against the elimination of American representation from the Cinematograph Films Council Advisory Group to the Board of Trade. This Council, after eliminating American representation, recommended the high quota adopted by the Board of Trade.[22]

These protests had no *immediate* effect: the quota remained at 45 percent.

Were theatres able to fulfill their obligations? The answer must include a brief account of how quota fulfillment is calculated. The 1948 Act provided that under conditions of great competition an exhibitor could apply for quota relief, and if granted, his theatre's quota would be lowered from the statutory 45 percent to a figure the Board of Trade considered reasonable. During the 1948–1949 period, of the 4,182 operating theatres, close to 1,500 were granted reduced quotas ranging from 40 to 10 percent. When these reliefs were computed with those theatres which had to adhere to the 45 percent quota, the national *average* quota was only 37 percent for first feature films. This average quota was achieved.

In early 1949, discussions were resumed between the British film industry and the government for the 1949–1950 quota. Although the British Film Producers Association (BFPA) recommended that the quota remain at 45 percent, the Board of Trade ordered a 40 percent quota. The BFPA stated in its annual report that "this must be regarded as a temporary set-back to continued expansion in the production field."[23] While the statutory quota was 40 percent, reliefs reduced it to an *average* quota of 33.6 percent. But even this mark could not be reached and British films managed to fill only 30.4 percent of average national screen time. Failure to achieve quota was caused primarily by a decrease in film production brought on by numerous unsuccessful ventures in the home market and by limited success in penetrating foreign markets.

In the following year, the 40 percent quota was reduced to a statutory 30 percent for first features, where it remains today. From 1956 the statutory quota has been continuously exceeded while the *average* quota (computed on the basis of reliefs) has been exceeded every year since 1951. It is interesting to note how the quotas have been achieved. Although British film production has remained fairly constant from year to year, quota fulfillment on the part of exhibitors has increased. This seemingly impossible situation has been brought about predominantly by the closing of theatres. As opposed to approximately 4,600 theatres operating at the end of 1950, there were less than 1,700 operating by 1966. With fewer theatres for British films to play in today, and given a relatively steady film supply over the years, each theatre is able to exhibit more British films than seventeen years ago.

The forty years of screen quota have worked successfully to assure the industry that "British" films will have the chance to be exhibited even in the face of competition from America. The experiment of the first quota from 1928 to 1938 demonstrated, according to one study, "that official support was not to be a temporary expedient but that henceforward, if production was to survive, then it could only do so as a protected industry."[24] It can be said parenthetically that the screen quota is something of a paradox in Great Britain today due to the extensive American investment in British film production. In one sense, the quota guarantees *American* companies producing in Britain a reserved place on British screens!

What is happening to European protective measures in the 1960's? Protection was needed in the past because of the great threat from the productive capacity of the American industry and the postwar shakiness of European production. However, American production has declined markedly, and, as far as Europeans are concerned, so has the threat. With fewer new American films available for export, European producers realize that their own competitive position has improved somewhat. Moreover, European industries have achieved some

TABLE 2

Feature Film Production in Selected Countries

Country	1950	1955	1960	1965
United States	383	254	154	153
Great Britain	125	110	122	90
France[1]	117	95	119	90
Italy[1]	98	114	141	121

1. Excludes coproductions having a majority foreign interest.

Sources: *The Film Daily Year Book of Motion Pictures*, Board of Trade, Centre National de la Cinématographie, and Associazione Nazionale Industrie Cinematografiche ed Affini

measure of economic stability. The import quota is virtually obsolete today because the production decline has eliminated the surplus of films which had often flooded the market. Table 2 shows that the production imbalance in the major countries has tended to level off.

In some respects, the movement toward trade liberalization in Europe has helped reduce barriers to film circulation. This is clearly the case in France where the old policy of protection has been replaced by one of cooperation. This new climate prompted a representative of an American distribution company to declare that today the import license is only "theoretical" and that almost all films can be brought into the country.

Neither should one overlook the liberal importation policies generated by the substantial American investment in French and Italian production. European authorities realize that American money flowing into local film production has helped to keep studios open, to provide jobs, and to supplement local sources of finance. This assistance to local production has been rewarded, at least in one way, through relaxation of trade barriers.

The screen quota is also becoming superfluous. British first features now occupy about 40 percent of screen time even though the statutory minimum is 30 percent. In Italy, exhibition of national films greatly surpasses the legal minimum of one hundred days each year. Authoritative people there believe the screen quota is not important now because local production can exceed it. The screen quota in France has been exceeded every year since 1955, and only narrowly missed in the two preceding years. By contrast, Spain, with a less developed film industry, not only has maintained its screen quota but increased it. By a government order in January, 1967, the quota was set at one day of Spanish films for every three days of dubbed foreign films. Previously, the ratio was one to four. Original version foreign films and those with subtitles are not covered by the decree.

The American policy on film importation also bears on liberalization in most European countries. Eric Johnston once declared:

> Now, we feel that this international market is so important to us that if we tried restrictions in America we would simply get further restrictions on our films overseas. If that should occur, then our dilemma would be a very serious one.
>
> So we feel that the best thing for us to do is to set an example, the right kind of example, and then urge our Government to try to get other countries to follow that example. In a sense we have been successful because when we started this policy back in 1946, the restrictions abroad against American motion pictures were infinitely greater than they are today.[25]

American policy has been against the establishment of any *official* barriers to foreign films. There has never been an import quota or a screen quota in the United States.

3: American Films in the European Market

To understand the position of American motion pictures in Europe, one must look at quantitative measures of various sorts. To do so also establishes the relationship between American films and those from other producing nations.

Several scales should be available for a broad and intensive analysis. Ideally, for a given European nation, one wants to know how many domestic and imported feature films were released, what companies distributed these films, the share of screen time achieved by various nationalities, and how the box office receipts were divided among them. A firm basis for analysis would exist if these data were available for all years since 1945, for all countries, and in a form suitable for cross-country examination.

Unfortunately, such a utopian condition does not exist, because each nation selects and makes available only the information it considers important.[1] Even when several nations seem to be measuring the same thing they may be using different yardsticks. On the elementary question of foreign films coming into a country, several standards exist. One nation may state this in terms of total meters of exposed film imported. Another nation may decide to tabulate the number of pictures that have actually gone through the customs office. A third may base its measure on the number submitted to censorship. And a fourth country may count the business licenses issued which permit films to be exhibited. None of these measures, however, really indicates the number of films *released* and put on the market (although they do provide clues). Further complications are introduced when the version of the film is considered. Is the subtitled version the one to be tabulated, the dubbed version, or both? And if the picture is a bipart or tripart coproduction, to which country is the film credited?

On financial matters, which are even more complex, there is a general dearth of reliable material. Universally, revenue figures are treated as business secrets. Even if a government bureau or a trade association is authorized to collect and tabulate such data, there is no assurance that they will be made public in meaningful form. Problems of definition become important because gross box office receipts are divided in many ways. One share remains with the exhibitor; another may go to the government's treasury as an entertainment tax; one part may be diverted to a national fund to help production; and still another portion is taken by distributors of newsreels and short films. The residue is for distributors of both domestic and imported feature films, and the distributors, in turn, pass a part of this share to producers or investors. Thus, it becomes essential to know whether figures refer to gross box office receipts, net receipts, or the distributor's share.

The statistical material in this discussion (presented in comparative tables following) is derived almost exclusively from official government or industry trade association figures. Of course, some information from other sources is available but in numerous cases this unofficial material lacks standardization and definition, and cannot be considered reliable.

The previous chapter pointed out that the quantity of American films in Europe has been the primary reason for the erection of protective schemes. Evidence to support this must consider the number of American pictures available for marketing in various nations. This is a two-fold measure, for it implies, first, a count of films imported annually and, second, the number actually released, or authorized to be released, by distributors for exhibition.

Concerning the number of films imported, data can be presented for Italy, the Netherlands, and Switzerland. On the second point, three similar measures are available from ten countries: films censored or authorized for exhibition in Denmark, Ireland, and Spain; films registered with the Board of Trade for distribution in the United Kingdom; and films released in Italy, West Germany, Austria, Sweden, Norway, and Finland.

Table 1, films imported by Italy, counts titles brought into the country whether they are in subtitled or dubbed form. The American industry in 1946 sent six hundred films to Italy, while in 1966 the number was only 155, about a 75 percent reduction. The data indicate that in the years immediately following World War II, large numbers of American films flowed into certain European markets. From 1946 to 1949 inclusive, the United States accounted for 2,277 of the 3,187 films imported by Italy, 71 percent of the total. The decade of the 1950's was one in which imports from America declined from near four hundred to slightly more than two hundred. By way of comparison with the four postwar years, importation of American films from 1963 to 1966 inclusive accounted for 651 of a total 1,196, or approximately 54 percent.

TABLE 1

ITALY

Nationality of Feature Films Imported

	1946	1947	1948	1949	1950	1951	1952	1953	1954	1955	
American	600	507	668	502	394	230	246	222	209	244	
British	57	78	91	110	49	18	31	31	41	40	
French	121	101	31	37	31	42	59	42	28	22	
West German	–	–	–	2	16	15	20	4	5	21	
Other	72	108	84	18	49	37	38	59	24	40	
Total	850	794	874	669	539	342	394	358	307	367	

	1956	1957	1958	1959	1960	1961	1962	1963	1964	1965	1966
American	242	253	267	223	167	160	150	188	156	152	155
British	44	55	51	42	49	45	35	46	56	36	22
French	39	35	43	49	38	48	33	46	16	24	22
West German	21	21	24	47	64	27	24	18	14	14	13
Other	36	26	30	51	90	60	49	40	59	63	56
Total	382	390	415	412	408	340	291	338	301	289	268

Source: Associazione Nazionale Industrie Cinematografiche ed Affini

The effectiveness of import restrictions in Italy is apparent. The Andreotti Act came into force in July, 1949, and placed a tax on imported dubbed films. From a high figure of 668 in 1948, imports of American pictures dropped to 502 in 1949 and 394 in 1950, the first full year during which the law was operative. A further decline occurred in 1951, resulting from negotiations between the MPEA and ANICA. The agreement reached by the two associations provided that a maximum of 285 dubbed American films could be imported annually into Italy, 225 by American distributors and the remainder by Italian distributors. While the data in Table 1 are not confined solely to dubbed versions, they do point out that overall importation was reduced substantially at the time the MPEA-ANICA agreement became final.

Italy abolished import restrictions in 1962. The reason is apparent in the figures for the importation of American films in 1960, 1961, and 1962. In those years, only 477 American pictures were brought into

TABLE 2

THE NETHERLANDS

Nationality of Feature Films Imported

	1946	1947	1948	1949	1950	1951	1952	1953	1954	1955
American	199	289	290	301	271	245	249	229	195	235
British	137	68	64	47	40	36	30	36	51	58
French	95	58	39	17	27	27	34	50	47	58
Italian	3	15	18	12	26	24	23	29	35	33
West German	–	–	–	7	16	24	47	37	44	45
Other	63	61	27	49	23	26	36	30	32	20
Total	497	491	438	433	403	382	419	411	404	449

	1956	1957	1958	1959	1960	1961	1962	1963	1964	1965	1966
American	243	230	240	197	139	123	113	118	114	107	124
British	39	72	69	74	77	61	67	73	75	66	66
French	67	64	49	52	65	67	79	72	61	65	60
Italian	42	31	16	21	24	47	68	64	57	59	80
West German	73	85	111	83	72	86	42	29	29	23	25
Other	21	26	23	28	22	32	27	29	22	33	34
Total	485	508	508	455	399	416	396	385	358	353	389

Source: Nederlandsche Bioscoop-Bond

the country. During the same period, the Italian industry produced more than six hundred feature films, some in conjunction with American companies.

Table 2 presents similar data for the Netherlands. The years with the largest importation of American films were 1947 through 1950. After that period, American pictures gradually declined to a low of 107 in 1965, less than 30 percent of all imports for the year. In contrast, American films in 1949 accounted for almost 70 percent of all imports.

Data for the importation of feature films in Switzerland are presented in Table 3. Prior to 1958, figures made available concerned

TABLE 3

SWITZERLAND

Nationality of Feature Films Imported

	1958	1959	1960	1961	1962	1963	1964	1965	1966
American	198	172	160	150	128	123	150	125	126
British	47	46	47	62	39	32	36	39	30
French	93	93	100	104	93	85	89	74	59
Italian	45	43	41	98	103	117	107	112	102
West German	103	108	83	92	61	68	47	46	57
Other	33	33	28	37	34	43	49	39	62
Total	519	495	459	543	458	468	478	435	436

Source: Annuaire Statistique de la Suisse, Bureau Fédéral de Statistique

only the total footage of imported films, not the actual number of them. However, even for the nine years covered in the table, the relative decline of films with American nationality is evident. In 1958, about four of every ten films imported were American. By 1966, this proportion dropped to about three out of ten. On the other hand, Italy has come up strongly in the last six years. The importation of Italian features reflects not only an increase in production but also the large numbers of Italian workers who have migrated to Switzerland and now constitute a substantial audience for Italian films.

The second broad indicator of films on the market can be considered now. This involves the number of pictures approved for exhibition or actually released. In one sense, this is a more meaningful way of gauging the extent to which American films have penetrated the European market. The effect of their number is felt first when films are released for exhibition.

The Danish data in Table 4, indicating the number of films submitted for censoring, reveal the effect of the MPEA's boycott of the

TABLE 4
DENMARK
Nationality of Feature Films Submitted for Censorship
(Years ending March 31)

	1947	1948	1949	1950	1951	1952	1953	1954	1955	1956
American	172	155	198	229	225	238	228	236	189	116
British	66	32	15	30	28	32	27	28	41	51
French	50	52	19	10	14	26	18	30	34	29
Italian	1	–	3	–	6	7	16	8	16	14
German	–	–	–	3	9	5	13	20	27	41
Swedish	20	21	7	18	14	16	16	23	22	15
Other	16	9	6	6	6	8	13	6	14	11
Total Foreign	325	269	248	296	302	332	331	351	343	277
Danish	10	14	8	10	13	12	16	13	11	13
Total	335	283	256	306	315	344	347	364	354	290

	1957	1958	1959	1960	1961	1962	1963	1964	1965	1966	1967
American	55	155	193	215	184	175	154	139	143	144	126
British	73	57	31	28	36	26	28	33	32	28	24
French	59	35	22	29	34	42	46	32	35	39	36
Italian	29	8	3	2	6	18	15	10	12	17	15
German	57	55	54	57	50	40	39	23	20	17	10
Swedish	13	12	8	6	6	4	9	6	9	11	8
Other	17	11	6	18	19	14	29	20	16	38	23
Total Foreign	303	333	317	355	335	319	320	263	267	294	242
Danish	16	17	14	16	17	24	19	21	17	18	17
Total	319	350	331	371	352	343	339	284	284	312	259

Source: Statens Filmcensur

market. In May, 1955, the American cartel declared a halt to its members' film shipments to Denmark in protest over rental fees which, it claimed, were too low. This boycott was not terminated officially until May, 1958. The number of films censored, of course, does not reflect the number actually released and exhibited but it is a good measure of the number imported.

After a slight drop to 116 films in the year ending March 31, 1956, American pictures submitted for censorship declined to fifty-five in the year ending March 31, 1957. The following year, there was a three-fold increase but even this cannot compare to the number in the years preceding the boycott. The increase in the 1957–58 period can be attributed to the fact that several exhibitors in Copenhagen decided to increase the rentals they were willing to pay for American pictures. The MPEA accepted these new terms and resumed shipping films, but only to these exhibitors. The data for the boycott years

TABLE 5

IRELAND

Nationality of Films[1] Submitted for Censorship

	1951	1952	1953	1954	1955	1956	1957	1958
American	454	391	406	320	351	336	326	350
British	53	61	82	137	100	90	96	122
French	3	10	7	13	7	26	26	26
Italian	3	4	10	16	6	13	12	11
German	–	1	1	1	2	3	8	6
Other	7	4	4	6	3	17	5	7
Total Foreign	520	471	510	493	469	485	473	522
Irish	–	2	1	–	1	–	2	3
Total	520	473	511	493	470	485	475	525
ITE	–	–	–	16	8	14	7	5

	1959	1960	1961	1962	1963	1964	1965	1966
American	292	237	231	203	193	206	175	191
British	107	147	129	105	103	85	73	55
French	16	19	16	14	19	11	10	20
Italian	10	26	19	21	27	18	21	28
German	12	12	7	6	6	3	2	8
Other	6	27	16	24	17	17	14	21
Total Foreign	443	468	418	373	365	340	295	323
Irish	3	4	2	3	2	3	1	3
Total	446	472	420	376	367	343	296	326
ITE	1	6	2	1	2	1	2	3

[1] Films of 2,000 feet or more in the following categories: Drama-variety, Interest-topical, Educational. The number of Interest-topical and Educational films is included in the total and also shown separately in the horizontal row marked ITE.
Source: Film Censor's Office

reveal another pertinent point. Imports from Great Britain, Germany, and France increased to offset the decline in the number of American features available. It would seem that the withdrawal of American pictures from the market gave new opportunities for other film producing nations to sell their productions in Denmark.

Data for Ireland in Table 5 indicate the number of films of two thousand feet or more submitted for censorship. There is no language barrier to the circulation of American films there, and, in the absence of other restrictions, American pictures are freely importable. The figures disclose the decline in the number of American features available. In 1951, of 520 films submitted for censoring, American films numbered 454, or 87 percent. By 1966, American features dropped to 191 out of 326, or only 59 percent. Of course, British producers also have found Ireland to be an attractive market.

Table 6 presents data on the number of feature films authorized for exhibition in Spain. It should be recalled from the previous chapter that the MPEA imposed a boycott of the Spanish market from mid-

TABLE 6

SPAIN

Nationality of Feature Films Authorized for Exhibition

	1946	1947	1948	1949	1950	1951	1952	1953	1954	1955
American	201	193	157	87	86	74	109	140	158	127
British	20	23	7	8	12	10	25	34	24	25
French	14	14	15	16	25	12	20	24	23	19
Italian	15	25	21	6	6	5	29	27	16	20
German	4	4	3	1	–	5	7	14	1	5
Mexican	30	29	44	15	26	34	35	29	23	17
Other	28	35	18	27	18	12	6	23	19	3
Total Foreign	312	323	265	160	173	152	231	291	264	216
Spanish	36	70	63	51	72	48	43	55	69	94
Total	348	393	328	211	245	200	274	346	333	310

	1956	1957	1958	1959	1960	1961	1962	1963	1964	1965	1966
American	70	48	51	93	99	95	98	109	137	116	111
British	38	36	28	19	20	26	22	30	40	37	48
French	32	32	24	20	29	32	25	47	36	35	37
Italian	54	41	35	28	21	29	35	39	32	27	29
German	8	27	16	17	18	20	15	35	16	10	14
Mexican	28	17	28	16	30	33	55	20	38	40	35
Other	10	23	27	21	16	32	25	49	32	47	36
Total Foreign	240	224	209	214	233	267	275	329	331	312	310
Spanish	93	64	80	73	78	91	89	98	105	138	160
Total	333	288	289	287	311	358	364	427	436	450	470

Source: Ministerio de Información y Turismo

1955 to 1958. The number of American films authorized for exhibition in 1956, 1957, and 1958 reflects this. During those years, only 169 American pictures were approved, which is only slightly more than the total for 1954 alone. In Spain, as was true during the boycott of Denmark, importation of films from Britain, France, and Italy increased during the boycott period. In the five years following 1958 the effect of the import quota is apparent, as an average of ninety-eight American films were authorized for exhibition each year. In the mid-1960's, liberalization of Spain's trade policy is reflected in the increase of films of American nationality.

A measure of films on the market in Great Britain is provided by Board of Trade registration figures in Table 7. Although nationality categories are not complete to the early postwar years, total imports are listed, and an important point can be drawn from them. In August, 1947, as a result of a 75 percent duty placed on imported films, the

TABLE 7

UNITED KINGDOM

Nationality of Films[1] Registered for Distribution
(Years Beginning April 1 Except 1961 and After)

	1946	1947	1948	1949	1950	1951	1952	1953	1954	1955	1956
American				392	391	424	362	329	305	284	286
French				22	30	18	41	28	25	29	41
Italian				7	15	17	20	10	24	17	21
German				4	2	2	3	5	–	4	6
French or Italian Coproductions[2]				–	–	–	1	–	–	3	4
Other				15	6	15	22	23	32	18	23
Total Foreign	367	301	403	440	444	476	449	395	386	355	381
British	107	170	119	131	125	114	117	138	149	110	107
Total	474	471	522	571	569	590	566	533	535	465	488

	1957	1958	1959	1960	1961	1962	1963	1964	1965	1966
American	321	267	229	160	164	148	146	135	120	146
French	42	37	36	44	56	45	31	22	15	22
Italian	18	10	13	23	24	31	58	33	26	23
German	5	5	15	13	10	12	8	6	4	2
French or Italian Coproductions[2]	1	4	3	3	10	5	5	34	51	44
Other	36	30	36	35	52	49	32	26	40	50
Total Foreign	423	353	332	278	316	290	280	256	256	287
British	138	121	122	122	120	116	110	98	90	85
Total	561	474	454	400	436	406	390	354	346	372

[1] Films of 3,000 feet or more.
[2] Coproductions in which one of the parties was either French or Italian.
Source: Board of Trade

MPEA declared a boycott of the British market. The registration year April 1, 1947, to March 31, 1948, covers the period of this seven-month boycott. The data indicate that imports did fall, although not substantially, from previous years. Of course, there is no way of knowing how many of the 301 foreign films in the 1947–48 period were registered before the import tax became effective and how many of these were American. Nor is there a way of determining what the magnitude of imports would have been had there been no duty.

One point does stand out, however. During the boycott period, British film production increased sharply, and 170 features were registered during the 1947–48 year. This mark has not been approached, let alone exceeded, since that time. It seems that the MPEA's decision to withhold films from the market spurred British film producers. An additional impetus came from the high screen quota of 45 percent set for the 1948–49 year.

On another matter, Table 7 repeats the decline in availability of new American pictures that has been evident for countries already examined. In 1949–50, the 392 American films accounted for 69 percent of the 571 films registered. In calendar year 1966, the 146 American pictures represented only 40 percent of the 372 registrations. If only imported films are considered for the same years, then American pictures in 1949–50 accounted for almost 89 percent of foreign registrations, but in 1966 they represented only 51 percent.

As the decline in production in the United States has resulted in the diminishing availability of new American films in the United Kingdom, importation of features from France and Italy has been increased. In the 1949–50 year, the twenty-nine films from these two countries represented only 6 percent of all imports registered. In 1966, the two exported eighty-nine films, including coproductions, to the United Kingdom, and these accounted for 31 percent of foreign registrations.

Data for Italy in Table 8 refer to the number of films in Italian version released annually from 1950 through 1965. "Italian version" means films with Italian language sound tracks—foreign films dubbed into Italian and Italy's own production. There are some differences between this table and Table 1. The latter presented figures for *imported* films, dubbed or subtitled. Table 8 gives data for *released* Italian language pictures. Furthermore, the importation of a certain film in, say, 1959, does not necessarily mean that it was released in Italy the same year.

The downward trend in the number of dubbed American releases

TABLE 8

ITALY

Nationality of "Italian Version" Films Released

	1950	1951	1952	1953	1954	1955	1956	1957
American	234	232	290	228	207	277	195	248
British	18	26	24	22	24	37	45	41
French	20	35	54	41	36	19	32	33
West German	1	5	10	4	5	17	13	18
Other	62	81	23	26	23	26	33	56
Total Foreign	335	379	401	321	295	376	318	396
Italian	104	107	148	166	201	133	105	129
Total	439	486	549	487	496	509	423	525

	1958	1959	1960	1961	1962	1963	1964	1965
American	238	215	181	144	132	166	152	140
British	45	38	45	45	39	34	53	34
French	39	33	24	38	42	35	27	18
West German	21	33	35	35	29	19	19	14
Other	20	38	52	46	42	29	51	60
Total Foreign	363	357	337	308	284	283	302	266
Italian	137	167	168	213	241	222	315	182
Total	500	524	505	521	525	505	617	448

Source: Associazione Nazionale Industrie Cinematografiche ed Affini

is clear. From a high of 290 in 1952, the figure for the United States falls to 140 in 1965. The pattern is repeated if American films are considered as a percentage of total films released for certain years. During 1950, 1951, and 1952, 756 dubbed American films were released out of a total 1,474. These American features accounted for 51 percent. In 1963, 1964, and 1965, there were 458 American releases out of 1,570. American films during that period represented only 29 percent of all releases.

The data reveal that Italy's own production has increased, due to American investment and the growth of coproduction among European nations. In 1950, 1951, and 1952, the 359 Italian pictures represented only 24 percent of the total number of releases. In 1963 through 1965, Italy released 719 features, 46 percent of the total, with the highest point in 1964.

Table 9, for feature films released in West Germany, reveals some similarities with the Italian market. During the sixteen years covered in the table, releases from the United States declined from about five out of ten films in 1951 to three out of ten in 1966. British and Italian pictures have increased numerically and proportionally. The number of French features released reached a peak in 1960 and has fallen off

TABLE 9
WEST GERMANY
Nationality of Films[1] Released

	1951	1952	1953	1954	1955	1956	1957	1958
American	216	261	224	201	234	206	226	232
British	29	17	12	27	27	37	49	51
French	40	40	40	39	35	45	47	47
Italian	29	22	35	40	26	24	36	19
French-Italian Coproductions	2	3	12	15	20	16	17	22
Austrian	21	17	17	13	19	25	25	23
Other	41	28	21	16	24	30	36	52
Total Foreign	378	388	361	351	385	383	436	446
West German	65	72	98	111	123	123	108	114
Total	443	460	459	462	508	506	544	560

	1959	1960	1961	1962	1963	1964	1965	1966
American	193	175	141	132	134	124	123	125
British	56	56	53	47	48	41	51	43
French	44	49	42	46	16	17	20	20
Italian	25	35	38	43	35	41	43	47
French-Italian Coproductions	26	52	46	54	51	63	46	44
Austrian	13	18	16	18	12	11	7	11
Other	54	53	62	53	58	53	52	70
Total Foreign	411	438	398	393	354	350	342	360
West German	105	97	82	66	60	71	59	65
Total	516	535	480	459	414	421	401	425

[1] Films of 1,600 meters or more, excluding television films.
Source: Spitzenorganisation der Filmwirtschaft

considerably since then. In one respect, this has been offset by the significant rise in French-Italian coproductions. In 1951, they accounted for less than 1 percent of total foreign releases while in 1966 they represented 10 percent. Taken as a unit, French, Italian, and French-Italian films accounted for a quarter of all releases in 1966.

Difficulties facing West Germany's own film industry are reflected in its feature production, and therefore in its releases. The number climbed steadily until the late 1950's when a reverse trend set in. In 1966, only sixty-five German films were released (half were coproduced), compared to 123 in 1955 and 1956 (less than a tenth were coproduced).

Data in Table 10 for Austria disclose that it has been a consistently good market for West German films. Few are produced which are not released there. Concerning American films in Austria, their high point occurred in the mid-1950's but they have since declined to about

TABLE 10

AUSTRIA

Nationality of Feature Films Released in Vienna

	1946	1947	1948	1949	1950	1951	1952	1953	1954	1955
American	52	31	59	150	204	184	192	180	219	229
British	21	11	30	34	40	32	26	25	25	18
French	43	39	36	19	22	23	28	25	32	42
Italian	7	–	–	3	11	11	27	10	25	31
West German	135	2	17	40	108	98	71	106	105	105
Other	84	39	44	34	40	35	48	44	25	15
Total Foreign	342	122	186	280	425	383	392	390	431	440
Austrian	29	14	24	26	17	23	19	25	22	29
Total	371	136	210	306	442	406	411	415	453	469

	1956	1957	1958	1959	1960	1961	1962	1963	1964	1965	1966
American	227	221	200	214	193	166	141	151	127	132	174
British	25	41	33	55	70	51	50	47	48	46	56
French	59	51	64	52	68	69	64	66	66	51	54
Italian	38	28	46	36	35	46	47	72	79	89	65
West German	122	116	118	118	98	89	71	54	62	52	65
Other	20	26	30	45	46	39	34	47	49	47	57
Total Foreign	491	483	491	520	510	460	407	437	431	417	471
Austrian	31	29	23	21	19	22	21	17	18	16	19
Total	522	512	514	541	529	482	428	454	449	433	490

Source: Osterreichische Gesellschaft für Filmwissenschaft

36 percent of all releases. The small number of them in the late 1940's might reflect reluctance on the part of American companies to export to a market from which they could not withdraw their earnings or spend them internally. This was true for West Germany, as a later chapter points out.

The number of films released annually in Sweden, Norway, and Finland are presented in Tables 11, 12, and 13, respectively. As for other European markets, the data here indicate the diminishing number of American releases. The most striking example is Finland where only ninety-four American features were released in 1966. This reflects our declining production as well as the reduction of theatres in Finland. There were 620 houses in 1958 but only 370 in 1966, thus creating a demand for fewer films. This also is apparent in the total number of releases which has fallen below the three hundred level during the last four years. Ten years earlier, more than four hundred films were available annually.

So far, data have concerned only the importation and release of American pictures in various European nations. It is unfortunate that

TABLE 11

SWEDEN

Nationality of Feature Films Released

	1950	1951	1952	1953	1954	1955	1956	1957	1958
American	192	213	201	190	179	163	183	178	182
British	37	46	41	39	49	52	42	54	67
French	27	24	27	20	29	32	30	50	39
Italian	5	7	10	15	14	16	13	13	11
West German	5	5	8	12	11	17	24	28	25
Danish	3	2	2	5	1	4	1	5	6
Norwegian	2	–	1	–	1	3	1	2	3
Finnish	2	1	2	2	1	–	2	–	1
Other	8	10	13	11	20	14	15	10	15
Total Foreign	281	308	305	294	305	301	311	340	349
Swedish	23	28	25	30	34	34	34	30	26
Total	304	336	330	324	339	335	345	370	375

	1959	1960	1961	1962	1963	1964	1965	1966	1967
American	182	138	125	127	107	107	105	97	108
British	47	50	49	45	52	45	54	46	42
French	44	49	49	44	30	45	41	32	44
Italian	16	14	31	38	40	29	20	21	55
West German	29	25	31	15	12	3	9	9	11
Danish	6	5	2	5	8	8	8	7	8
Norwegian	–	1	3	–	2	–	–	–	1
Finnish	–	–	–	2	–	3	–	1	2
Other	21	19	15	25	13	14	21	10	22
Total Foreign	345	301	305	301	264	254	258	223	293
Swedish	17	20	15	16	18	20	21	20	19
Total	362	321	320	317	282	274	279	243	312

Source: Sveriges Biografagareforbund and Sveriges Filmuthyrareforening

figures going back to 1946 are not obtainable for some countries. But based upon the evidence available, a few comments can be made.

The peak years for the importation, censorship, or release of films with American nationality occur between 1946 and 1951 for eight countries: Spain, Italy, the Netherlands, Norway, Finland, the United Kingdom, Ireland, and Sweden. For Denmark, the peak falls in the year between April 1, 1951, and March 31, 1952, thus overlapping significantly the period for the other eight. West Germany, although a special case because of the Occupation, received its greatest annual supply of American pictures in 1952. Even Austria registered a small peak in 1950, although the major one occurred five years later.

On this basis, it can be seen that the postwar wave of American exportation to Europe reached its climax within six years after the end

TABLE 12

NORWAY

Nationality of Feature Films Released

	1946	1947	1948	1949	1950	1951	1952	1953	1954	1955
American	179	227	177	181	253	234	244	198	197	178
British	60	55	62	53	44	55	46	45	51	46
French	33	36	49	19	28	17	19	29	38	28
Italian	–	–	3	13	10	11	13	16	20	26
German	–	–	1	4	20	8	9	4	14	28
Swedish	63	53	43	31	23	27	25	26	31	31
Danish	11	12	9	6	14	12	15	14	12	10
Other	21	15	12	18	18	20	10	17	10	15
Total Foreign	367	398	356	325	410	384	381	349	373	362
Norwegian	6	3	6	3	5	11	14	11	19	8
Total	373	401	362	328	415	395	395	360	392	370

	1956	1957	1958	1959	1960	1961	1962	1963	1964	1965	1966
American	187	189	202	157	137	164	164	180	144	157	131
British	41	56	62	67	48	64	44	56	45	52	64
French	30	47	33	39	26	45	44	45	34	46	35
Italian	19	9	8	8	17	35	21	18	12	15	30
German	30	41	39	45	43	47	38	20	11	12	16
Swedish	26	24	26	29	13	17	19	9	14	16	25
Danish	6	12	11	13	14	16	18	16	11	13	17
Other	16	8	19	25	22	29	20	35	22	25	27
Total Foreign	355	386	400	383	320	417	368	379	293	336	345
Norwegian	13	11	14	10	11	11	5	6	9	12	9
Total	368	397	414	393	331	428	373	385	302	348	354

Source: Kommunale Kinematografers Landsforbund

of hostilities. Yet this was precisely the period when American film production began declining. According to *Film Daily Year Book of Motion Pictures*, American releases in the United States during the 1941–45 period averaged 425 films annually. But between 1946 and 1950, an average of only 370 pictures were released each year. This suggests that Hollywood was sending to some European countries films made during the war which could not have been exported when new, because of hostilities. This was also the time of relatively free access to many European markets before trade barriers were erected.

Hollywood production slumped steadily until 1954 when it hit a trough with only 253 films. From 1955 through 1957, there was a temporary recovery in production and this is reflected in the flow of films to Europe. The 1957 peak in the United States (300 films) was reflected in 1957 or 1958 in virtually all nations under consideration. Of course, the MPEA boycotts of Spain and Denmark held down the quantity of American features in those countries.

TABLE 13

FINLAND

Nationality of Feature Films Released

	1946	1947	1948	1949	1950	1951	1952	1953	1954	1955	1956
American[1]	157	184	197	230	272	264	263	233	198	197	202
British	24	43	31	28	26	24	26	34	33	36	38
French	16	17	29	19	12	12	13	19	28	49	43
Italian	–	–	2	–	1	1	7	13	23	22	34
West German	–	3	3	8	10	12	24	15	17	27	40
Swedish	26	26	26	20	16	12	15	7	14	11	12
Other	26	26	38	36	40	39	30	39	34	31	30
Total Foreign	249	299	326	341	377	364	378	360	347	373	399
Finnish	14	15	16	15	14	19	29	24	28	29	17
Total	263	314	342	356	391	383	407	384	375	402	416

	1957	1958	1959	1960	1961	1962	1963	1964	1965	1966	1967
American[1]	224	199	187	139	142	104	100	113	107	94	129
British	35	41	46	36	50	43	42	44	45	39	33
French	48	46	49	43	60	62	45	32	34	40	43
Italian	22	11	15	18	40	50	32	18	11	27	27
West German	35	37	30	49	51	30	19	10	17	20	12
Swedish	7	11	12	11	12	10	8	9	8	6	13
Other	22	15	39	34	41	42	52	41	28	30	37
Total Foreign	393	360	378	330	396	341	298	267	250	256	294
Finnish	21	17	14	18	18	20	12	8	7	7	3
Total	414	377	392	348	414	361	310	275	257	263	297

[1] Figures for the United States prior to 1961 may include some non American films released by American distributors.
Source: Suomen Filmvuokraajaliitto and Suomen Elokuvatoimistojen Liitto

In 1958, American production began a steady decline that was to be more serious than the short dips which had preceded. From the early 1950's, many countries on the continent had been importing annually between 200 and 250 American films. In 1958, American production fell below 250 and in 1959 below 200. To exhibitors who had come to depend upon a steady flow of American pictures, the decline presented problems. Rather than with an oversupply, they were faced with a shortage. Film producing nations of Europe, of course, increased their own exportation to help fill the gap. American producers responded, not by increasing production, but by reissuing old films.

For example, data for 1960 indicate that in addition to Ireland and the United Kingdom, the major markets of Italy and West Germany, and the smaller markets of Switzerland, Denmark, and Austria were receiving *more* American features than were released in the United States (154). American producers, through their distributors, sought to maximize profit on their investments, not by producing more, but by rereleasing their films. In this way, the production decline put American producers in a more favorable position. Europe could absorb not only their new films but some of their old ones as well. Such was also the case with Great Britain between 1954 and 1963. Even though the number of theatres declined from about 4,500 to less than 2,500 in that decade, 2,310 American pictures were registered. Meanwhile in the United States, only 2,060 American films were reported to have been released.

Another factor bearing on the matter has to do with the nationality attributed to particular films. Although a later chapter discusses this in more detail, it should be noted here that the nationality can vary as a film circulates from country to country. This problem has become severe during the 1960's with increased American investment in European production. A film shot in Italy, for example, might well have Italian nationality in that country. But when the same film is exported to, say, Norway, it might be considered American because of the extensive American investment in it. Thus, a film *not* made in the United States can carry American nationality. Furthermore, when it is released in this country, in all likelihood it will be recognized here as a foreign film. Considered on this basis, it is not surprising that some countries can see more "American" films than America can.

Throughout Europe films from the United States have been present in greater numbers than have local films. But granting their number, how have they fared at the box office relative to their competitors? Little evidence is obtainable to answer this question, but a small conjecture can be made. Of interest is the share of the box office accruing to American films for it is this share which is denied to producers in European nations.

In recent years, Italy has been the largest non-English-speaking market for American films. Table 14 indicates that American pictures in 1965 had a gross box office of $104,700,000 in Italy, or 41 percent of the total. In percentage terms, this is the smallest share of the box office American films have had since Italy began publishing statistics on this matter in 1950. In that year, American pictures captured 67 percent of the gross but this amounted to only $68,300,000.

The data reveal that American earnings have not kept pace with the growing Italian box office. This has more than doubled since 1950, while American earnings have increased only about 50 percent. On the other hand, an interesting point becomes apparent relative to data in Table 8. While the number of American releases has declined from 234 in 1950 to 140 in 1965, the American share of the gross receipts has increased from about $68,000,000 to almost $105,000,000 during the same period. An increase in the number of tickets sold is not necessarily the answer. While a peak was hit in 1955 with 819,000,000 admissions, the number for 1950, 662,000,000, is little different from the 1965 figure of 663,000,000. Neither is higher rental terms an entirely adequate explanation, because the figures under consideration here are gross box office receipts. The rental an exhibitor must pay for a film is not always reflected in gross revenues for the theatre.

TABLE 14

ITALY

Division of Gross Box Office Receipts
($000,000)

	1950	1951	1952	1953	1954	1955	1956	1957
American	68.3	74.1	77.8	86.6	94.3	108.3	116.7	106.3
British	4.3	3.7	4.3	4.7	5.4	6.5	7.8	9.7
French	1.7	3.5	4.2	3.9	3.7	3.2	4.3	5.4
Other	2.8	3.1	3.3	3.1	4.0	3.7	4.1	4.9
Italian	24.3	32.8	44.3	52.9	60.9	65.0	52.7	54.2
Total	101.4	117.2	133.9	151.2	168.3	186.7	185.6	180.5

	1958	1959	1960	1961	1962	1963	1964	1965
American	97.9	94.7	88.8	92.2	89.0	95.5	105.9	104.7
British	10.3	10.5	9.5	10.5	10.4	10.2	13.5	18.5
French	5.0	5.8	5.1	4.5	4.3	7.0	4.8	3.3
Other	6.3	8.6	11.1	10.3	9.4	9.3	8.2	8.4
Italian	57.8	67.2	80.3	84.7	100.3	103.9	109.3	119.7
Total	177.3	186.8	194.8	202.2	213.4	225.9	241.7	254.6

Source: Associazione Nazionale Industrie Cinematografiche ed Affini

Two explanations are possible. First, the number of new films entering a market may not be consistent with the number of films already in circulation. In Italy in 1965, there were about 3,000 American films of all ages available for exhibition, a figure hardly different from that of the early 1950's. Thus, while the number of *new* American films declined, the total supply has remained quite constant. Second, the price of admission has increased. The average ticket price in Italy in 1956 was about 148 lire but by 1965 the average had become 240 lire. So a greater American gross could reflect a stable reservoir of films and a higher admission price.

Since 1950, Italian features have experienced a five-fold increase in their gross earnings. In that year they earned about $24,000,000 while in 1965 they grossed almost $120,000,000. Their percentage share of the total box office has increased from only 24 percent in 1950 to 47 percent in 1965. Included, of course, would be some films produced with American investment which would be "Italian" in Italy but perhaps another nationality elsewhere.

Productions from Great Britain also have been doing better than in 1950. They grossed $4,000,000 in that year in contrast to more than $18,000,000 in 1965. The current mediocre earnings for France are somewhat deceptive. In recent years, the majority of French films have been coproduced, chiefly with Italy. When released in Italy, revenues accruing to them are credited to the Italian category. In 1965, for example, almost 70 "Italian" films were, in reality, "Italian-French" productions.

Data in Table 14 referring to the gross box office can provide an indication of the distributors' share of receipts. Generally, at least 30 percent of the gross reverts to the distributor after deductions are made.[2] In other words, 30 percent of $104,700,000 (gross for American pictures in 1965), or $31,400,000, is the approximate share going to companies distributing American pictures. (Almost all important American films, however, are handled by American companies.) When this calculation is applied to the total gross for American films from 1950 to 1965, then the distributors' share becomes about $450,300,000.

France is another major market for American films, although Table 15 indicates that French pictures consistently have had a better aggregate box office value in their home market than American features. In 1966 for example, French films earned almost twice as much as American films. This contrasts sharply with Italy, for Table 14 disclosed that American pictures have earned more money there than Italian films with the exception of the last three years. The share of the gross French box office for French films has shifted mildly around the 50 percent level with 1965 representing the high point, 55 percent. The American share has declined from 37 percent in 1952 to 28 percent in 1965.

The average distributors' share of the gross box office receipts in France is about 33 percent. On the basis of an American gross in 1966 of $45,300,000, the distributors of American films received about $14,900,000. However, unofficial American industry figures declare that revenues accruing to American *companies* in France for the year were about $23,000,000. The difference can be accounted for in two ways. In addition to American films, these companies also distribute non-American pictures and their earnings would be credited toward the $23,000,000. Second, there is American investment in French film production. Revenue from this source would not be reflected in box office receipts for American films but would be tabulated in the earnings of American companies in France.

From 1952 to 1966 inclusive, American pictures in France have accounted for about $643,400,000 of the total gross box office. On the basis of a 33 percent share reverting to distributors, American films have earned approximately $212,300,000. This is less than net earnings for American pictures in Italy. But the gross box office in France

TABLE 15

FRANCE

Division of Gross Box Office Receipts
($000,000)

	1952	1953	1954	1955	1956	1957	1958
American	40.0	41.4	43.9	45.7	46.9	41.7	37.3
British	4.1	4.5	5.2	4.3	5.2	6.0	8.3
Italian	5.9	8.3	9.4	11.7	9.0	4.8	3.6
German[1]							
Other	4.5	6.3	7.3	8.0	8.6	9.4	11.6
French	54.2	56.8	62.8	66.8	70.6	67.0	59.6
Total	108.7	117.3	128.6	136.5	140.3	128.9	120.4

	1959	1960	1961	1962	1963	1964	1965	1966
American	38.2	37.6	38.1	45.1	50.0	48.7	43.5	45.3
British	5.8	7.1	5.5	3.6	6.5	9.7	14.0	12.9
Italian	3.2	5.4	6.8	7.5	8.9	8.6	6.8	7.7
German[1]		6.3	5.1	3.8	2.6	2.2	1.8	2.0
Other	11.3	6.3	6.7	8.6	8.3	6.8	6.1	6.8
French	62.3	71.7	69.3	72.6	74.1	79.1	88.3	84.8
Total	120.8	134.4	131.5	141.2	150.4	155.1	160.5	159.5

[1] Receipts for German films are included in the "Other" category prior to 1960.
Source: Centre National de la Cinématographie

is considerably smaller than in Italy and French films in France consistently have captured about half the gross.

The United Kingdom is the largest foreign market for the American film industry. Unofficial American industry figures indicate that companies earned about $48,000,000 there in 1966 (in contrast to about $23,000,000 in France and $33,000,000 in Italy). Earnings of American films, however, can only be estimated because data from the British government are presented for "British" films and all "foreign" films—there being no tabulation of the nationality components of "foreign" earnings.

Table 16 presents gross theatre receipts and the distributors' share divided between British and foreign pictures. Rental figures for 1965 and 1966 have not been released by the Board of Trade. An outstanding feature is the marked decline in gross receipts from $294,600,000 in 1950 to $166,400,000 in 1966. The drop is even more striking when the 1966 figure is compared to the peak year of 1954 when receipts were $308,000,000. But revenues accruing to British films have not suffered a similar fate. Even though paid admissions are

TABLE 16

UNITED KINGDOM

Rentals Charged for British and Foreign Films[1]
($000,000)

	1950	1951	1952	1953	1954	1955	1956	1957	
Rentals for foreign films	46.8	47.6	48.2	45.9	45.9	47.3	44.0	37.5	
Rentals for British films	19.0	17.6	18.5	20.2	22.4	20.2	21.3	22.1	
Gross theatre receipts	294.6	303.2	307.7	304.6	308.0	296.2	291.8	260.1	

	1958	1959	1960	1961	1962	1963	1964	1965	1966
Rentals for foreign films	36.4	31.9	34.0	32.1	32.1	27.1	28.5		
Rentals for British films	23.5	22.1	23.8	26.3	22.5	24.7	25.4		
Gross theatre receipts	233.5	189.0	178.2	167.5	159.3	154.3	161.1	172.7	166.4

[1] Rentals charged in 1965 and 1966 have not been made public.
Source: Board of Trade

down, British films have earned more than $20,000,000 annually since 1953. In contrast, the rentals for foreign films are now less than two-thirds what they were in 1953. Moreover, the share taken by films with American nationality is probably less than it was in the early 1950's. Then, practically all imported films were American but in 1965 only half were American.

West Germany is another important market for American films. Although earnings by nationality are not available for the years before 1955, Table 17 indicates that in each year except 1966 American pictures received more than $20,000,000 from the box office. As is the case in other countries, films from Great Britain and Italy have a better box office value today than in the mid-1950's. An interesting point about the West German market is that Austrian films also are

TABLE 17

WEST GERMANY

Division of Distributors' Share of Box Office Receipts

($000,000)

	1955	1956	1957	1958	1959	1960	1961	1962	1963	1964	1965	1966
American	23.1	24.2	25.2	22.9	21.5	23.2	24.6	24.9	24.1	24.0	20.3	17.9
British	1.4	1.4	2.7	5.5	4.2	3.5	3.5	3.3	4.7	3.6	8.1	9.3
French	3.6	3.9	5.7	5.6	6.4	7.0	7.2	5.9	3.7	3.8	4.3	3.5
Italian	2.6	2.7	1.8	2.3	2.5	3.9	4.8	5.9	5.5	6.3	5.2	6.7
Austrian	6.1	8.4	8.4	6.0	5.2	4.3	4.5	4.9	3.7	3.0	2.6	2.6
Other	.9	1.1	1.2	3.2	2.9	3.1	3.9	3.5	2.7	6.8	6.7	7.4
West German	33.9	37.2	41.0	41.5	37.8	31.3	23.4	19.8	19.4	17.6	19.1	16.5
Total	71.6	78.9	86.0	87.0	80.5	76.3	71.9	68.2	63.8	65.1	66.3	63.9

Source: Spitzenorganisation der Filmwirtschaft

important and their earnings compare favorably with those of the major film producing nations of Europe.

So far, revenues accruing to American pictures in only the larger European nations have been examined here. The survey now considers two of the smaller markets, Denmark and the Netherlands. In these countries, American pictures are faced with different competitive circumstances because each produces very few films.

TABLE 18
DENMARK
Division of Distributors' Share of Box Office Receipts
($000,000)

	1950	1951	1952	1953	1954	1955	1956	1957
American	1.3	1.4	1.4	1.4	1.4	1.1	.6	.7
British	.2	.2	.2	.2	.2	.3	.4	.4
French	—	.1	.1	.2	.2	.2	.3	.3
Italian	—	—	—	.1	.1	.1	.2	.1
West German	—	—	.1	.1	.2	.3	.3	.5
Swedish	.1	.1	.1	.1	.1	.1	.1	.1
Other	—	—	—	—	—	.1	.1	.1
Danish	.5	.6	.7	.7	.7	.8	.8	1.0
Total	2.1	2.4	2.6	2.8	2.9	3.0	2.8	3.2

	1958	1959	1960	1961	1962	1963	1964	1965	1966
American	1.4	1.8	1.7	1.4	1.4	1.5	2.2	2.7	3.0
British	.4	.3	.2	.2	.4	.1	.4	.3	.3
French	.2	.2	.2	.3	.2	.3	.2	.4	.4
Italian	—	—	.1	—	.1	—	.1	.1	.1
West German	.5	.4	.5	.4	.3	.3	.2	.2	.2
Swedish	—	.1	.1	.1	.1	.1	.2	.1	.1
Other	.1	.1	—	—	—	—	—	.1	—
Danish	.9	.8	.9	1.3	1.2	1.4	1.0	1.3	2.1
Total	3.5	3.7	3.7	3.7	3.7	3.7	4.3	5.2	6.2

Source: Government Statistics Department

The division of the distributors' share of the Danish box office is given in Table 18. Even though it has been increasing since 1950, the American portion has not kept pace. In 1950, the $1,300,000 reverting to distributors of American films accounted for 62 percent of the total share. In 1966, the $3,000,000 earned by American pictures represented only 48 percent of the total distributors' share.

The effect on American earnings of the MPEA's boycott of the Danish market is visible in the data. From an amount of $1,400,000 in preboycott 1954, American earnings slid to $1,100,000 in 1955, dropped to $600,000 in 1956, increased by $100,000 in 1957, and recovered to $1,400,000 in 1958. While it is impossible to determine what earnings would have been had there been no boycott, an estimate can be offered based on earnings during the previous years. From 1951 to 1954 inclusive, American pictures returned annually to their distributors a consistent $1,400,000. Assuming this would have been the amount in 1955, 1956, and 1957, then earnings should have been $4,200,000 for these three years. In reality, they were only

TABLE 19

THE NETHERLANDS

Division of Net Box Office Receipts
($000,000)

	1947	1949	1951	1952	1953	1954	1955	1956	1957
American	8.4	7.5	7.2	7.2	6.5	7.5	8.1	8.4	7.3
British	2.5	.9	1.2	.9	1.3	1.3	1.1	1.5	1.8
French	1.5	.3	.6	.8	1.5	1.7	1.9	2.2	2.3
Italian	.1	.3	.5	.6	.7	1.2	1.3	1.5	1.3
West German[1]			.5	.9	.7	1.0	1.3	2.2	3.3
Other	.5	.9	.7	.7	.6	.5	.4	.4	.4
Dutch	.2	.2	.1	.1	.4	.1	.6	.3	.1
Total	13.2	10.1	10.8	11.2	11.7	13.3	14.7	16.5	16.5

	1958	1959	1960	1961	1962	1963	1964	1965	1966
American	6.8	6.4	6.2	6.5	7.0	7.7	7.3	7.4	7.8
British	2.5	2.2	2.1	2.5	2.1	2.3	3.0	4.2	4.1
French	2.2	1.8	1.8	2.4	2.3	2.1	2.4	2.9	3.4
Italian	.6	.4	.7	.9	2.1	2.4	1.9	1.5	1.9
West German[1]	3.9	3.3	3.1	2.4	1.8	1.3	1.0	1.0	.9
Other	.2	.5	1.0	.9	.5	.4	.6	.6	1.0
Dutch	.8	.3	.6	.5	.4	1.1	1.1	.1	.3
Total	17.0	14.9	15.5	16.1	16.2	17.3	17.3	17.7	19.4

[1] Earnings of West German films are included in the "Other" category in 1947 and 1949.
Source: Based upon data from Nederlandsche Bioscoop-Bond

$2,400,000. On this basis, the boycott cost American companies $1,800,000 in film rentals. The data in Table 18 reveal that the loss to America was a gain for other countries. Earnings of German, French, British, and Danish films increased during the boycott years.

Table 19 presents the net box office receipts for the Netherlands. As far as American earnings are concerned, the situation there is not very different from that in other countries. American films have lost ground at the box office as their actual, as well as percentage, share of the market has declined. In 1947, American pictures had net receipts of $8,400,000 in contrast to the 1966 amount of $7,800,000. Their

percentage share of the market has declined from a high of 74 percent
in 1949 to 40 percent in 1966.

In the late 1950's, an important portion of the Dutch box office
went to West German films. In 1951, the first year for which West
German earnings are given, they accounted for only $500,000 of the
net. In 1958, West German films earned $3,900,000. Since then,
their revenues have been shrinking; this reflects the trying conditions
through which their film industry has been going.

TABLE 20

FRANCE

Distribution Companies and Share of Market

	1956	1957	1958	1959	1960	1961	1962	1963	1964	1965
Total number of distributors	171	171	159	158	154	152	152	161	162	146
Local and regional	155	155	143	145	141	139	139	151	152	136
National	16	16	16	13	13	13	13	10	10	10
National Distributors										
French companies	8	8	8	6	6	6	6	3	3	3
% Share of total business	30.0	30.3	31.5	30.1	32.3	30.3	29.5	13.7	15.8	15.5
% Share of French film business	50.0	50.0	55.0	51.0	52.0	50.0	51.6	26.2	27.4	26.4
American companies	8	8	8	7	7	7	7	7	7	7
% Share of total business	36.0	33.1	33.8	32.9	32.0	33.6	34.5	38.1	39.9	35.0
% Share of American film business	90.0	90.0	90.0	90.0	91.0	91.0	84.7	83.7	83.1	79.4

Source: Centre National de la Cinématographie

This survey of American films in Europe has covered the number
of them available in markets and the revenue accruing from exhibition. Now a third element will be examined—the operation of American distribution companies. Data on this subject is rather spotty but
some points stand out.

Table 20 presents a breakdown of the distribution business in
France during recent years. Between 1956 and 1965, the total number
of distributors in the country declined from 171 to 146. Only a small
fraction of this number, however, are national companies servicing the
entire country. Of the sixteen national distributors operating in 1956
through 1958, eight were French and eight were American. By 1965,

only three French national distributors remained, but seven American companies were still operating. The concentration of business around national companies is apparent in the data. For the years considered, these companies accounted for at least half of the total distribution business in France although they represented only 6 to 10 percent of the operating companies.

Considering American distributors—they have accounted for about 5 percent of all companies but they have had a one-third share of total

TABLE 21

NORWAY

Films Distributed by American Companies

	1946	1947	1948	1949	1950	1951	1952	1953	1954	1955
Warners	4	28	11	20	25	24	17	28	17	21
Universal	24	23	25	23	28	30	24	23	22	23
Paramount[1]	16	29	15	18	22	23	31	27	21	17
M.G.M.[2]	24	21	22	28	32	30	23	16	38	23
Fox	18	24	22	29	27	33	31	34	29	33
Total	86	125	95	118	134	140	126	128	127	117
Total Films	373	401	362	328	415	395	395	360	392	370

	1956	1957	1958	1959	1960	1961	1962	1963	1964	1965	1966
Warners	19	17	24	13	14	13	46	26	33	34	38
Universal	18	24	25	11	12	17	16	27	22	23	20
Paramount[1]	16	15									
M.G.M.[2]	35	30	49	49	42	48					
Fox	28	32	30	24	28	36	58	67	44	19	20
Total	116	118	128	97	96	114	120	120	99	76	78
Total Films	368	397	414	393	331	428	373	363	342	348	354

[1] From April, 1958, to September, 1961, Paramount films were distributed by M.G.M. and later by Warner Bros. A/S.

[2] From March, 1962, to September, 1964, M.G.M. films were distributed by Fox and later by Fotorama.

Source: Kommunale Kinematografers Landsforbund

business. Moreover, they have a virtual monopoly on the distribution of important American films. The data point out that in recent years at least 80 percent of the business flowing from distribution of American pictures fell to American companies.

Table 21 summarizes the activities of American distributors operating in Norway. From 1946 through 1966, they handled more than 2,300 films, approximately 30 percent of the total 7,900. The data reveal that in recent years there has been a slight decline in the number of pictures distributed by these companies. But it is not as great as the drop in Hollywood's production. It appears that American companies are now acquiring non-American films for distribution to offset the contraction of Hollywood's supply. It also reflects the growing American investment in foreign film production which gives such companies distribution rights to them.

Four snapshots of film distribution in the United Kingdom are provided in Table 22. One interesting feature is the number of British films handled by American distributors. In 1947, seven American companies distributed 45 percent of all films registered but only 6 percent of the British pictures. In 1951, hardly any change is apparent. But between 1951 and 1958, a significant modification occurred in the policy of American companies. Although their share of all films remained fairly constant, they increased their distribution of British films and handled about a quarter of them. By 1967, American companies were distributing slightly less than half of all British pictures.

The list of distributors in 1967 lacks R.K.O., which dropped out of business, but includes Disney and Warner-Pathé. Concerning the latter, Warner Brothers acted independently until 1959 when, with Associated British-Pathé, it formed Warner-Pathé, with each company owning half. One could contend that Warner-Pathé should not be listed with American distributors. However, Associated British-Pathé is a subsidiary of Associated British Picture Corporation and a quarter of ABPC's ordinary shares are in the hands of Warner Brothers. Thus, the half ownership of Warner-Pathé and the quarter ownership of ABPC gives Warner Brothers an important position in this distribution company. (Between 1945 and 1961, Warner holdings of ABPC amounted to 37.5 percent.) Nonetheless, even if Warner-Pathé is excluded from the America list, the trend toward American distribution of British films is still valid, because 1967 saw 29 percent of them being handled by American companies.

The increased distribution of British films by American companies after 1951 reflects the number of them produced by American firms or financed with American money. This also is the period during which the British production subsidy plan went into effect.

Another dimension can be added to our considerations by data from West Germany showing the ages of American films released in Europe. In examining figures on the number of American features released in a certain country during a given year, one is apt to assume that films offered in, say, 1960, were produced in either that year or the one preceding. The data in Table 23, presenting the production year of films released in West Germany in 1964, indicate quite a different pattern.

TABLE 22

UNITED KINGDOM

Films[1] Registered for Distribution by Selected Companies
(Years Ending March 31)

	1947		1951		1958		1967	
	All	British	All	British	All	British	All	British
Total registered	350	81	566	128	561	136	364	84
20th Century-Fox	24	2	35	3	49	5	21	4
Columbia	41	1	71	4	41	10	24	5
M.G.M.	23	–	36	1	33	8	26	2
Paramount	15	–	23	–	20	–	23	6
United Artists	13	1	17	1	51	7	30	6
R.K.O.	23	1	20	1	16	1		
Disney							7	1
Warners	18	–	28	1	33	4		
Warner-Pathé							38	15
Total for above companies	157	5	230	11	243	35	169	39
Percent registered by above companies	44.9%	6.2%	40.6%	8.6%	43.3%	25.7%	46.4%	46.3%

[1] Films of 3,000 feet or more.

Source: 1947 and 1967: The Board of Trade Journal. (The Journal resumed publication of registrations in July, 1946. The 1947 period, therefore, reflects registrations from July 9, 1946 to March 31, 1947.) 1951 and 1958: Political and Economic Planning, The British Film Industry 1958 (London: Political and Economic Planning, 1958)

Of course, there is bound to be a time lag between completion of production and first release. A generous estimate would allow two years. However, if a film were produced in the United States in 1958 and not released in the German market until 1964, one would have to conclude that it was held back deliberately or that a shortage of new product in 1964 offered the chance to resurrect this picture.

Table 23 points out that of the 124 American releases in 1964,

TABLE 23

WEST GERMANY

Production Year of Feature Films Released in 1964

	Pre-1940	1940–1944	1945–1949	1950–1954	1955–1959	1960	1961	1962	1963	1964
American	4	2	2	9	5	2	–	8	58	34
British	1	–	–	–	1	1	2	2	25	9
French	–	–	–	–	–	1	2	5	5	4
Italian	–	–	–	–	–	3	6	12	19	1
French-Italian Coproductions	–	–	–	–	–	1	1	5	41	15
Other	1	–	–	–	5	5	7	8	21	17
Total Foreign	6	2	2	9	11	13	18	40	169	80
West German	3	–	–	–	–	–	1	–	17	53
Total	9	2	2	9	11	13	19	40	186	133

Source: Spitzenorganisation der Filmwirtschaft

twenty-four were produced in 1961 or earlier. Of these twenty-four films, seventeen were made prior to 1955 with four being in the pre-1940 period. It is apparent that films released in a given year are not necessarily new ones and that some may have needed dusting off before they were reissued, also that films released in 1958 are not necessarily withdrawn in 1959. They continue to be available, and when added to films released in following years, the total grows into a large pool. In a sense, data on the number of annual releases obscure this reservoir of already released films, a group which is considerably larger than the number of new films entering the market each year.

Table 24 presents the number of films in circulation annually in France. The data disclose that the quantity of films in release has fluctuated between a low of about 3,300 and a high of almost 4,100. In 1966, there were 4,078 films available for exhibition, more than 1,100 of them being American pictures of various ages. The total number also includes almost 1,500 French features.

A logical question is: When were all these films released? The

TABLE 24

FRANCE

Nationality of Films in Circulation

	1951	*1952*	*1953*	*1954*	*1955*	*1956*	*1957*	*1958*
American	1,482	1,431	1,301	1,224	1,130	1,122	1,136	1,123
British[1]		196	178	175	166	168	192	211
Italian	170	213	221	253	272	285	270	262
West German[2]								
Other	570	470	559	619	717	752	746	774
Total Foreign	2,222	2,310	2,259	2,271	2,285	2,327	2,344	2,370
French	1,491	1,264	1,098	1,078	1,098	1,115	1,105	1,12 0
Total	3,713	3,574	3,357	3,349	3,383	3,442	3,449	3,490

	1959	*1960*	*1961*	*1962*	*1963*	*1964*	*1965*	*1966*
American	1,116	1,072	1,034	1,061	1,019	1,036	1,095	1,131
British[1]	202	222	232	220	223	242	236	255
Italian	268	240	228	236	257	280	304	314
West German[2]		366	367	360	337	332	316	300
Other	789	495	515	522	520	580	586	611
Total Foreign	2,375	2,395	2,376	2,399	2,356	2,470	2,537	2,611
French	1,138	1,185	1,231	1,302	1,348	1,394	1,452	1,467
Total	3,513	3,580	3,607	3,701	3,704	3,864	3,989	4,078

[1] In 1951, the number of British films circulating was not separately tabulated and is included in the "Other" classification.

[2] From 1951 to 1959 inclusive, the numbers of German films circulating were not separately tabulated. They are included in the "Other" classification.

Source: Centre National de la Cinématographie

answer is provided in Table 25 which indicates the number of films circulating in 1966 broken down by the year of their first release. American films of all ages accounted for 1,131 of the 4,078. This American total was composed of 313 pictures released in 1964 and later, and 818 released for the first time before 1964. The latter figure represents 72 percent of American features exhibited in France during 1966. On the other hand, this same group of pre-1964 films accounted for only 33 percent of the spectators for all American pictures, 36 percent of the performances, and 38 percent of the taxable receipts. On this basis, it is clear that new American films, although accounting for only a quarter of American pictures on the market, get the lion's share of the business.[3]

One point remains to be considered before this chapter is concluded. It is the total revenue accruing to pictures with American nationality. Sufficient data are at our disposal about the major markets of the United Kingdom, Italy, France, and West Germany to permit a calculation of the amount of money American films have returned to their distributors during the fifteen-year period 1951 to 1965. While British data do not permit a precise tabulation of net earnings of American films there, enough is known about that market to estimate conservatively that rentals for American features have averaged about $35,000,000 annually for the period under consideration.

From the four markets, and based upon data already presented, American films have returned to their distributors at least $1,500,000,000 from 1951 to 1965 inclusive. In consideration of the

TABLE 25

FRANCE

Year of First Release of Films Circulating in 1966

	Pre-1960	1960	1961	1962	1963	1964	1965	1966
American	484	78	73	102	81	109	113	91
British	80	19	23	18	20	34	31	30
Italian	43	17	35	43	54	44	37	41
German	68	55	44	32	36	37	17	11
Other	184	64	48	52	66	76	58	63
Total Foreign	859	233	223	247	257	300	256	236
French	510	113	134	160	137	143	146	124
Total	1,369	346	357	407	394	443	402	360

Source: Centre National de la Cinématographie

smaller markets of Finland, Sweden, Norway, Denmark, the Netherlands, Belgium, Switzerland, Austria, Ireland, Spain, and Portugal, the figure should be increased by at least $350,000,000. The combined total for these fifteen years then would become almost $1,900,000,000. This is the sum reverting to distributors of American films (mainly American companies); and, of course, a share of it would go to producers.

The figure does not represent the earnings of American companies nor the amount actually remitted to the United States, both being impossible to determine. It should be stressed that this estimate is on the conservative side. Rentals for individual American films have increased in recent years, with some getting as much as 70 percent of the gross in key theatres in certain countries. These high rental rates obviously are diminished in size when the *average* share of the gross going to distributors is the basis of calculation.

Nevertheless, the money earned by American films represents some loss of revenue to European producers. This amount cannot be estimated in any practical way. The fact that American films are on the market and that they have drawn considerable sums from European box offices means that European producers have that much less opportunity to broaden the base on which they must amortize their investments. However, one new market for European films has opened recently and the next chapter considers it.

4: European Films in the American Market

The United States, with 200,000,000 people speaking the same language and spending billions on entertainment, is the world's wealthiest film market. To the European producer, it is a market without a screen quota or an import quota. Officially, the United States is a free market, and a film from Sweden or Italy has as much opportunity of being released as a Hollywood production. This large, rich, easily accessible market, when viewed superficially, gives the impression that a foreign producer merely has to export to the United States and watch the money flow back to him. For the British producer, it would seem easiest of all because he has no language problem with which to contend and does not have to face dubbing or subtitling costs.

Admittedly, this view of the market has not been supported by reality. The United States has been one of the most difficult markets for European films to enter. Until the early 1950's, the American film industry was producing pictures in such quantity that there was generally a sufficient supply to fill the demands of exhibitors in the United States. When demand exceeded output, old films were available for reissue. This condition had its foundation in the vertically integrated film industry in which large companies owned production, distribution, and exhibition facilities. The monopolistic structure of the industry and the coordination between exhibition and production assured a continuous flow of product. Studios were geared to quantities of production based upon what the company-owned houses could absorb. Horizontal coordination helped to provide stability for major distribution companies which did not own such chains. Due to the ownership pattern of theatres, there was little desire to import films and little if any screen time available in which to show them. American producers had their own film investments to amortize and this could not be done if their theatres were playing foreign pictures. When American companies were attracted by a foreign actor, director, or technical expert, they usually brought him to Hollywood to make films rather than import the films he had made in Europe. The structure of the industry was based upon the mass production of films exploited profitably in company-owned theatres and block booked into independent houses. To introduce foreign films would have meant disrupting the production-distribution-exhibition chain and voluntarily giving away a portion of the box office to foreign producers. In monopolizing the home market, American companies were following the dictates of economic self-interest.

This policy had other implications for foreign films. As long as they were not being exhibited widely, they remained in the category of the "untried and unproven." Who would be willing to gamble on importing a film, dubbing or subtitling it, then advertising it, without any precedents? Few people in the industry could even guess how a given foreign film would do at the box office—if it could get wide bookings. In short, there were no indications that large scale importation and distribution of foreign pictures could be a profitable business.

As foreign films remained unknown, so did their stars. In a market where films are sold to the public on the basis of actors' names, there is slight chance for any film which cannot be publicized in this way. If an American distributor located an excellent foreign film and considered acquiring it for the United States market, he would certainly think about its merchandising possibilities. When the actor's name is unknown, there is that much less to be said about a film, and it must be brought to the public's attention in other ways, predominantly through the exploitation of sexual themes.[1]

The integrated companies' policy of monopolizing the market had other consequences. Since the introduction of sound, American audiences had consumed a steady diet of American accent sound tracks. These audiences grew accustomed to hear American English spoken from the screen in perfect synchronization with lip movements of actors because they had little opportunity to hear anything else. True, some foreign actors speaking English did become popular with American audiences, but these exceptions existed because their accents were often vital to the roles they played and the images they created. If non-English foreign films were to be introduced, they had to be subtitled or dubbed. Subtitling requires the audience to read the translated text of what the actors are saying. To certain types of audiences, this procedure is cumbersome and distracting.[2] Experienced film importers readily acknowledge that subtitled films lack wide-spread box office appeal. The alternative is dubbing, the substitution of an American sound track for the original. This solves much of the problem but only if the dubbing is precisely matched to lip movements, often impossible to achieve. Dubbing has been adopted predominantly for films and prints sent into wide distribution and is practically mandatory for television as the subtitles are often lost below the bottom of the home screen. Nevertheless, language has not been the main reason for the spotty success of foreign films in the United States.

In the face of these barriers to the importation and circulation of foreign pictures, many have had rentals of more than $1,000,000 in the American market, although this generally has occurred only during the last ten years. A series of events changed the market structure in the United States to make it more fertile for foreign films. The most obvious has been the decline in the number of films made in Hollywood, with today's production less than half of what it was twenty years ago. Even though many theatres have closed, the current level of production does not fill American screen time, and television has stolen the market for reissues. The gap between exhibition's demand and Hollywood's supply is being filled by foreign films.

The antitrust decisions against vertically integrated film companies, while being linked with production declines, broke the production-distribution-exhibition chain which had prevailed for decades. Exhibition was forced to stand alone and monopolies of theatres were dissolved.[3] The business of exhibition became solely to exhibit, rather than to provide the assured outlet for Hollywood's producers. The end of vertical integration made exhibition policy one of outright self-interest—exhibitors would play any film that was likely to draw patrons. In the words of the industry: "If films made by Eskimos would bring in money, exhibitors would play them."

At the time when the production decline and the new exhibition independence helped to open the United States to foreign films, weekly attendance here was declining rapidly. Scapegoats were sought and found to explain the diminishing audience, and the content of Hollywood's production was one not overlooked. With the spread of television, even the uncritical eye could see that programs made for TV were similar to (Grade B) movies in content and that the Matinee Theatre and the Late Show brought stars into the living room. But there was one important difference; after the initial investment in the receiver, television was free. With competitive free entertainment being offered, exhibitors reasoned that perhaps the public was tiring of paying for Hollywood's traditional content, so well spelled out in the old Production Code. Acquisition of foreign films offered the chance to experiment in luring the missing millions of viewers back to theatres. Foreign films with fresh (and flesh) appeal were called upon to revitalize theatre programs. This experiment produced mixed results, for some foreign films brought in attractive revenues while many others failed to display any box office value.

With the exhibitor's new freedom to select, theatre owners had to devise ways of merchandising foreign films to a public which had hardly been exposed to them. Edward L. Hyman, vice president of United Paramount Theatres, speaking to a gathering of exhibitors in 1954, declared that because of the film shortage "it might be wise for exhibitors in this country to consider ways and means of popularizing the foreign film." In introducing foreign films, he said, they would be "seeking to establish an audience where there has been none before," and that they ought to "proceed with patience and foresight." Mr. Hyman felt exhibitors should consider opening theatres "that will present art and foreign pictures in a small way—until such time as the idea has expanded. . . ." He told the theatre operator: "You are a pioneer bringing a new entertainment form to many people and people don't develop tastes over night."[4]

Other factors contributed to the increased importation and success of foreign films, among them being the modification in policy of the Hollywood majors. During the years after World War II, American film earnings in Europe were not permitted to be taken to the United States. As we have seen, this stemmed from the balance of payments problem facing European nations and their desire not to export currency. Anxious to market their films in Europe, the American companies had essentially three alternatives for the disposal of their revenues. First, they could leave their earnings in blocked accounts and wait until remittance to the United States was permitted. Second, they could purchase foreign goods and ship them to the United States where they could be sold for dollars. Or, finally, they could produce films abroad. The American companies took mostly the third alternative and thereby brought about significant changes in their production policies.

At the time of this decision, American producers became aware that their domestic market was no longer providing the bulk of revenue for their films. They recognized that Europe, the major overseas market, was rivalling the United States in the amount of earnings their own films generated. Perhaps in an attempt to secure the American position in Europe, producers increased the use of foreign stars in their films. The names of foreign stars incorporated in American productions, initially a move to enhance the attraction of American films abroad, soon became known to American audiences. This was a definite benefit for the foreign film in the United States because American audiences began to recognize the same names in non-American pictures.[5]

American producers, in using their blocked earnings, came to realize the advantages of shooting films in Europe. There were authentic locales available (the Riviera, for instance, being impossible to duplicate), labor costs were often less (film crews and armies of extras could be hired cheaply), and the absence of daily supervision by company management (made difficult by distance) provided a little more liberty. In addition, some European governments offered subsidies to domestic film production providing a picture met certain qualifications. American producers availed themselves of this by joining with European producers in the making of films which were technically American but legally "French," "Italian," or "British." The American financial stake in these pictures dictated that they be brought into the American market for exploitation. Again, American companies were acting according to their self-interest, but how different this self-interest had become! Until the early 1950's, it called for keeping foreign films out of the American market so that investment in domestic production could be amortized more quickly. Before the end of the 1950's, producers' self-interest demanded that foreign films be imported so that their investment in *them* could be amortized.

As American producers were joining hands with European producers, so were American distributors and to a smaller extent, exhibitors. To insure the acquisition of potential box office attractions, American distributing companies began offering distribution guarantees to secure at least the right to handle foreign films in the United States. This is a form of production financing in which a distributor advances a portion of the expected box office revenue in exchange for the distribution rights in particular markets. The acquisition of films in this way reflects the short supply of American pictures. The American distributing companies, insufficiently supplied by their own production affiliates, turn to nonaffiliates and secure films from them to fill out the lists which they offer to exhibitors. The widespread use of this method of financing today by American companies indicates they recognize the box office power of European-made films. It also means that they have brought into the American market more and more foreign films because they have a direct financial interest in them.

In some cases, major Hollywood companies acquired subsidiaries to import and distribute foreign films in the United States. The subsidiary is also a useful device for avoiding restrictions of the Production Code Administration and for handling pictures (American or foreign) which have received low or condemned ratings from the Legion of Decency or its successor, the National Catholic Office for Motion Pictures. In each case, the parent company can truthfully declare that it is not distributing films of questionable morality, while, through its subsidiary, it can participate in the box office revenues accruing to these films.

Lopert Pictures, affiliated with United Artists, was the distributor of *Never On Sunday*, a film released in the United States without the Production Code Administration's approval seal and with a condemned rating from the Legion of Decency. Completed at a reported cost of about $150,000, *Never On Sunday* had gross rentals in the United States of about $4,000,000. More recently, Lopert distributed *Phaedra, That Man from Rio,* and *The Knack.* Kingsley-International, which was an affiliate of Columbia Pictures, was responsible for American release of *And God Created Woman,* the French film which made Brigitte Bardot a star in this market.

In at least one instance, an American exhibitor became active in bringing foreign films into the United States. The scope of operation, however, went beyond mere importation, for it also involved production financing. Continental Distributing was established in the early 1950's by Walter Reade to acquire foreign films for his Baronet Theatre in New York City. (Reade now operates almost fifty theatres, predominantly in the eastern part of the United States.) The original purpose of Continental was soon obscured by the company's policy of distributing its imports to other theatres. To stabilize the flow of product, Reade, through Continental, began investing in foreign film production. Continental has brought a number of important and impressive films to the United States. They include two Alec Guinness pictures, *To Paris With Love* and *The Lady Killers, Gervaise, The Entertainer, The Mark, Saturday Night and Sunday Morning, A Taste of Honey, Room at the Top,* and Jacques Tati's *Mon Oncle.* Several of these films were partially financed by Continental and many are now in television distribution in the United States.

It would seem that foreign films are taking a portion of the American box office and making it more difficult for American producers to recoup their investments in their own home market. Eric Johnston once observed that "this rising foreign competition has come at a time when the financial position of the domestic industry has been adversely affected by a combination of factors. . . ."[6] It is true, of course, that pure foreign films have made inroads at the American box office. But an equally valid point is that the foreign pictures playing in the American market are here because American companies have brought them. It is not a simple case of competition between American and foreign films. It is a matter of "runaway investment" which is as real as "runaway production." The latter term describes the practice of American companies which prefer to shoot a film abroad rather than in Hollywood's own studios. "Runaway investment" refers to American companies' investing their money in *foreign* film production, production which is foreign-based to begin with and probably never would take place in Hollywood.

The point is that there is an American investment in these films, whether they are American films shot on location abroad or true foreign films made in their native countries—although the distinction is increasingly difficult to draw. In reviewing the role of American investment in foreign production, one would have to conclude that the foreign-made films which have achieved the widest circulation and the most significant financial returns in this country have been those in which American companies have had direct monetary interests. What is happening is the increased channeling of American money into foreign-produced films which were restricted in the United States market until the early 1950's.

The American majors, with the only worldwide film distribution system, have had a virtual monopoly of distribution in the American market. This control has consequences for the circulation of foreign films in the United States (and in other markets as well). Before the majors actively began acquiring non-American pictures, foreign producers faced the very real problem of achieving wide distribution and promotion in the United States. There existed, of course, a corps of small independent distributors working within cities or areas who were experienced in importing films. In New York City thirty years ago, a handful of theatres did exhibit subtitled films, and exhibition was often arranged for them in a few theatres in other metropolitan areas. There were other distributors, but their experience came almost exclusively from importing original versions which were shown without subtitles or dubbed sound tracks to theatres serving ethnic minorities. In this way, a substantial number of Mexican, Chinese, Greek, German, and Japanese films were imported annually, but their circulation was limited.

Foreign producers who sought access to the United States were confronted with a problem of means. The independents who had been importing films were not geared, either in staff or finances, to launch broad promotion and distribution work. The majors, on the other hand, were organized to do this, but they were not interested in bothering with foreign-made films as long as Hollywood was maintaining its productive capacity.

The lack of an adequate distribution organization in the United States for foreign pictures was one problem which had to be solved. Few foreign distributors were large enough to be willing to undertake a venture of this size, for it meant starting an organization that might be larger than the ones existing in their home markets. One company, however, elected to try. The Rank Organisation, through its managing director John Davis, consistently charged that vested interests in the United States were at work to discourage the importation, distribution, and exhibition of foreign, notably British, films. In early 1957, the Rank Organisation announced that it was establishing Rank Film Distributors of America (RFDA) to penetrate the United States market while by-passing American companies. By March of that year, ten offices had been set up and theatres were leased in key cities to play Rank products. *Variety* reported:

> There is no question in the mind of American observers that the Rank willingness to lease houses in cities where he feels he isn't getting proper release is a wise one and could pay dividends. . . . [The] only question raised . . . is whether the Rank product is strong enough to meet the competition on a continuous basis.[7]

The Rank Organisation did not expect immediate profits from its expansion move and recognized that it would take time to establish itself in the American market. By mid-1958, RFDA had more than one dozen offices in the United States even though industry rumors insisted that the company was absorbing great business losses. In March, 1959, after a two-year experiment, the Rank Organisation announced that "owing to difficulties existing in the industry" it was closing its offices in the United States.[8] The statement revealed that Lopert Pictures had been engaged to distribute films which Rank already had available in the American market.

At the annual Rank stockholders meeting in September, 1959, John Davis declined to reveal how much the Organisation had lost in its attempt to penetrate the United States market. He told stockholders:

> Unfortunately, after 18 months operation it became clear there was no reasonable prospect of achieving a profitable operation . . . and it was decided to terminate our losses, full provision for which has been made in the accounts. Our attempts to open up this valuable market for British films through our own distribution organisation have thus failed, but I feel that at the time we commenced the venture we were justified in our efforts. Unfortunately, the trend of the industry has been against us.[9]

It was felt that many films Rank brought to the United States were simply not good box office material here. In contrast to *Pursuit of the Graf Spee,* which reportedly had rentals close to $500,000, a large number of other Rank films did not earn more than $50,000 or $75,000. One other factor possibly contributing to the collapse of RFDA was the large overhead caused by the operation of more than a dozen offices throughout the United States. It is known that during the months immediately preceding the halt in operation, Rank undertook stringent economy moves by reducing staffs and closing several of its branch offices. The unsuccessful attempt by Rank to penetrate the market by establishing its own distribution system has been one of the few large scale efforts in this direction by European producers. They realize that if they want to sell their products in the United States they must work through American distributors, either the independents or the majors. This sore experience is behind the current thought in Europe which looks toward an amalgamation of several key European companies to establish a competitive distribution chain, not only in the United States, but world-wide.

The British film industry has not been the only one interested in penetrating the American market. Several years before the Rank effort, the Italian film industry had made an abortive invasion but had relied upon American companies for financial support.

The Italian expansion move can be traced to early 1951 when the MPEA was negotiating with the Italian industry for a film trade agreement on the importation of American pictures in Italy. In February of that year, the Italian industry, supported by the government, demanded that financial returns on their films in the United States be guaranteed. The Italians asked American companies to distribute some thirty films annually with a guaranteed net return averaging about $40,000 per film. The MPEA rejected this proposal and negotiations became deadlocked.

Three months passed before an agreement could be reached between the MPEA and ANICA. The resulting pact, effective in July, 1951, and running for two years, declared that 12.5 percent of American earnings in Italy were to be paid to a new Italian company. One of its functions was to be importing Italian films for the United States market. In essence, this agreement authorized American companies operating in Italy to indirectly subsidize the circulation of Italian films in this market. Apparently nothing of this nature had been done before. The new company, Italian Film Export (IFE), was supposed to become a dollar earner for Italy, which was facing a serious balance of payments problem. A trade source in the United States reported:

> American companies are anxious that IFE get going full force, since they feel the pact is advantageous to them. They think that by creating dollar income for the Italians through exhibition of their [pictures] in the U. S., the government in Rome will be encouraged to allow [American companies] to withdraw all or most of their [blocked] earnings there. Should IFE not prove effective, there's a likelihood the government won't permit its continuance and cut off the funds now being converted as part of the subsidy deal.[10]

IEF began operating in the American market by publicizing Italian pictures and by having Italian film stars make personal appearances. By the end of 1952, it had also established a subsidiary, IFE Releasing Corporation, to handle the distribution of Italian pictures. Producers in Italy were not obligated to channel their films through IFE although the company hoped to attract them by offering specialized knowledge of Italian film making and broad promotional work.

In early 1953, negotiations were resumed between the MPEA and ANICA for a new film agreement to replace the one expiring in June, 1953. The MPEA opposed a further subsidy. On the other hand, the Italians insisted that the subsidy be continued, although they were willing to reduce the amount from 12.5 to 10 percent of American earnings. Meanwhile, independent film distributors in the United States were growing unhappy over the role of IFE. The Independent Motion Picture Distributors Association of America (IMPDAA) charged that IFE was acquiring the good Italian films for the American market and distributing these on terms which the independents could not meet. IMPDAA contended that IFE was not interested in making a profit and was willing to pay Italian producers higher fees for their films. The MPEA had not liked the 1951 subsidy arrangement but had accepted it in exchange for Italian concessions on other points. In 1953, the MPEA found itself the target of charges from IMPDAA, which claimed the MPEA was subsidizing IFE, and the target of proposals from the Italians who wanted the subsidy to be continued. The dilemma was that the MPEA was being charged with restraining competition, yet if it discontinued its policy of subsidization, it might face further restrictions in the Italian market, which was worth at least $15,000,000 annually at that time.

The MPEA was able to devise a compromise that seemed to suit all parties except itself. It agreed to continue the payments to IFE but at a rate of 10 percent of American earnings in Italy. The MPEA demanded, and the Italians agreed, that the money could not be used for the distribution of Italian pictures in the United States—it could be used only for promotional work. This agreement was to become effective in July, 1953, and run for one year.

Later in 1953, independent American distributors, renewing their charges that IFE was competing unfairly, again brought their case to the MPEA. The MPEA reportedly responded that it had understood the subsidy paid under the 1951 agreement was to be used only for promoting and publicizing Italian pictures, not for distribution. The MPEA declared that it was surprised when IFE organized its distribution subsidiary in 1952. Nonetheless, when the 1951 agreement was announced in the American trade press, there was clear reference to IFE acting as a distributor in addition to a film promoter. In August, 1951, *Variety* reported:

> Several former top sales [executives] for major American companies are reportedly under consideration by the recently-formed co-op of Italian film producers to head a nationwide distribution organization for Italo films in the U. S. Setup will be financed, in effect, by Hollywood, with a potential of $3,000,000. . . .
>
> Organization, to be known as Italian Film Export (IFE), is an outgrowth of the Italo-U. S. film pact which became effective July 1. Under that agreement a sum equal to 12½ percent of their earnings in Italy . . . is to be advanced by American distribs to Italian producers for establishment of the distribution and promotion organization in the U. S.[11]

In February, 1954, the Independent Motion Picture Distributors Association of America brought its case to the Federal Trade Commission. The independents declared that the subsidized IFE, by distributing Italian films, was interfering with "free and fair competition" and that "a monopoly in the distribution of such films" was being approached. The complaint stated that "the manner in which IFE has been subsidized is also, in the opinion of IMPDAA, a violation of law" because "funds derived from a United States export association [MPEA] were utilized to lessen competition within the United States."[12] While IMPDAA's charges seemed to implicate the MPEA on one hand, they tended to absolve the MPEA on another by declaring that "IMPDAA does not contend that MPEA intended or even suspected that its funds would be utilized by IFE to subsidize the distribution of films in the U.S."[13] It would appear that the independents either accepted the MPEA's contention that it knew nothing about IFE's distribution activities, or that they reached an entente with the MPEA. Conceivably, the agreement could have resulted in the complaint against IFE but was worded to make MPEA appear innocent of the affair. The anticipated outcome could have been an FTC ruling that MPEA subsidies were illegal and had to stop. This would serve the purpose of IMPDAA while extracting the MPEA from the subsidy arrangement which it had never liked.

At the time IMPDAA made its charges to the FTC, the MPEA was preparing to resume negotiations with the Italian industry for a new agreement to replace the one expiring in June, 1954. These negotiations produced the 1954 film agreement which formally ended MPEA's payments to IFE. In reporting the details of the new pact, *Variety* noted:

> Elimination of the subsidy is a major victory for the Americans who have pointed out to the Italians that, due to a variety of circumstances including Federal Trade Commission pressure, they'll no longer be in a position to grant the aid.[14]

It appears that IMPDAA's complaint to the Federal Trade Commission had brought desirable results for itself and the MPEA.[15]

The 1954 pact officially terminated the relationship between the American majors and IFE. For three years, the MPEA had been subsidizing the Italian film industry in its efforts to penetrate the American market. Eric Johnston estimated that during this period the MPEA had paid between $4,000,000 and $4,500,000 to the Italians.[16] In one sense, this can be considered the price Americans had to pay for the privilege of doing business in Italy. If they had not agreed to the subsidy, probably they would have faced severe restrictions on their films in the Italian market. The affair also indicates that the MPEA was so concerned about its position in Italy as to agree to the subsidy even though this allegedly jeopardized the position of independent distributors in the United States. As for IFE, sources in the American industry believe that while the company did make an effort to penetrate the market it was never paticularly successful in generating bigger box offices for Italian films. Some observers believe that IFE Releasing was not even a money-making subsidiary for IFE and that few dollars were ever remitted to Italy. In 1955 IFE closed its dubbing studio in New York, and in the months following the entire IFE structure underwent organizational changes. Subsequently, export promotion for the Italian film industry became a function of a newly created official body, Unitalia, which now operates on a worldwide basis. IFE, as it was originally established in 1951, no longer exists.

At the time the MPEA was involved with IFE, the French realized they too might be able to obtain a subsidy from American companies to penetrate this market more extensively. The French plan was announced as early as July, 1951, and called for the MPEA to donate approximately a quarter of a million dollars to finance an organization which would promote and release French films in the United States. The proposal was not pursued seriously until the following year when discussions took place concerning a new film agreement covering the circulation of American films in France. In contrast to negotiations in Italy which were carried on between the MPEA and ANICA, those in France were conducted on the governmental level with American State Department representatives there, assisted by the MPEA, bargaining with the French government for a film agreement.

Negotiations in early 1952 became deadlocked when the French insisted that, in exchange for increasing the importation of American films, the MPEA agree to pay a subsidy to French producers so their films could be promoted more extensively in America. The MPEA and the State Department rejected the proposal, the latter believing that the film subsidy would set a bad precedent for other industries.

During the summer of 1952, the French revised their demands by withdrawing the subsidy proposal and replacing it with a "discount" plan. Details of the plan are somewhat vague but apparently it was to bring at least $250,000 to French producers, the amount originally said to be needed for the creation of a French film office in the United States. While the sum would not come directly from American companies' earnings (as it did in Italy), the arrangements were such that

American companies would have earnings $250,000 less than if there had been no "discount." In this form, the agreement probably was more palatable to the State Department as it expressly did not involve a direct subsidy. Moreover, the pact between France and the United States is said to have specified that the money could not be used for distributing French films in the American market, but only for promotion and publicity.

Whether the arrangements with France constituted a subsidy is a moot point. In any event, the French obtained money from American companies to penetrate this market. There was at least one group, however, which did consider this to be a subsidy. The president of the Society of Independent Motion Picture Producers (SIMPP), Ellis Arnall, brought the matter to the State Department. In a letter to the then Secretary of State John Foster Dulles, Mr. Arnall asked whether the terms of the agreement with France were "in line with the general economic and foreign policies of the government." Mr. Arnall, a former governor of Georgia, declared that the pact enabled the French to obtain funds from the MPEA

> to use in an unrestricted fashion for the production, exploitation, advertisement or even the exhibition of French pictures in the U. S. as well as in other countries in competition with pictures of American producers who are not members of the MPEA to their injury and detriment.[17]

He charged that the agreement amounted to a purchase by the MPEA of economic privileges from the French government, privileges denied to American competitors of the MPEA who also desired to do business in France. He declared that SIMPP wished to be advised whether "such subsidy arrangements have the approbation and approval of the Department of State."

It is important to distinguish Mr. Arnall's charges from those IMPDAA made against the MPEA's relations with IFE. IMPDAA was concerned lest IFE monopolize the distribution of Italian pictures in the United States. Mr. Arnall and SIMPP charged that money which found its way to the French industry was being used to support distribution of French films in the American and other world markets.

The MPEA responded to the complaint by denying that it was subsidizing French films. It declared that the money, representing "the settlement of an outstanding debt," was being paid to an agency of the French government which could dispose of it in any way it saw fit.[18] In addition, the MPEA said that the State Department had been kept fully informed of this arrangement and had not expressed disapproval of it.

Mr. Arnall's charges to the State Department apparently brought no result as the pact continued to be operative. This meant that the State Department was in tacit agreement with the principle of American companies' paying tribute for the privilege of operating in certain foreign countries. It also reflected the State Department's concern with the propaganda value of American films and its desire to see that they be circulated abroad with as few restraints as possible. It is known that "subsidies" similar to the one executed with France existed in other countries. The arrangement with France helped to secure the position of MPEA companies in that country and allegedly worked to support the circulation of French films in foreign markets at the expense of pictures from independent American producers.

Did French films in the United States benefit from this plan? Eric Johnston said in 1954 that the MPEA paid about a quarter of a million dollars to the French, an amount "hardly enough for them to set up any distribution organization" in the American market.[19] He declared he did not know what the French intended to do with the money but he thought they would use it to promote their films in the United States. The payment to the French government, he said, was a necessary compromise which had to be made during the negotiations for a film agreement.[20]

An increase in French film earnings in the United States as a result of the "subsidy" is unlikely. Jacques Flaud, then the director of the Centre National de la Cinématographie, declared in 1956 that the French considered their returns from the American market to be insignificant. He was quoted as saying that "even if they improved 100 percent, they would still be ridiculously small."[21] This was supported later the same year by a report from France's Economic Council, an advisory group composed of industrial, governmental, and labor union representatives. The Council's report on the film industry recommended, among other points, an export policy based on "equitable and reciprocal exchanges" which would do away with a "shocking lack of proportion." The report pointed to the "still insufficient" returns from the foreign markets and, as if speaking about the American market, declared:

> It is abnormal and unjust that certain foreign countries are able to make enormous receipts in France . . . while their market rejects all reciprocal exchange and remains closed to French pictures.

(In 1956, American films in France returned to their distributors approximately $15,500,000 while French films in the United States reportedly earned only $2,200,000.) The report continued:

> . . . in regard to the American market, impenetrable to French films, particular encouragement should be given to French companies who would attempt opening this market with a university circuit. If this circuit would, financially speaking, bring no immediate profit . . . it would at least create customers for French pictures later, say in five or ten years.[22]

The Council's report also recommended financial aid to French companies which sought to operate showcase theatres in the United States.

Thus, the three major European film industries, the British, the Italian and, to a lesser extent, the French, had developed plans and organizations for penetrating the American market and for bringing wider circulation to their films. Each of these formal attempts collapsed or was replaced by a modified structure. While these efforts may have failed to bring greater immediate revenues for European films, they have succeeded in the long run by introducing previously "unknown quantities" to the American public.

The road for foreign films in the United States has not been easy, yet it must be admitted that they have made progress. The advance can be attributed to several things. There has been the outstanding success of a handful of foreign films which have attracted public and industry attention, significant box office returns, and great critical acclaim. At the same time, foreign industries have been constantly pushing to get more of their products into the American market. This has coincided with a subtle reeducation of the American audience and the American industry—the producer, distributor, and exhibitor. In addition, the policy of the American majors has undergone a significant change which is directly related to the decline in availability of Hollywood films. The interaction of these factors has generated a market condition in which foreign films are now a fairly consistent offering in the nation's theatres. Moreover, as the supply of Hollywood films dwindles because of television's demand for programming material, foreign-made films are finding their way to the home screen.

As for statistical material pertaining to the circulation of foreign films in the American market, it must again be recognized at the outset that there are no *official* or precise tabulations available. European governments often report transfers of film earnings from the

United States but this hardly gives a clue to actual box office receipts. Moreover, the United States government, unlike most in Europe, does not maintain checks on box office receipts by nationality nor on the number of films imported. This lack of reliable data is regrettable. Even the American industry, as far as can be determined, does not maintain records on the circulation and earnings of foreign films.

Evidently the only estimates are those published by *Variety*, but even they exist only for 1956 through 1964. In itself, this indicates two trends. First, it is quite probable that the revenue earning ability of foreign films was so limited in the early 1950's that the American trade press did not bother compiling and reporting the results. For example, *Variety* noted in reporting foreign film activities in 1956 that "foreign grosses in U. S. have never been published until now."[23] Second, discontinuance of *Variety* surveys after 1964 points to the increasing difficulty of determining exactly what is a foreign film. It is impossible in many cases to differentiate the source of financing in the increasingly complex production arrangements involving American and foreign companies. While this might not be true for, say, Swedish pictures, it is the case for British, Italian, and French films. Without a workable standard for determining precisely what makes a film "foreign," it becomes impractical to try to estimate earnings.

Variety tabulations have spotlighted this problem.[24] From 1959 to 1964, foreign films include those either wholly or partially financed by American interests and which met nationality requirements of the countries in which they were made. The same might also be true for the 1958 data. Although *Variety* made no explicit statement that year, it recognized as "British" *Bridge on the River Kwai*, a film produced by Sam Spiegel and distributed by Columbia, which had gross rentals of more than $14,000,000 in the United States. The 1957 data, by contrast, do not include a number of American-financed British films, even though they met nationality requirements. In 1956, *Variety* made no mention of the problem in reporting its findings.

Variety obtained its figures by questioning film importers. It is possible that a few distributors have not been checked (or declined to cooperate) and so the data should be considered as representing the minimum number of films imported. As for earnings, there might be a tendency on the part of some importers to swell their stated revenues to paint a healthy picture. On the other hand, some importers and their earnings might have been missed.

Another point for caution is that *Variety*'s tabulations refer to the

American *and Canadian* markets. Unfortunately, there is no way to determine the portion of earnings or the number of films for only the American market. It is reasonable to assume, though, that a film dubbed or subtitled in English would be released in both markets. Regarding earnings, the situation is somewhat more difficult because it is not known whether Canadian movie-going habits differ from those in the United States, or if rental arrangements differ. Of course, the population ratio of the United States and Canada is approximately 10 to 1, and based upon this it is to be expected that the great majority

TABLE 1

Foreign Films in Circulation in the United States-Canadian Market[1]

	1956[2]	1957	1958	1959	1960	1961	1962	1963	1964
British	50	93	76	116	135	146	122	77	83
French	38	61	46	78	105	90	97	91	60
Italian	52	160	48	96	116	79	89	93	60
German	74	51	52	81	72	69	63	55	55
Swedish	3	3	3	9	15	20	17	22	8
Danish	–	–	7	4	3	3	5	2	1
Greek	12	35	2	53	31	56	38	83	55
Russian	31	9	12	59	50	61	89	98	108
Spanish	–	3	–	–	15	13	24	13	18
Japanese	6	301	296	218	226	274	176	156	165
Mexican	107	116	116	106	96	104	101	88	93
Other	–	–	3	4	11	27	19	27	22
Total	373	832	661	824	875	942	840	805	728
Distributors Surveyed	24	28	38	39	45	44	48	49	46

[1] Chinese films not included.
[2] Data for 1956 pertain only to films released that year.
Source: Variety, January 30, 1957; April 9, 1958; April 15, 1959; April 20, 1960; April 26, 1961; May 2, 1962; May 8, 1963; April 29, 1964; May 12, 1965

of rentals accruing to a film would come from the American market. Possible exceptions might exist for British and French films which could earn proportionately more revenue in Canada because of the country's ties to Great Britain and the large French-speaking population. There are, however, many independent distributors in Canada who import pictures directly from Great Britain and France. The earnings of these films would not be reflected in the *Variety* tabulation because it covers only American distributors. Nevertheless, in examining the total revenues, one cannot help being impressed by their smallness even though they come from two markets.

Table 1 shows the number of foreign films in circulation in the United States-Canadian market from 1956, while Table 2 reports the estimated revenues which they earned for their distributors. The latter table indicates a clear difference between 1957 and 1958 for the earnings of "British" films. In 1957, excluding American-financed pictures, "British" films earned about $6,300,000. The following year, including American-financed films, "British" pictures returned almost $27,200,000 to their distributors. British earnings hit a peak in 1964 with a reported $49,100,000 in rentals which includes significant returns for *From Russia With Love*, *Tom Jones*, and *A Hard Day's Night*, all involving participation by United Artists. The peak year for

TABLE 2

Division by Nationality of Distributors' Share of Foreign Film
Box Office Receipts in the United States-Canadian Market[1]
($,000)

	1956	1957	1958	1959	1960	1961	1962	1963	1964
British	1,747	6,347	27,167	18,644	22,975	40,967	24,027	37,455	49,098
French	2,230	3,176	8,346	5,188	5,190	3,040	6,424	4,567	2,951
Italian	2,319	1,768	1,508	9,720	12,266	11,149	8,885	17,233	9,396
German	282	266	509	662	1,233	1,857	1,020	483	1,930
Swedish	80	37	97	477	635	2,104	520	451	557
Danish	–	–	48	32	44	130	1,119	38	47
Greek	16	88	34	107	110	3,113	896	964	152
Russian	194	75	30	175	1,833	767	384	354	104
Spanish	–	12	–	–	89	502	964	1,400	1,481
Japanese	248	932	933	1,160	2,014	1,772	1,695	2,359	1,124
Mexican	3,017	3,206	3,301	3,201	3,277	3,427	3,235	3,330	3,340
Other	–	–	19	260	624	350	260	708	722
Total	10,132	15,908	41,992	39,626	50,291	69,178	49,428	69,342	70,902

[1] Chinese films not included.
Source: Variety, January 30, 1957; April 9, 1958; April 15, 1959; April 20, 1960; April 26, 1961;
May 2, 1962; May 8, 1963; April 29, 1964; May 12, 1965

French earnings, 1958, shows a considerable jump from the previous year. The increase from $3,200,000 to $8,300,000 can be attributed almost entirely to Brigitte Bardot and the film in which she appeared, *And God Created Woman*, which had rentals of approximately $4,000,000. Italian films have hit two earning peaks in the American market for the years considered. In 1960, they had estimated rentals of more than $12,200,000, although about a third of this was earned by only four pictures. They starred strongman Steve Reeves in a series of Hercules-type films. In 1963, Italian pictures returned more than $17,200,000 to their distributors, about three-quarters of this amount being earned by spectaculars such as *Barabbas* and *Sodom and Gomorrah* in which American companies had investments. The phenomenal success of Greek films in 1961 is somewhat deceptive because all but about $100,000 was earned by *Never On Sunday*.

Other significant points are apparent. The data reveal that from 1958 to 1964, foreign films (including those financed by American interests) returned to their distributors an estimated $390,000,000. Foreign film earnings in the United States-Canadian market are compared in Table 3 with earnings of films with American nationality in certain European countries. While 1958 through 1964 are the high points for European earnings in this market, they are not necessarily the peak years for American earnings in Europe. Moreover, in the case of Italy and France, the distributor's share for American films was calculated at 30 percent and 33 percent, respectively, of the gross receipts, figures admittedly low for many films. The contrast in earn-

TABLE 3

Comparison of Rentals; French, Italian, and German
Films in the Combined United States-Canadian
Market; Films with American Nationality in the
French, Italian, and German Markets, 1958 to 1964
($000,000)

	French	Italian	German
Rentals in U. S.- Canadian Market	35.7	70.2	7.7
American Rentals in Foreign Markets,	97.4	221.3	165.2

Source: Table 2, Chapter 4; and Tables 14, 15 and 17, Chapter 3

ings is more striking because the average ticket price in the United States during the period considered approached $.80 while that for France, Italy, and West Germany was only about $.40.

Before this discussion of foreign films in the United States-Canadian market is concluded, the role of the major American distributors must be considered. Table 4 indicates the number of films handled by ten (eleven in 1963 and 1964) major American distributors and the estimated rentals accruing to these films, and contrasts them with the activities of independent distributors. *Variety* did not provide tabulations of major vs. independent until 1960. The ten or eleven major distributors questioned by the trade journal represent less than a third of the total number of distributors surveyed. Although they have distributed no more than a quarter of the foreign films, they have earned between half and three-quarters of the total estimated rentals, with the most impressive shares being in 1963 and 1964. To a great extent, this reflects the fact that the majors, by virtue of their greater monetary reserves and sources of funds, are able to buy into or finance

TABLE 4

American Majors' Share of Foreign Imports and Earnings in the United States-Canadian Market[1]

($,000)

	1960		1961		1962		1963		1964	
	Films	Rentals	Films	Rentals	Films	Rentals	Films	Rentals	Films	Rentals
British	30	17,487	33	34,266	22	18,381	29	33,143	42	44,060
French	2	810	3	846	2	665	11	1,285	4	603
Italian	24	11,228	12	5,188	14	4,880	21	12,452	13	3,000
German	2	574	5	1,205	3	600	—	—	3	1,730
Spanish	—	—	1	400	13	700	13	1,400	17	1,311
Mexican	—	—	—	—	20	700	87	3,300	93	3,340
Other	9	2,107	8	4,850	5	1,415	19	1,685	11	950
Majors' Total	67	32,206	62	46,755	79	27,341	180	53,265	183	54,994
Total	875	50,291	942	69,178	840	49,427	805	69,342	728	70,902
Majors' share in percent	7.7%	64.0%	6.6%	67.6%	9.4%	55.3%	22.4%	76.8%	25.1%	77.6%

[1] Major companies: American International, Allied Artists, Columbia, Metro-Goldwyn-Mayer, Paramount, Twentieth Century-Fox, Universal, United Artists, Warner Brothers, and Buena Vista. Azteca, a distributor of Spanish language films, is considered a major in 1963 and 1964.

Source: *Variety*, April 26, 1961; May 2, 1962; May 8, 1963; April 29, 1964; May 12, 1965.

outright large-scale foreign productions with name stars who attract higher box office revenues. As a recent example, United Artists' *Goldfinger* (a "British" film) is reported to have been rented in the United States for as much as 80 percent of a theatre's gross[25] while the same company's *Thunderball* is said to have hit a maximum rental of 90 percent of the gross in some theatres.[26] In this way, it is not surprising that the latter film reportedly recovered its $15,000,000 cost after only seven weeks in release in the United States and Canada.

The position of the majors also reflects the kind of foreign films which have been distributed by the independents. Generally, they have been of the "art house" type—likely to play in a more restricted and limited market.[27] The independents normally operate on smaller budgets and are able to devote less money to acquiring and promoting their films. In recent years, it appears that the popularity of "nonart" foreign films has eclipsed that of the "art" film and this has had an impact on distributors. A few small independents have left the business, while some others are moving into the less "arty" films. This does not mean that "art" film distribution is dead. However, the independents who wish to compete with the majors can find themselves at a serious disadvantage because with rising production costs overseas, more money is needed to be a coproducer. In addition, foreign producers are asking higher prices for American distribution rights to their films. Gone are the days when American rights could be bought for a few thousand dollars. With foreign film content changing due to the investment pattern of the majors, it seems that the "art" film is declining in importance. Although small independents might never be completely squeezed out of business, it appears that many of them are finding it increasingly difficult to stay in. Like many other economic activities, film distribution is moving toward fewer, but larger, companies.

In the United States today, there is a fairly wide market for some kinds of foreign pictures where practically none existed fifteen years ago because of the structure and policy of the American industry. Their position here will continue to be solidified not only by their occasional unique tone and content, but also by the continued American investment in them. As long as producers hold to their practice of making a relatively small number of pictures in Hollywood, there will be room in the American market for the foreign-made film. Moreover, American audiences have demonstrated at the box office that they are willing to pay to see non-American pictures, although in many cases the audience probably does not realize it is seeing a film made abroad. As European-made films continue to have success in the United States, American companies will be more likely to invest in them. This will increase the problem of defining the nationalities of films and accelerate the vanishing of what little dividing line remains today.

5: The Foreign Policy
of the American Film Industry:
Monopoly and Free Trade

For many American industries, export trade is a sideline. This is not the case for the American motion picture industry, because without the foreign market the American film industry as we know it today would collapse.

To facilitate operation overseas and to secure markets, the American industry has had to develop a foreign policy and to build and structure an organization to carry out this policy. These measures have been developed over decades, many through trial and error, others through positive planning. The industry has explicitly stated little about its foreign policy. Yet a policy is clearly evident when one studies the foreign operations of the industry, for certain principles, objectives, and tactics appear and reappear.

Aside from field offices maintained abroad by individual companies, foreign affairs of the major American companies are centered in the Motion Picture Export Association, an arm of the Motion Picture Association of America. The MPEA was organized as a legal cartel and registered in 1946 under provisions of the Webb-Pomerene Export Trade Act of 1918. This act provides qualified exemptions for American business from prohibitions in the Sherman Act of 1890 and the Federal Trade Commission and Clayton Acts of 1914, but only insofar as the business of the associated enterprises relates to export trade. The MPEA is one of the more than two-hundred associations and organizations which have registered during the last fifty years with the Federal Trade Commission under the Webb-Pomerene Act

Generally, a registered association can act as the sole export sales agent for its members, set prices and terms of trade for sale of its members' products abroad, and make arrangements for the distribution of these products in overseas markets.

The MPEA facilitates overseas activities of its members in a variety of ways by expanding and keeping open foreign film markets, expediting transfers of earnings to the United States, reducing restrictions imposed on the distribution of American films through direct negotiations and "other appropriate means," disseminating information of interest to members about trading conditions abroad, negotiating film import agreements, and in some cases, negotiating rental terms.[1] The association has been referred to as "The Little State Department" because its functions, scope, and methods are not unlike those of the Department of State. It maintains an office in the United States as well as an extensive network of offices in key film markets. It negotiates, compromises, threatens, and bargains to achieve its objectives. It tries to win friends and to influence local policy. It even has been known to give "foreign aid" in the form of loans and subsidies and to bolster employment in foreign industries by virtue of American film production in those countries. The MPEA embodies the interests of businessmen and diplomats (some who have actually represented our government), whose principles and methods have clashed occasionally: on the one hand, business may be demanding a swift resolution of a particular problem; on the other, diplomacy would call for negotiation and compromise. The blend of these viewpoints has not produced uniform success for the MPEA in overcoming foreign difficulties for statesmanship—has, on occasion, given way to the approach favored by company management.

To be effective in its foreign activities, the American film industry has to present a united front, ideally in the form of the MPEA whose mission is to represent the companies belonging to it. Solidarity is essential in negotiation, as only in this way can the MPEA hope to achieve the best possible operating conditions for its members. When ranks are split, the MPEA bargaining position is weakened, as it ceases to speak for an entire industry. The opponent of the MPEA, whether it is the French Centre National de la Cinématographie, Italy's ANICA, or another comparable body, recognizes when unity is lacking among the Americans, and is better able to press its demands without compromise.

Disunity within the MPEA can be fatal, especially when major markets are at stake which can yield $20,000,000 or $30,000,000 annually for American films. On a worldwide scale, the lack of a solid front can be more costly. More than a decade ago, Eric Johnston, the late president of the MPEA, claimed that American companies would lose $100,000,000 a year if ever they resorted to individualism in dealing with foreign countries. He was quoted as stating:

> Our pictures fill about 60 percent of the screen time in foreign countries. When any one of them wants to impose restrictions I can go to the Finance Minister, not threateningly, but to simply state that our films keep more than half of the theatres open. This means employment and a bolstering factor for the economy of whichever country is involved. And I can tell the Finance Minister of the tax revenue which these theatres yield.
>
> But if only two or three American companies were to accept the restrictions on their own, my argument with the Finance Minister would lose its weight. My position would be an impossible one if our ranks are to be broken. We must have the uniformity of policy.[2]

It would seem that not only is uniformity necessary for the execution of policy, it has become a policy in itself. The MPEA has stressed this point continuously, although momentary economic gains for individual companies have sometimes overridden the MPEA's call for a solid front. The trade press has observed that even though the American companies are joined in the MPEA framework they often maintain an individual and competitive manner of operation. The observation added that this type of policy is

> absolutely geared to the need of the instant moment, without much consideration either for the overall European pattern, the benefits of unity or the economic shape of things to come.
>
> . . . With the squeeze on harder than ever to produce revenue, the companies in Europe aren't beyond pulling the rug from beneath one another's feet.[3]

This is illustrated, perhaps, by events which occurred during the MPEA's boycott of the Danish and Spanish markets. The official declaration of the MPEA was that member companies were halting all shipments of films and that they would no longer distribute American pictures until grievances had been eliminated. The plan was to withdraw American films from the market, create a product shortage, and cut heavily into exhibition revenues. The idea, however, did not function as conceived because some American companies franchised Spanish distributors to handle their films, while in Denmark a number of films were made available to a Danish distributor by an American company.

Uniformity of view is complementary to the monopoly foundation upon which the MPEA operates, for the organization, under the Webb-Pomerene Act, is entitled to represent overseas the combined interests of American film companies who are supposed to be competitive in the United States market. While the MPEA strives toward monopoly in its activities, it also pursues the doctrines of competition, free trade, and free enterprise. These tenets are not necessarily at odds with monopoly for, in reality, they work to create market conditions overseas which are healthy for American companies. Free trade slogans and certain activities of the MPEA work to eliminate restrictions on the importation and circulation of American films in foreign markets. Reduction of barriers means easier access to the market for American pictures and a greater opportunity to exploit them. The unified export activities of the industry, when and where they can be obtained, facilitate a greater hold on the market and also operate to discourage any subsequent restrictions which might be contemplated.

The companies view screen quotas and import quotas as restrictions on free trade, that is, restrictions on the free flow of American films into markets. There is also evidence to suggest that companies have, at times, looked unfavorably upon programs of foreign governments which support local film production through subsidies and rebates to producers. The belief was that the combination of quotas and production assistance permitted foreign industries to operate with a competitive advantage over American films brought into these markets. Quotas limited importation and reserved a portion of exhibition time for local films, while subsidies permitted local producers to make films which could compete with American products.

The vice president in charge of foreign distribution for United Artists discussed these measures before a United States Senate committee in 1956. He dealt specifically with Italy, as an example, and revealed how Italian film producers benefit from a subsidy program. The vice president said that this "has not served to create a healthy industry." He added:

> It is my considered opinion that subsidies and artificially created market conditions only serve to subsidize mediocrity, and the public will not patronize such a medium to the extent necessary to keep it healthy. The freer the market in all phases of its operation, the healthier is the state of affairs that will exist. Only a free market

allows ability to be the test of whether a producer, distributor or
exhibitor can meet competition and prosper or fail according to the
results of his efforts.[4]

This verbalization of the free enterprise philosophy applied on an
international scale calls for a completely free marketplace in which
goods of different origin can compete for public favor. In centering
purely on economic and business considerations, the view overlooks
the fact that film is, in addition, a vehicle of creative and cultural
expression. The film has been turned into a business commodity by
those people who have come to control it, but this does not, and
cannot, negate its role as a carrier of images, ideas, and ideals. In many
countries, due to economic factors which have been imposed on the
film, it has perforce been considered in business terms only. From an
economic view, film production in these countries may not be a
"healthy industry" but the value of film as a nationalizing medium
makes it worthy of state support in order for production to continue.

The contention that "a free market allows ability to be the test"
may seem plausible, but only in a business context. The American
industry, in its campaign against restrictions in overseas markets, is
clearly following its own economic interests, because these restrictions
have been devised almost solely to protect foreign industries from
being crippled or put out of business. The MPEA, legally empowered
to monopolize export business for its members, in combination with
demands for free trading in foreign markets, has become a two-
pronged instrument of policy. On the one hand, there is pressure for
the elimination of trade barriers, and on the other there is an organization whose purpose it is to enter and secure foreign markets for
American films. With restrictions inoperative and foreign industries
in a poor competitive position, the organized American industry could
become as strongly entrenched abroad as it has been in its own
domestic market.

The development of the European Economic Community (EEC)
has posed a problem for the American industry. In general, the
Common Market aims to reduce barriers over a period of years so
there can be an increased flow of goods, services, capital, and labor
among its members. A key objective of the Community is the elimination of internal trade restrictions, which is to provide the impetus for
augmenting the circulation of commodities. In the First and Second
Directives pertaining to film of the EEC Council, steps have been
taken in this direction. Import quotas applying to films made by

member nations were eliminated by the end of 1966 while mandatory screen quotas applying only to national films were expanded to include films made in any EEC country.

The American industry constantly has favored elimination of restrictions and on this point it could be said that the aim of the Community is seemingly parallel to that of the American industry. However, the problem exists as to how the Community will treat American films (or other non-Community films) and, more importantly, American investment in Community pictures. Indeed, EEC policy on these points is still in the developmental stage. The response of the American industry to the EEC has not been uniform because the trade policies of the Community could both favor and work against the interests of American companies.

Eric Johnston strongly endorsed the principle of the Common Market in a speech in 1958. He declared that expanded American economic activity depended, in part, upon the functioning of the European Economic Community. Not only did he support the EEC, but he went further and advocated similar trade blocs in Asia, Africa, and Latin America. It is not clear whether Mr. Johnston was speaking as president of the MPEA or as an economic advisor to President Eisenhower—he held the two positions simultaneously. The position of the MPEA, however, has been that any measures which contribute to greater overall economic stability and security in Europe must in the long run benefit American business, including American film business.[5]

Unofficial industry opinion in the past has not been as optimistic, since it realized that reduction of western Europe's internal restrictions could mean an increase of external restrictions. But this has not materialized in the realm of the film. Nonetheless, a belief within the American industry has been that those people in Europe who favor applying Community principles to film would like to better their competitive position at the expense of the American film. In 1959, *Variety* reported that MPEA executives

> are now acknowledging more or less publicly what heretofore was strictly private opinion, that is, that the real purpose of the Common Market re films was a united defense against the domination of the U. S. motion picture on the European screen.[6]

The article disclosed that one MPEA executive claimed he did not see what the Common Market could hope to obtain for the betterment of the European film industry that might not be attained as easily outside the Community structure. He believed the only things EEC could provide were the mechanics and rationale for imposing more restrictions on the importation of American films. The executive was reported as saying that film industry people in Europe

> aren't really interested in liberalizing trade. They're principally interested in building up some kind of defense against U. S. films. Despite all the talk, neither tariffs, nor quotas, nor taxes, is the bugaboo. *The bugaboo is the U. S. film.*[7] [Italics mine]

While a defense against American *films* might have been important a decade ago, the more pressing problem today is a defense against American *economic control* of European production and distribution. Although the American companies may be influential when individual European countries generate policy for their own film industries, their influence on a supra-national level is not as great and they can only assume the role of powerful, interested observers. Because of this, and the uncertainty which has prevailed concerning the film industry's position within the Community framework, the American industry has recognized that it must adapt itself to probable changes in the European film industry's structure.

American film companies have one overriding *raison d'être*: they are in business to make motion pictures which make money. They owe allegiance to the profit motive as long as it does not conflict with the laws, policies, or wishes of the American government. Loyalty to profit does not put them beyond producing pictures in foreign countries; in fact, it encourages them. This being so, they find themselves free to shoot films abroad as well as to invest in foreign-made films which are legally not American but "French" or "Italian," for example. This is important as far as the Common Market's application to the film industry is concerned, for it is one method by which American industry can coexist with an organization which might have initiated policy unfavorable to the importation of films from the United States.

The American industry's policy *vis-à-vis* the Common Market has not been developed as a frontal assault on trade barriers which the Community could erect. Rather, it has been aimed at bypassing possible restrictions by a flanking movement. This entails direct and indirect investment in European film production, which removes the "American" label from a film and substitutes the nationality of the country in which the film was made. By this means, American companies can have their films, their revenues, but not the restrictions which may apply to them. While the threat of Common Market restrictions has not been the primary motive for this new stream of investment, it undoubtedly has been one of the contributing reasons for it.

How demands for free trade and a monopolistically organized export business work together is evident from events which have occurred in Africa and its newly independent nations. While colonial policies were in force, the African market was serviced from parent countries in Europe. As the colonial status was erased and African dependencies became nations, the flow of motion pictures began to restructure itself and opportunities appeared to develop new markets. The American industry's attention to Africa, however, did not start when new nations were born. This only added new interest and urgency to a plan which had been under consideration for almost a decade and which had been developed under a different rationale.

As early as 1952, Eric Johnston noted that American companies should begin considering how to exploit new markets rather than rely solely on existing ones for revenue. He felt that some markets were then yielding as much as they could and that American companies should not exhaust themselves trying to extract a few additional dollars when the effort could be applied better in virgin areas. Mr. Johnston declared that American companies would do well to look to such markets as Africa and the Far East where, as he emphasized, the theatre-going habit was still in its infancy. He believed that these areas offered potentially wealthy markets.[8] A year later, Mr. Johnston stressed the point again, saying that while Europe was still a major source of revenue, it was rapidly becoming a static market. In discussing Europe's ability to yield revenue, he declared that "we have to fight for it, but we should begin to concentrate more attention on other great markets like South America, Asia, the Middle East and Africa" even though initially "they may be low income areas."[9]

Significant action apparently was not taken on these proposals until 1959—a fact which suggests that the companies' policy might have been decidedly short range in contrast to that of the administrative and diplomatic side of the industry, which had urged action at least seven years earlier. In 1959, MPEA representatives were authorized to make an inspection tour of the west African market. According to the association, the annual revenue accruing to American companies from that market at the time was around $125,000. It was believed that with proper handling, the area could be made to yield a good deal more. (The prediction was well-founded, because by 1966 the west African market was worth close to $500,000 to American companies.)

During 1960, Eric Johnston toured the African market to survey exhibition facilities and to contact African government officials. One reported purpose of the tour was to study measures which might work to restrict the circulation of American films in the area. In noting that independence meant a restructuring of the film distribution process, *Variety* reported:

> With the coming of independence, and the rising tide of national-ism, these old distribution patterns are bound to change, and the result could be chaos unless the U. S. film industry can convince local government chiefs of the economic importance of trade as unrestrictive as possible. In Guinea, for example, [an American executive] said, there already have been moves by the government to take over all film distribution as a government function.
> "In such a situation," [the executive] asked, "doesn't it make sense to have someone like Johnston go right to the top man and talk the matter over? In many cases, there's no one beneath the top man who is empowered to handle the problem."

In this case, the MPEA pressed for elimination of restrictions, whether they were actual or potential. *Variety* continued to report this anonymous American executive's remarks, and in discussing trade barriers, added:

> Typical of the kind of "protectionist" and/or unrealistic thinking in many of these areas . . . was that to be found in one newly independent African country . . . which has decided to build its own film industry by placing prohibitive taxes on all foreign distributors. . . .
> The Johnston tour is designed to check this sort of situation, if possible, before it starts.

The anonymous executive was quoted as saying that "we have to make them aware of the U. S. film industry and of the fact that we are interested in the futures of their countries."[10]

After his tour, Mr. Johnston indicated that Africa offered a substan-tial opportunity for the development of a new American film market and predicted that revenue could be considerably larger than it was at the time. Before 1960 ended, the MPEA had authorized a committee to consider developing a corporation for exploiting the west African market. The major functions of the new association were to be distrib-uting films of member companies, developing exhibition facilities, and initiating a program of government relations. The last point can be construed as including attempts to head-off threatened restrictions on American films and to reduce those barriers which already existed.

In less than nine months' time, a new company was born and incorporated under Delaware laws. The American Motion Picture Export Company (Africa), was established and registered under the Webb-Pomerene Export Trade Act to coordinate the export business of the American film industry in the west African market. Participating companies included Columbia, M.G.M., Paramount, United Artists, Twentieth Century-Fox, Buena Vista, and Warner Brothers. While technically separate from the MPAA and the MPEA, AMPEC-Africa drew its officials and administrative personnel from these organizations. The expressed function of AMPEC-Africa was the distribution of American pictures in Liberia, Nigeria, Gambia, Ghana, and Sierre Leone, although the company could move into other areas by unanimous vote of its directors. Member companies licensed the corporation to distribute their films in this market and to act as the sole bargaining agent and representative. The new company had the power to accept or reject rental offers from exhibitors and to control the number of films on the market.[11] The structure of AMPEC-Africa is such that it works to monopolize the supply of American pictures and can turn the flow on, or off, as conditions warrant.

The importance of the African market to the United States today is probably not as much economic as it is political. This follows indications from American industry sources that the United States government has not been entirely passive while the film industry has been trying to gain and maintain a foothold in west Africa. It has been suggested that propaganda considerations of the American government were part of the motives behind the American film companies' movement into this area.

AMPEC-Africa's activities, when viewed not only in economic but in political terms, offer a contrast to what many believe are more pressing needs in Africa. In January and February, 1962, a meeting at the UNESCO Headquarters in Paris discussed informational needs on the African continent. The official report declared that the participants

> agreed that concerted action should be taken to develop the media [press, radio, television, and film] in all African countries, particularly in rural areas, and promote their effective use as a means of information and education for the people.[12]

Specifically concerning film, the report suggested that African countries wishing to develop film production should study "problems of policy and priorities in view of the aims to be achieved and the resources at their disposal." The report recommended that "policies should be determined chiefly in the light of the contribution which films could make to education," considering the "urgency of educational problems in Africa."

In discussing film production in Africa, the report declared that "encouragement and support to national film units" should be given "in order to promote rapid development of the production and distribution of films that are truly African in style and content." The UNESCO conference did not ignore ways and means of supporting local film production. It recommended:

> Governments should take all possible measures to assure the expansion of national film production. They might consider levying an import tax on foreign films commercially distributed in their countries.

While UNESCO was suggesting an import duty, American companies were working to prevent the implementation of such a measure. The same anonymous American film executive cited earlier mentioned this point. He said that because most national markets in Africa were too small to make it feasible to supply each with their own prints of Hollywood films,

> . . . it is vital that distribs be able to send prints from one area to another *without payment* [*of*] *border taxes or duties.* If they should be imposed—and it's always a danger since such duties look like an easy source of income—film trade in such areas would come to a halt.[13] (Italics mine)

The stake the American companies have in this problem is evident. The more they have to pay for duties and taxes, the less they can withdraw from the market. Furthermore, if such levies were used to support local film production, the American companies would be indirectly assisting small potential competitors.

The monopolistic element in the American industry's foreign policy is detectable in another geographic area. While it is not a major market, the experience the American companies gained there perhaps was useful for the move into west Africa.

Malta, a tiny island with some 300,000 inhabitants, has about three dozen film theatres, and the market is clearly too small for the major distributors to set up their own offices there. Following World War II, two small Maltese companies managed to acquire control of the cinema business on the island. It is said they illegally acquired prints of films and were distributing these without making payments to the films' producers. Because Malta is a British-controlled island and had been serviced with films from distributing companies in London, British distributors decided to press the case and regain the market. The Kinematograph Renters Society (KRS), an organization of British distributing companies, brought action against the two Maltese firms, and, in effect, put them out of business. To secure control over the island, KRS established the Malta United Film Company in 1947 to organize and monopolize the flow of films into the market. The company, however was not a strictly British undertaking, as American distributing companies have subsidiaries in Britain which are members of KRS. In practice then, the Malta Company was a joint venture between British distributors and the United Kingdom subsidiaries of American distributors. The MPEA was not officially involved in the venture, although individual companies were free to become parties to it.

The members of KRS, which account for virtually all the business in the British market, license the Malta Company to distribute their films in the Maltese market. In exchange for this service, the company receives a commission on the rental fees. With few exceptions, the Malta Company handles all English-speaking films entering the market and, as a trade source stated, has a monopoly of the film distribution business in Malta worth about $400,000 annually.

An earlier chapter (2) concerning European restrictions of film importation reserved discussion of West Germany until later. That market can be considered now to see how events there coincide with the American industry's foreign policy. By 1950, difficulties facing the German film industry had grown to such magnitude that ways were sought which might bring any measure of relief. Credit for production was hard to obtain as banks were lending money at high interest rates for industrial purposes with less risk than film production. In West Berlin alone, forty-three out of fifty-seven production companies had not made a single film by 1950.[14] Moreover, on a number of occasions, film studios in Munich had been idle for months at a time because no company had the capital to produce. Film importation was high, the United States being the chief supplier, and little screen time was available for German pictures even if they could be produced.

The high importation of films alarmed the German industry and the Spitzenorganisation der Filmwirtschaft pressed the government for measures to regulate the number of imports.

In March, 1950, the West German government proposed that importation of American films be curtailed sharply and demanded that American companies limit themselves to bringing only one hundred pictures into the market annually. Shortly before this, the American distributors had agreed on a yearly ceiling of about 160 films. The reduction asked by the government threatened to hinder the operations of the American companies and was construed by the latter as a move to block their easy access to the West German market.[15] At this time, the Allied High Commission maintained authority over the West German parliament's legislative powers. The Commission could veto items approved by the parliament if it felt they did not contribute to the reconstruction and rehabilitation of Germany, or if they violated the Commission's own laws.

The occupation statutes, enacted in September, 1949, included Law Five on "Freedom of Press, Radio, Information, and Entertainment." The proposal of the West German government was brought to the Commission's attention and in June, 1950, the High Commission rejected the parliament's plan for officially limiting importation of American films. In its rejection, the Commission declared that film was an information and entertainment medium and that Law Five applied to matters concerning film importation. This appeared to end the immediate threat of governmentally imposed quotas on American feature pictures.

Law Five, however, was vague in its reference to film and did not refer explicitly to importation. Article I of the law provided that:

> The German press, radio and other information media shall be free . . . , [and that the] Allied High Commission reserves the right to cancel or annul any measure, governmental, political, administrative, or financial, which threatens such freedom.[16]

The law did not give the Allied High Commission power to reject West German government proposals for import quotas when such imports were threatening economic hardship for that country's film industry. Moreover, the law did not make it mandatory for the Commission to invalidate measures pertaining to film approved by the West German government. Thus, the Commission's right to decide against import quotas was questionable and there was no assurance the Commission would repeat its action if the West German government brought the matter up again.

This apparently was recognized by the American film industry, for its subsequent activities demonstrated that it was not entirely satisfied with the June decision of the High Commission. In October, 1950, representatives of the MPEA visited the State Department in Washington to impress upon it the propaganda value of American films for rebuilding West Germany. An implicit aim of the mission was to win State Department approval for the principle of unrestricted access to the West German market. By couching the matter in a political and propaganda framework which was closer to State Department thinking, the film executives hoped to get official support for their campaign. If free access to the West German market could be guaranteed, then the economic aims of the film industry, and the political aims of the government, would be fulfilled.

The MPEA argued that "Germany is the focal point in the current battle of ideologies" and that while millions of dollars were being spent on Voice of America programs, it would be "illogical to restrict the powerful message that American pictures could carry to the Western Zone" of Germany.[17] MPEA representatives declared this message was in danger of being hindered in West Germany through the desire of its industry to protect itself against Hollywood competition. They felt that if the State Department really wanted to assure maximum exposure of the American message, then the Department would have no alternative but to instruct the High Commission to prohibit any further measures which would restrict importation of American pictures. The MPEA contended that unregulated importation would not mean a flooding of the West German market as the Germans insisted.

Shortly after, the State Department instructed the U. S. High Commission that it preferred to see no quota on the importation of American films. This reinforced the June decision of the High Commission and set a policy for future action. It also meant that Hollywood's economic interests were bound inextricably with Washington's political interests and that both parties could work together, when they wanted to, with mutual support. The State Department's decision further indicated that governmental policy, at least in this case, was implicitly in favor of supporting the export business of American companies even when it seemingly threatened to bring hardship to foreign competitors in a country the United States was trying to rebuild.

Without an official quota, the industry was at liberty to determine what it thought constituted a suitable number of American pictures in West Germany, considering the box office potential and the general economic state of the market. While the American government opposed on political grounds West Germany's initiating a quota, the American industry was free to impose on economic grounds a quota itself.

As MPEA representatives were presenting their case in Washington for a quotaless West German market, other MPEA representatives were negotiating with the Spitzenorganisation der Filmwirtschaft to reach a voluntary quota on American films in Germany. The number agreed upon was approximately two-hundred, a small increase over the previous year's amount and substantially more than the West German government thought the market could absorb. This informal self-controlled importation, known as the "Gentlemen's Agreement," called for the MPEA to try to keep annual imports to the agreed-upon ceiling, although there was no penalty if imports exceeded it. From the standpoint of the West German industry, "this was not successful," according to one writer. Henry P. Pilgert, in a publication of the U. S. High Commissioner for Germany, declared that "foreign competition continued to plague the German motion picture industry . . . since many of the companies did not adhere to their self-imposed quotas. . . ."[18]

The agreements executed after 1950 generally were negotiated in an atmosphere of stress. Groups within the West German industry, notably producers, demanded that the MPEA voluntarily agree to restrict imports to below the two-hundred figure. The MPEA, backed by the State Department and its representatives in West Germany, rejected such proposals on economic and political grounds. In 1954, for example, the German industry asked that American imports be limited to 160 and that certain taxes be levied on the earnings of American pictures in the market. Neither proposal materialized. In later years, West Germany tried to set an age limit on American films to discourage the importation of old pictures previously unreleased in the West German market. This plan also was thwarted. In addition, the West German industry hoped to obtain reciprocity by being guaranteed the distribution of German films in America, or a subsidy which would enable the industry to establish a distribution and publicity office in the United States. This proposal, to quote an American industry representative, was "shot down immediately."

The success of the American program is evident because at no time has the importation of American films officially been limited in West Germany. The only restriction which has ever applied was the "Gentlemen's Agreement," a voluntary measure permitting American companies to bring into the German market almost twice the number of films they had been bringing into France where import controls were officially operative. In reality, the American industry had free access to the German market. The campaign in Germany was of a preventive nature, designed to head off restrictions before they could become official.

This should not imply that efforts against potential restrictions were unique to the West German market or that they functioned only in the immediate postwar years. The 1959 film agreement between the MPEA and Italy, for example, called for similar protection in that market. An appendix to the agreement bound Italian film authorities to take all steps necessary with the Italian government to insure that there would be no changes in Italian film legislation which would affect unfavorably activities of the MPEA and its members in Italy. Moreover, the Italian film industry, through ANICA, pledged to abstain from demanding legislative measures which would further restrict or place new burdens on the importation, dubbing, or distribution of films belonging to MPEA member companies.[19]

In 1953, Henry P. Pilgert wrote that "the German motion picture industry is still in a state of uncertainty and insolvency."[20] That statement could be made now with as much truth. The second war, in destroying the German war machine, also largely destroyed the film industry which had helped to support it. The absence of film strength in postwar West Germany gave the American industry an opportunity to attempt imposing its own conditions in the market. One writer, formerly attached to the headquarters of the United States Forces in the European Theatre, has contended that the

> [American] industry, through its European representatives in Paris and on the staff of Military Government in Germany as distribution experts, made serious efforts to convince occupation authorities that it be allowed to establish what would in effect have amounted to a monopoly of not only motion picture distribution, but of production and the ownership of theatres as well. The industry even interposed objections to the showing of German films for fear of competition. The industry was induced to oppose the showing of German films by a desire to have its own control of the market in Germany.[21]

When the last twenty years of European film history is reviewed today, the usual conclusion is that West Germany has failed to show a vital artistic and a viable economic production force. Ordinarily, this is attributed to the flight of film people from Germany in the 1930's, the moral drain on the country due to the war, and the reconstruction difficulties after the war. However, one must add to this list the foreign policy of the American industry, for it too was significant in shaping the postwar film climate in Germany, as well as in other nations.

6: The Foreign Policy of the American Film Industry: Representation and Revenue

Revenue from foreign markets is so essential to our film production companies that, as we have noted earlier, Eric Johnston once declared: "any action that would materially cut down on this foreign income would . . . threaten economic disaster for the American motion picture industry."[1] Thus the securing of favorable operating conditions abroad has become an essential policy consideration of American companies. One way of achieving these conditions is through membership in foreign industry trade associations. But while American companies generally are members of European film groups, European industries have no representation in American trade organizations. This indicates the relatively small business done in the United States by foreign films, and that European producers who reach the American market have their films distributed by American companies.

Membership in a foreign industry association has important implications. A clue to these is evident if a situation is imagined in which, say, the French industry were a major supplier of films for the American market and these regularly obtained at least a 40 percent share of the market revenue. By virtue of its position in the United States, the French industry would have substantial representation in the Motion Picture Association of America and (assuming the French also were shooting films here) in the producers' association. The French, seeking to consolidate their position in the American market, would actively pursue a policy within these associations which would contribute to maintaining or increasing their security and their share of the box office revenue. Because they were powerful, the French would be consulted within the American market on such policy matters as distribution procedures, rental terms, censorship problems, taxation, advertising regulations, relations with television, import restrictions, and policy recommendations to the American government. French opinion also would be solicited on production matters which could comprise employment of non-American actors, directors, producers, and technicians, labor union problems in general, and export procedures for joint Franco-American productions. In effect, the French would be partially (and perhaps occasionally completely) responsible for policy decisions affecting the American industry and the American market. In addition, because of exhibition dependence upon their films, the French would be able to extract compromises so that the French position in the market would not be threatened.

This is a hypothetical situation for the American market, but it represents quite accurately the conditions in many European countries. It would be untrue, of course, to claim that the American voice is dominant everywhere in European industry affairs and that it is directed solely against interests of local competitors. In some instances, American membership in trade groups is compulsory. Moreover, American interests may run parallel to local interests and a triumph for the American view is a triumph for all. This is usually true in regard to film distribution and rental terms. In disputes with European exhibitors, American distributors align themselves with their European counterparts and the unity of view may be more than exhibitors can cope with.

The alliance of American and local interests has worked, on occasion, for the mutual gain of both parties. Italy, perhaps, typifies this most clearly. In 1954, Eitel Monaco, the director of Italy's film industry association, ANICA, expressed the hope that the cordial relationship between the American and Italian industries would develop from "a simple commercial interchange to a happy status of genuine co-production."[2] Since that time, relations between the two industries have developed extensively. Not only have American companies done a considerable amount of shooting in Italian studios, but they have participated directly in making Italian films by providing production financing and also by distributing them. The same general conditions would hold true for Anglo-American film relations, although those have a longer history.

The advantages to be gained by belonging to a trade association are rather uneven when one examines the entire European industry.

American membership in these groups can be compelled, and this is a means of controlling the activities of the American companies. Spain provides an example of this, because all distributing companies must belong to the Grupo Sindical de Distribucion Cinematografica. If a company is not a member, it receives no permission to distribute films and cannot operate. The Grupo is also the organization which recommends to the Spanish government how baremo points should be allocated and how import licenses should be distributed to members. Representatives of American companies declare that they really have little weight in formulating internal policy in Spain. In talking about Spanish distributors, one American representative stated that "they dominate everything, they are dominant in their own market." The situation in Spain is such that even the MPEA does not maintain a formal organization, office, or staff there. When conditions warrant, the MPEA will have its representative in another country go to Spain temporarily for negotiations or it will attempt to resolve difficulties by working through the American embassy in Spain.[3] It is said that Spanish authorities do not like "little groups" and want to have all the distributing companies within a single organization. The only connection among the American companies operating in Spain is an MPEA "informal board" which meets as required to consider the American position in the country and to develop a common opinion among the member companies. Nonetheless, the American industry has little to say directly about what is being done in the Spanish market. The evidence to support this is the baremo system by which the American companies receive consideration no different from that accorded to Spanish distributors.

The Netherlands is another country where membership in the local film industry organization is compulsory. The difference from Spain, however, is that the Netherlands has a much smaller film production industry and that controls on the distribution of American pictures have not reached the level they have in the Spanish market. The overall industry association in the Netherlands is the Bioscoop-Bond, essentially a "closed shop" as far as trade and business are concerned. The Bioscoop-Bond brings together, under a single roof, production, distribution, and exhibition. Members are pledged to do business only with members. If American companies do not belong to the Bioscoop-Bond, Dutch theatres will not exhibit their films. Organizing and regulating the film trade in the Netherlands in this fashion insures economic stability of the local industry by controlling the number of theatres and the distribution terms on which films are offered. The strength of the Bond is such that it can bargain effectively with the American industry. In the late 1940's, tension developed between the MPEA and the Bond, resulting in an MPEA withdrawal from the Bond. Rather than risk losing this market, American companies returned, outside the formal MPEA structure, and became members of the trade association.

Policy within the Bond's distributors' section has been determined by balloting, one vote per office. An American company with only a single office is given one vote while a small Dutch distributor with, say, two offices would receive two votes. By means of this system, local companies which may have a business turnover less than that of American distributors actually have a greater voice in determining policy. In the same way, the Bond's Board of Directors has had a membership of nine, but only two of them have been representatives of American companies. A source within the Netherlands declared that the Americans always will have a minority voice because "things are arranged that way." The result, as far as policy and business are concerned, is that Americans "cannot do what they want to."

To discover whether the American view is necessarily at odds with that of a local industry one must take into account the structure of the film industry itself. Interests of producers and distributors generally are opposed to those of exhibitors because the latter want to keep as great a share as possible of the box office revenue, while the former want to obtain as much as possible. A struggle often results with producers and distributors aligned against exhibitors. These general points can be illustrated by referring to conditions in France.

The distributors' group, Fédération Nationale des Distributeurs de Films, is composed of three types of distributors: American companies, French companies serving the entire country, and the many smaller French companies serving regions or small areas. As France is a major overseas market for American films, one would expect that difficulties often would arise between French and American interests and that the distributors' association would be the place where they were aired. This has not been the case, however. Officials within the French film industry declare there are few policy differences between American and French distributors because all distributors have common aims, and nationality really makes no difference. Their interests are sufficiently alike to generate uniform objectives and strategy. When conflict does appear, it often is between distributors and exhibitors.

A form of block booking, for example, is not practiced by the

Americans only or by the French distributors only. Both nationalities have used it, and for the same purpose—to guarantee the placing of as many of their films as possible. Concerning rental terms, distributors regardless of nationality prefer to offer films on a percentage basis, while exhibitors prefer to rent pictures for a flat fee. Thus, many differences which do exist within the industry would be there even if American companies were not present, because they are built into the structure of it. The battles are between wholesaler and retailer.

But this does not deny that American companies are powerful and can be instrumental in affecting policy decisions. When movements are started which could threaten their position in overseas markets, they are resourceful and can bring sufficient pressure in the appropriate places to reduce the potential harm. The role American companies play in financially supporting foreign trade associations is one through which such pressure can be exerted. In Belgium, for example, the Chambre Syndicale Belge de la Cinématographie receives more than half its operating funds from American companies which belong to it. This association is composed of three units: American companies, French companies, and local independents. Each member contributes to the association a fee based on its business turnover. In recent years, American companies have contributed about 60 percent of the association's operating funds, the French companies about 25 percent, while the remainder has come from the independents. The voting process within the organization is not based on revenue contributed; rather each of the three groups has one vote on the council which makes final decisions on distribution policy questions. Although American companies are numerically inferior as far as number of offices maintained is concerned, they have a one-third voice in determining policy for the organization, and the same weight in balloting as the three dozen French companies.

While this is true for the formal structure of the organization, the American voice is even stronger if the association is considered on an informal basis. An American industry representative in Europe declared that officials of the association clearly recognize the power and position the American companies have in the Belgian market. He noted that the association's leadership is aware of the American companies' opinions and has not actively pursued matters which would work against their interests. This spokesman felt the money contributed by American companies for support of the association was a factor which carried great weight with its leadership. In addition, when policy was developed for all distributors, it was observed that it generally originated with American companies and that others merely followed, recognizing that what was good for Americans also would be good for them. It seems that because American companies supply the most films and are the greatest money earners in the Belgian market, they are in a position to deal more effectively with exhibitors than the smaller and weaker French and independent distributors.

The drive by American distributors for higher film rental fees has been linked in some cases with their membership in local trade associations. As the number of American produced films declined and the investment in them increased, American companies found that returns from box offices across Europe were inadequate to support this more costly style of production. While rental terms of 30 or 35 percent of the exhibitor's gross may have sufficed when film budgets were small, they have been deemed inadequate for multimillion dollar pictures. So, American distributors have pressed for greater portions of the total box office revenue.

In Switzerland in the early 1960's the exhibitors' and distributors' associations were locked in battle for more than three years over film rental fees. Exhibitors had agreed among themselves not to accept a film for which rentals would be more than 50 percent of gross receipts. This rate was the ceiling for "special" films, generally longer, more extravagant, and more costly than "regular" pictures which were rented at a lower percentage. While exhibitors had established this ceiling, distributors were engaged in trying to destroy it completely, or at least moving it to a higher level of, perhaps, 60 or 70 percent. When negotiations between exhibitors and distributors reached an impasse, the matter was taken to Swiss courts by the distributors' association. It is reported in Switzerland that about half the funds collected to support the campaign came from American distributors. In the Association Suisse des Distributeurs de Films, however, there were some forty members but only seven of these were American distributors or representatives of American distributors. These companies, by virtue of American leadership in the realm of expensive film making, had the most to gain from a victory and were the greatest financial contributors to the action.

The campaign for higher rental terms also has existed in Norway. Immediately after World War II, there was a drive among Norwegian distributors for an increase in the rental fee which was 30 percent of the exhibitors' gross regardless of the type of film being offered.

American films were entering Norway on a restricted basis due to currency exchange difficulties within the country but were also being rented for 30 percent.

In late 1946, an American request for a higher rental percentage was rejected, but rather than lose the market completely, American companies continued to send films to Norway on the prevailing terms. But agitation for higher terms continued, and in the early 1950's, as one source stated, the MPEA "officially" joined the fight by calling on the American State Department and the American embassy in Oslo for assistance. Extensive discussions were held on the governmental level, several steps above the usual distributor-exhibitor level. Involved were representatives of the State Department and embassy and representatives of the Norske Bank, and the Norwegian government. After what has been called "strenuous negotiation," the rental fee was increased from 30 to 40 percent of the exhibitor's gross with a possibility that "special" films could receive 45 percent. This price structure became effective in 1953 and has prevailed since that time.

When the increase of rentals was approved by the Norwegian government, it had to instruct theatres to accept the new terms distributors would be asking. The theatres, many of them municipally owned and operated, had no choice but to agree to the new rental structure. Tied to the higher fees was a stipulation by the Norwegians that American films offered in other markets would be offered in Norway. This meant that a film which might be rented for 65 percent elsewhere had to be offered in Norway even though it could receive no more than 45 percent. There were occasional attempts by American companies to withhold films from Norway because of this ceiling. One American major elected to withhold a film, but the municipally-owned theatres countered by refusing to exhibit all other films from this distributor. As a result, the company was out of the market for several months, but finally returned and agreed to offer the film for the maximum rental.

The successful campaign for higher rentals can be attributed largely to the activities of the American companies and the assistance they received from the American government. American distributors were able to muster enough force in appropriate places, something which Norwegian distributors were not able, or did not want, to do. However, the change in the price structure has benefitted both American and Norwegian distributors. The feeling within the film industry in Norway is that the change in rentals never would have happened without pressure by the American companies. One person, in fact, declared that "we have to thank them [the Americans] for what they have done."

The Norwegian episode was mirrored a few years later in Denmark and in that campaign the American industry revealed another plank in its program for foreign operation—the boycott. The drive in Denmark began very much as it did in Norway. American distributors asked local exhibitors for an increase in film rentals from the 30 percent rate which prevailed. Danish exhibitors refused. The position of the MPEA was that the price structure in Denmark was below that existing in Norway and Sweden and that it would be difficult to continue to get 40 percent in those markets when Danes were getting the same films for 30 percent.

Discussions between American distributors and Danish exhibitors brought little result. To break the deadlock, the MPEA declared that its members would no longer offer films for exhibition in the Danish market. This move, announced in May, 1955, was based on the belief that starving the theatres in Denmark would bring them quickly into line. The MPEA felt that withholding American films from the market would create a shortage, that attendance would fall, and that admission revenue also would tumble. The American companies believed they could sacrifice the returns they were getting from Denmark (about $1,000,000 a year), but that Danish exhibitors could not cope with the lack of American films. American distributors expected the boycott to last three months at the longest.

The MPEA, however, failed to recognize several points. First, the production of Britain, France, and Italy was substantial enough to fill that portion of screen time which had been occupied by American films. In effect, the boycott did not create a shortage of films; it only created a shortage of American films. Second, while MPEA members were obliged not to do business in Denmark, there was no such restraint on American independents. The boycott, therefore, did not completely block the exhibition of American films because independents successfully rented a limited number of them. Finally, the shortage of American films gave added incentive to Danish producers. Without competition from a great number of American pictures, local producers captured a greater share of box office revenue which strengthened their position in the market.

The mechanics of resolving the problem in Denmark were strikingly similar to those in Norway. When distributor-exhibitor negotiation failed, the MPEA took its case to higher levels—the Danish government. The argument reportedly employed by the MPEA was that American films actually helped strengthen the local film industry. Perhaps the words used were the same as those spoken by MPEA executive vice president Ralph Hetzel when he told an industry conference in the United States that

> . . . the time has come, now that the post-war era of distorted economies is coming to a close, to make it clear to those countries who represent the overseas market for American films that the export of U. S. films provides a healthy and much-needed stimulus for their own economies.

Mr. Hetzel believed that when it is demonstrated to "responsible foreign officials that a free flow of American films is a boon to the native theatrical industry" by providing it with more exhibition revenue, then "their attitude towards American film imports will become much more liberal."[4]

Termination of the boycott has been attributed largely to discussions between the American ambassador to Denmark on the one hand, and the Danish Prime Minister, Finance Minister, and head of the exhibitors' association on the other. They yielded an increase in rentals whereby Danish threatres were to be divided into three classes, the first to pay 40 percent, the second 36, and the third 30. In addition, each company could offer two pictures per year on a freely negotiable basis with rentals as high as 70 percent of the exhibitor's gross.

The boycott of the Danish market ended in May, 1958, three years after American companies withdrew. It had lasted considerably longer than anyone might have imagined and while it achieved its goal of higher rentals it revealed that boycotts, if they could be used at all, were risky. The trade press reported that the "bitter fact is that the industry can no longer afford to impose embargoes" because it can no longer "muster the kind of unity that's needed [and] can't afford to take the kind of losses which the quitting of markets entails." The report observed that the boycott of Denmark (and the simultaneous one of Spain) exposed "a growing weakness of MPEA" and the fact that "it's possible to play the various companies against one another."[5] What the report did not mention, but what is equally valid, is that the decline in American film production meant there were fewer American pictures to withhold from markets. The numerical dependence upon American films is diminishing and future boycotts will be ineffective if the purpose is to starve foreign exhibitors for the American product.

While the campaign in Denmark was conducted outside the distributors' association and centered on increasing rentals, American membership in local trade groups has been used in other countries to head-off moves which could hinder activities of American distributors. The importance of belonging was brought to light as early as 1950 when American distributors in West Germany applied for membership in the Spitzenorganisation der Filmwirtschaft (SPIO), the central trade association for the German film industry. American companies felt membership in SPIO would be vital for their position in the market because the association's

> job is to make recommendations to the German government on all things affecting films. The Americans, as members, have a full vote equal to that of any of the German delegates and thus have a right to cast a veto, as all decisions must be unanimous.

In addition to voting power, American companies thought of other benefits. Belonging to SPIO meant that Americans

> at all times know what the German industryites are thinking and planning and can head off any recommendation to the Reich government that appears dangerous to American interests. It amounts to a veto before the fact, and the companies are very pleased that they have been able to get into SPIO at all.

American distributors were convinced that their joining SPIO would "result in improved German-American film relations"—especially because the Germans "have always been leaders in . . . protecting their own industry at the expense of Hollywood."[6]

These statements are not mere theoretical observations of the power American companies could hold in the German market. On the contrary, they demonstrate the technique American distributors have used to secure a firm position there. While the above comments were made in 1950, the following decade of activity demonstrated that belonging could be a useful tool in the American industry's foreign policy. In 1960, the MPEA representative in West Germany told a trade journalist that there were "continuing efforts on the part of some protectionists to curb our position" in Germany. However, he went on to declare:

> I feel that while we have to be alert against any moves to trim our position, nonetheless *we can be reasonably confident that we can thwart any such moves.*[7] (Italics mine)

More recently, an American representative in Germany declared that if there were ever a showdown in the distributors' section of SPIO, American members could block any policy they felt was unfavorable to their interests. This source indicated that through annual dues paid to the distributors' section, American companies were indirectly supporting SPIO.

The advantages of association membership also were demonstrated in the United Kingdom when the government and the industry were drafting the 1960 Films Act. This legislation was to replace earlier laws which regulated the film industry in the United Kingdom. An important part of the Act was the definition of a "British" film, for on it hinged the subsidy allocated to producers. On this point, American companies had a direct interest, for their subsidiaries in Britain were making pictures which at that time were meeting the official and legal requirements for being labeled "British." As such, they were eligible for government-approved subsidization. Any modification in the definition of a "British" picture which would make it more difficult for films of American companies to acquire this label would work against the interests of American producers.

In 1958, the British Film Producers Association (BFPA) submitted a memorandum to the Board of Trade setting forth its position on the proposed legislation. Among other points, the BFPA felt the "British" label should not be awarded on the same basis as it had been in the past. The Association believed that employment of non-British directors and producers should be more limited, and that this, when applied stringently, would make it more difficult for the productions of some companies to be declared "British" and have access to the aid fund. The BFPA declared it was improper for all films to have the advantages of the production subsidy, an implicit attack upon American companies who produced "British" films and drew payments from the production assistance fund. The Association believed the subsidy should be used in the way in which it was originally intended—to support the production of *British* films, not to support overseas shooting by American companies. The BFPA recommended to the Board of Trade that in order to have a film declared "British"

> . . . all the producers and directors of a film, except one, by whatever titles they may be described, must be of British nationality wherever domiciled, or if not of British nationality, ordinarily resident in the Dominions. We also urge that if one person on his own fills the position of sole producer and sole director, he must

fulfil one or the other of these requirements; i.e., he cannot be the one person as mentioned above who need not fulfil them.[8]

This suggestion struck at American companies who, although employing the legal minimum number of British technicians and actors in their films, had often used American producers and directors. It meant that British nationals, nominally at least, would have more control over "British" film production and perhaps that more British producers and directors would be employed. According to an American industry representative in London, the BFPA recommendation was "dead against our interests" for it would have placed new obstacles in the path of drawing on the British subsidy fund.

That this was the intent of the suggestion was apparent when the Federation of British Film Makers (FBFM) submitted its recommendations to the Board of Trade. The FBFM, criticizing the Association's memorandum, stated it was designed to "impede Anglo-American co-operation" and could be regarded as a "retrograde step" for the British film industry. In outlining the need of occasionally employing more than one foreign producer and director, the Federation declared:

> There are some cases, not large in number but generally of considerable importance, when finance will be available for a film with a foreign producer and a foreign director but will not be available otherwise. We think it quite unreasonable that drastic action should be taken because of a handful of cases. . . . We simply cannot afford to drive away from our studios these important [Anglo-American] productions.[9]

The key to understanding the position taken by the Federation, ostensibly an organization for British producers, is contained in the group's annual report for 1958–59:

> A second reason for the formation of the Federation was the feeling that an important body of makers of British films had been isolated because they had American finance or distribution. With a membership that includes representatives of some of the major Anglo-American organisations, *the Federation has helped greatly to influence the climate of opinion* and to reduce the old suspicions and hostility. In its submission to the Board of Trade last year, in the further submissions of this year, and in many detailed ways the Federation feels confident that it has done a great deal to encourage the development of Anglo-American co-production.[10] (Italics mine)

It would seem that the organization was a vehicle for the dissemination of opinion favorable to American interests in the United Kingdom.

With the Federation taking a public stand opposing the BFPA's recommendation, other parties were at work on different levels. The trade press reported in December, 1959, that Board of Trade officials had been meeting with certain unnamed "leaders from various sections of the British film industry" who explained to the Board that the BFPA's proposal could be "interpreted as having un-American connotation."[11] To make certain that the BFPA's suggestion would not be adopted, pressure was brought to bear directly on the Association. A film industry source in Britain has revealed that a statement was presented to the BFPA by an influential American representative. It is reported to have pointed out that certain American companies had recently joined the Association and it requested the BFPA to amend its position regarding employment of foreign producers and directors. A short time later, the Association withdrew its recommendation to the Board of Trade and the proposed limitation did not find its way into the 1960 Films Act. Some of the companies which joined the BFPA between March, 1959, and March, 1960, are Twentieth Century-Fox Productions Ltd., Walt Disney Productions Ltd., United Artists Corporation Ltd., and Warner Brothers Productions Ltd.[12]

While rental fees and foreign legislation have been important, blocked earnings also have received priority attention in the American industry. The serious balance of payments situation in the decade after World War II caused European governments to prohibit American companies from withdrawing the money their films had earned. When it is remembered that some markets could yield more than $20,000,000 annually, it is apparent that sizable amounts of earnings were blocked overseas. Initially, this created a problem for American producers because they were denied access to their earnings—the money required to repay loans, to pay for future production costs, and to show a profit.

The industry dealt with the problem in several ways which included using frozen revenue for investment in foreign non-film industries, for investment overseas in film production and allied industries, and for the support of overseas offices and business operations. Another way of disposing of blocked earnings was through what the industry termed compensation deals. This was a broad heading embracing various methods of exchanging blocked currencies for other currency and eventually American dollars. The exchanges were not based on par value but involved certain discounts which a middleman took as commission for arranging the transfer. The companies lost some money, but on balance, felt they had most of the revenues their films had earned. In many cases, the compensation deals became elaborate and, in addition to exchanges of money, included the buying and selling of goods unrelated to the film business.

The extent to which American companies have gone to withdraw their frozen revenue was disclosed in a dialogue between Eric Johnston and Senator J. William Fulbright in 1953.

> SENATOR FULBRIGHT: I was a little surprised that you were able to sell $200,000,000 worth of movies. I don't know where they get the dollars for that when there are so many things that they want. . . .
> MR. JOHNSTON: As you know, Senator, we carry on very extensive trading operations all over the world in order to get our money out. We have done such things as buy wood pulp in Scandinavia for kroner, shipped it to Italy in exchange for lire, and there we have used the lire to build or rebuild ships to go overseas to be sold for American dollars; we even raised a sunken French tanker in the harbor of Marseilles and repaired it, paying for it with French francs, and shipping it to the United States where it was sold for dollars; we have made Scotch-type whisky in Chile, sold it in America for American dollars. All in all, we have a very extensive organization constantly working to get our dollars over the hurdles that beset you nowadays in foreign trade.
> SENATOR FULBRIGHT: You are very ingenious.
> MR. JOHNSTON: We have to be. That is the only way we can get our money out, I will assure you.[13]

Other arrangements with blocked earnings centered on the ship-building business in Italy. Beginning in 1953, as part of film agreements between the Italian and American industries, provisions were made for the use of blocked American revenues. The initial agreement provided that about 25 percent of these earnings could be invested by American companies in Italy's semi-official shipbuilding company, Finmeccanica. The company then guaranteed to repay a certain amount of American dollars, but at a discounted rate, which was reported to be about 14 percent. Evidence suggests that the American companies used this arrangement on several occasions and for substantial sums. By July, 1954, American companies were said to have just completed their third compensation deal with Finmeccanica for $1,000,000.[14] Fourteen months later, it was reported that deals with Finmeccanica had yielded around $6,000,000 for the Americans and that negotiations were under way for additional transfers of $3,000,000.[15]

This method of withdrawing funds was perpetuated and written into later film agreements. The pacts permitted American companies to dispose of their blocked Italian earnings not only through the building of ships but also in the construction of hotels or other works of national interest to Italy.[16] The agreements, as did earlier ones, authorized American companies to spend their blocked funds by investing in Italian film production. That American companies at that time were disposing of sizable portions of their earnings through compensation deals, and not through local film industry investments, was apparent when the director of ANICA brought the situation to light. In early 1958, Eitel Monaco suggested that compensation deals through Finmeccanica be ended because blocked earnings, originally intended for financing local film production, were being absorbed by shipbuilding and other non-cinema efforts. The problem eventually was resolved as Italy began to liberalize the remittance of American earnings, and by 1960 it was reported that hardly any American revenues were still blocked. In the same year, a source in Italy revealed that during the preceding ten years American film companies had channeled as much as $40,000,000 through shipbuilding deals.[17]

In other countries where earnings were frozen, American companies had opportunities to convert their funds through non-film-industry channels. In Great Britain, as a provision of the film agreements, American companies had permission to use their earnings for the "acquisition of real estate, the construction or renovation of buildings, participation in approved industrial or commercial enterprises, construction, acquisition and operation of hotels" and for participation "in travel and transportation agencies designed to facilitate and encourage tourist travel."[18]

The 1948 film trade agreement between the French and American governments also provided for the disposal of blocked American earnings in other than film industry enterprises. Frozen funds could be used for the "purchase of long term stock shares," the "purchase of French industrial values . . . , investment in French industrial or commercial businesses," and for the "purchase, with a view to export, of goods and materials . . . considered by the French government as being profitable to the French economy."[19] In the case of Great Britain and France, it is believed that the largest share of blocked earnings was used for film industry purposes including the expenses of American location shooting and direct investment in British and French film production.

The American film industry's foreign policy, as it pertains to matters of representation and revenue, has brought the companies into contact with overseas trade associations, into conflict with foreign economic interests, into close quarters with European governments, and into involvement in noncinema industrial activities. The American film industry is truly an international business.

7 : The American Film Industry and the American Government in Postwar Germany

Broadly speaking, the relationship of the government and the film industry is one of mutual support. The government perpetuates the environment in which all industry operates, and industry has an interest in preserving the existing social order. The film industry, which reaches man's mind and emotions, can be a powerful ally of government and the economic order, both at home and abroad. The belief that film is a useful instrument of propaganda evolved in government circles during the last world war and grew to maturity in the late 1940's and early 1950's. At this time, occupation forces in West Germany sought to reeducate the German people. How was the difficult task of destroying Nazi ideas and inculcating those of democratic capitalism to be accomplished? How was Communism to be combatted? American films, embodying "our" point of view, seemed an instrument which could be aimed at both opponents.

Relations between government and the film industry are tenuous, however, as their aims may not always coincide. The profit motive on the one hand, and the political motive on the other, may pull the two apart. When the objectives of the two groups are similar, however, they may work together actively for mutual gain. Even when their ultimate purposes are different they may tend to use identical means, resulting in an alliance between private and public interests.

There have been repeated pleas for emphasis on film as a propaganda tool. As early as March, 1950, Senator William Benton, in calling for a "Marshall Plan in the field of ideas," urged more recognition of the role film could play in the government's propaganda work. In a Senate speech, he discussed film, radio, and printed matter, claiming that "for all practical purposes, it may be said we are not using them at all." He declared:

> Their impact today, in our interests, is that of a midget. I make an exception of the Hollywood motion picture, with its varying types of impact. They do have the potential strength of a giant, and my plea today is that we give them a chance. Nothing equals the motion picture in its capacity for gripping and holding masses of people, and communicating information and attitudes in vivid, remarkable form. . . . We need to get the pictures. We do not have them now. We need to show them. Their impact can indeed change the fact of history.[1]

Senator Benton introduced a resolution asking that "the international propagation of the democratic creed be made an instrument of national policy. . . ."

With governmental needs favorable to employment of film for propaganda purposes, the film industry was quick to support this policy. If the government actively pursued a wider dispersal of American films throughout the world, the industry was likely to gain in a business sense from the additional revenue such dispersal brings. The dual advantages were recognized by the film industry, for it realized that a push from the government could be useful in developing new markets and for making old ones yield attractive revenue. To assist the drive for favorable operating conditions abroad, the industry had to follow up the government's belief that film could be useful for propaganda. Spyros Skouras of Twentieth Century-Fox once urged the industry to "work harder and harder to create [a] missionary spirit." "This will not only be of great importance to the motion picture industry economically," he said, "but it will also enable us to diligently discharge the sacred duty of our great medium to help enlighten humanity." Skouras added that

> it is a solemn responsibility of our industry to increase motion picture outlets throughout the free world because it has been shown that no medium can play a greater part than the motion picture in indoctrinating people into the free way of life and instilling in them a compelling desire for freedom and hope for a brighter future. Therefore, we as an industry can play an infinitely important part in the worldwide ideological struggle for the minds of men and confound the Communist propagandists.[2]

The Skouras statement is a call to the industry to have its films circulated more widely so that profits can be larger and Communism can be defeated.

While the government was quite explicit about why it wanted to have American films circulated abroad, the industry preferred to verbalize its own aims even though in tacit agreement with those of the government. The film companies have not actively enunciated the overt propaganda qualities of their products because, basically, they prefer to maintain their own control over content and not be confronted with the charge that they are shaping content to conform with government directives. The companies often cooperate with the government by erasing from their films undesirable elements rather than by purposely injecting types of content which propaganda would call for. The belief behind this is that films already convey "our" point of view and that no further positive steps need be taken to emphasize it.

Such thinking reflects the basically business orientation of the companies, for their initial allegiance is to the production of films which will draw audiences and generate revenue. If the same pictures also can carry a message beneficial to the government, so much the better. Basic conceptualizations of the social role of communications in America are involved. There has been a tradition of freedom of communication and separation of government from the operation and content of mass communication. This "hands off" policy—freedom of the press—is reflected in the distance between the film industry and the government when production values and content are involved.

Eric Johnston once declared that "Hollywood is not in the business of grinding out pictures neatly labeled for use as weapons in the propaganda war." "Hollywood is in the entertainment business," he added, "and that's precisely why our films are loved and believed by people abroad."[3] This concisely states the film companies' belief that a closing of the gap between industry and government is not likely to be useful for either party because credibility will decline and possibly revenue. Hollywood has been intent on stressing that its pictures can do a good job abroad within the production framework in which they are currently being made. There is also the suspicion that if Hollywood agrees to government planning of content with foreign audiences in mind, the next step could be planning of content with domestic audiences in mind.[4]

That Hollywood wants to cooperate, but independently, is implied in a statement Eric Johnston made to a Senate committee in 1953.

Pictures give an idea of America which it is difficult to portray in any other way, and the reason, the main reason, we think, is because *our pictures are not obvious propaganda.* They are completely free pictures, and they reflect the freedom under which they are made and the freedom under which they are shown.[5] (Italics mine)

. . . We have advised foreign managers to be careful and set up some criteria as to what pictures should be sent to areas and they have done that on their own. I know they have a keen awareness . . . of what pictures should go into what areas, and whether a picture is harmful and whether it will do a great deal of good. They are doing the screening themselves. . . . There are a good many of our pictures that are not shown overseas. . . .[6]

Senator J. William Fulbright was on the committee which heard Mr. Johnston's statement. In light of the film executive's comment, Senator Fulbright pushed the matter further and the following dialogue resulted:

SENATOR FULBRIGHT: What determines whether a picture is sold abroad or not? It is a commercial determination, is it not—what you think will sell?
MR. JOHNSTON: Yes. Drama sells abroad better, but I am not an expert. . . .
SENATOR FULBRIGHT: You don't have to describe it. What I mean is that your test, the criterion you use, is whether or not it will make money. Isn't that your objective?
MR. JOHNSTON: Of course, we are a commercial enterprise.[7]

Hollywood cooperates with Washington but only to the extent that it does not forfeit its autonomy. A vice president of Paramount Pictures, in discussing film production, has stated that

. . . we try to find out whether the subject matter that we are handling would be an offensive matter in the area where our Government is having problems, and, if so, not to do it. We try, where we can, to inject things that will be an expression of friendliness in relation to that country and those people. We do that as Americans. We do not do it under the demand or under the control of anybody in the Government.[8]

There is another element involved in this problem of propaganda and it is the obvious fact that American audiences also have to see these films. This involves a matter of balance and emphasis in film making, for a picture made with foreign audiences in mind can flop at home just as the reverse can be true. That the industry has to consider both ends is apparent in two statements made by Y. Frank Freeman, a vice president of Paramount. In testimony to a Senate committee in 1956, Mr. Freeman said:

> Paramount and all of the other companies must produce motion pictures which will have universal appeal. . . . Thus, the American motion picture is international and will so remain. . . .[9]

A few minutes later he declared:

> We have always designed our pictures primarily and essentially for the American market, and the record of all producers will, I think, show that.[10]

The extent and success of cooperation between industry and government when profit and propaganda motives are at stake is illustrated by events in postwar Germany. In considering Germany, the Allied Powers believed that simply to disarm the country would not be enough. They felt that eradication of "her false ideologies of superior nationhood and the right to make war for purpose of territorial acquisition [were] just as important as curtailing Germany's physical ability to make war."[11] This aim called for an intensive program of propaganda designed to reeducate Germany and for controls over all media of communication. Products and representatives of American media were enlisted in this campaign for the messages they carried and the know-how they could offer.

The American film industry had in its libraries thousands of pictures which could be placed at the disposal of the Military Government for use in the reeducation campaign. In recalling this period and its problems, Eric Johnston once observed:

> In response to urgent requests of top United States occupation officials, American feature pictures were sent into Germany . . . as soon as the fighting stopped. . . . American leaders recognized that these non-propaganda pictures would assist during the critical postwar period in conveying to the people of the occupied areas an understanding of American life and democratic institutions. The films were the first real contact between America and the former enemy. . . . The film industry provided the pictures at no profit to itself but rather at an actual loss for out-of-pocket expenses.[12]

> I don't know of any industry giving away cloth or clothes or steel or anything, but we gave away films, not only gave them away but paid for the means of showing them in dollars out of our own pockets, at an expense of about $500,000 a year.[13]

On the surface, Mr. Johnston's statement claims that the film industry was an active participant with the government and that the industry's role was philanthropic, not profit seeking as one would expect. These assertions, however, must be matched with the record.

The exhibition of films was prohibited in Germany until the end of July, 1945, when twenty theatres were allowed to open in the American zone. By the middle of September, about fifty theatres were operating and showing American films with German subtitles. The program for the reopening of houses, however, did not proceed as rapidly as was desired. One writer, active in Military Government affairs at the time, has stated that "the real difficulty in getting more motion picture houses opened lay in the short supply of films."[14] The Military Government did not have enough different pictures from which to select, and of those it did have, there was a shortage of prints. Even though theatres could be reopened, there were not enough films available to show in them.

The problem might have been solved except for "the inability of the American motion picture industry to co-operate along policy lines laid down by the United States Government for the occupation of Germany."[15] The film industry and particularly the majors, by controlling the reservoir of thousands of pictures, hoped to receive concessions from the Military Government which would give it a dominant position in the German market. In partial response to this strategy, military officials decided they would have to authorize the exhibition of certain German films which had been declared politically harmless. Thus, in December, 1945, a small number of German features began to be shown to alleviate the film shortage.

In exchange for providing more films, the American industry was making demands on the Military Government which "were so inconsistent with occupation policy" that the industry and the military "failed to reach a mutually satisfactory agreement."[16] The basis of industry demands centered on how it would be paid for its films, and how it could dispose of these earnings. Under the Military Government's program, revenues from the exhibition of American films in West Germany were held in blocked accounts with the Military Government. It had to approve plans the companies had for withdrawing and spending these reichsmarks which had value only in

Germany. What the companies did not like was that they could not convert their marks into dollars and that the Military Government would not approve their plans for spending them in the German market.

Because of the difficulties of retrieving exhibition earnings, the American industry was not willing to increase its flow of films to Germany to aid the reeducation program. A source within the American industry has revealed that between July, 1945, and December, 1946, only forty-three features were offered to the Military Government. By May, 1947, almost two years after the end of hostilities, only fifty American films had been released in Germany out of the thousands in Hollywood libraries. The "urgent requests" of Military Government officials were answered by the industry with a trickle of films.

Late in 1945, General Robert A. McClure had a number of conferences with film industry leaders in the United States in an effort to resolve the difficulties which were then impeding the reeducation program. When General McClure returned to Germany, he could report little except that the industry had shown a desire to "utilize the military occupation to establish an exclusive position for American films and American distribution machinery."[17] He felt the government had only a moral obligation to aid the companies, and then only if they cooperated with its policies and objectives. By the summer of 1946, it became increasingly apparent that the film industry was not likely to yield, and might ultimately refuse to make any films available to the Military Government.

There were several demands made by the American companies on occupation authorities. The MPEA insisted that only it should have the right to export to Germany and that only its members should be permitted to release films. "This ran straight into strong opposition from Military Government," according to one writer, "which wanted to include independent producers in order to obtain the best product."[18] The MPEA, legally empowered to monopolize the export business for the American industry, was attempting to force this privilege on the Military Government, but during a period when it hardly seemed justified.

The companies also were demanding that they be allowed to use their frozen marks for what amounted to economic penetration of the West German film industry. The companies asked to buy theatres in Germany, to produce newsreels for use in Germany and elsewhere, and to buy German raw stock to make prints of their own pictures. In addition, the American companies expressed an interest in obtaining the Bavarian Filmkunst studios for their own production purposes. The Military Government, meanwhile, had prohibited American companies from purchasing or investing in real estate and from buying items in short supply such as automobiles and typewriters.

These and other proposals made by the American industry ran contrary to the objectives the Military Government had in mind. The latter called for the rebuilding of a film industry that would be German in operation and in financial support as well as politically and economically independent. The Military Government felt the industry had to be rebuilt as a German enterprise, not as an American subsidiary, and that there should be no favoritism involved in occupation policies. As a step toward this, German film makers with non-Nazi records were encouraged to ask the Military Government for permission to start production companies.

Hollywood continued to use its control of films as a bargaining weapon. Military officials found themselves in a somewhat helpless position because they needed pictures and these could be made available only by the companies. When finally the policy was reformulated it allowed American companies to engage in production and distribution of films in the American zone of Germany. However, it continued to forbid American investment in theatres, and prohibited the acquisition of German raw stock for the making of prints for export trade. The effect of the new policy adopted by the Military Government was to give American companies entry into two of the three levels of the German film industry—production and distribution—and to establish a virtual monopoly of film distribution in the American zone. Plans for film production in Germany by American companies were never undertaken on a large scale, for reasons to be discussed in a later chapter.

In February, 1948, the MPEA officially began distributing American films in West Germany, taking over the function of the Information Services Division of the Military Government. The MPEA expanded its own organization and established seven main branches to service theatres in the American, British, and French zones. The earnings of American films, however, continued to be frozen, but instead of going into an account under the Military Government, they fell into an MPEA account. Regardless, the question of withdrawing money from the market was unsettled and the American industry was still wondering how it would convert reichsmarks into dollars.

This problem touched other American media doing business in Germany, notably the print media. Some American authors, for example, were reluctant to sell German publication rights to their work because they could not draw on their blocked earnings. This was a definite obstacle for the reeducation program, and officials in Washington took steps to remedy it. In 1948, the Informational Media Guaranty Program (IMG) was started as part of the Economic Cooperation Administration. The program permitted the converting of certain foreign currencies into dollars at attractive rates, providing the information materials earning the money reflected the best elements of American life. This was a decided advantage to the film companies for it allowed them to distribute and exhibit their pictures in difficult currency areas with complete assurance that some of the resulting revenue would be available to them in dollars. Implicitly, it expanded the number of markets which could be exploited by the American industry, and put an "official" label on Hollywood's work. American films could then go forward with the rank of ambassador.

At the time the IMG program was being launched, German currency underwent a reform and the official unit became the deutsche mark. This ended the Military Government's official control over the former reichsmark and the occupation mark. However, conversion of the new marks into dollars on the open market was not authorized and the MPEA companies would have continued to face the frozen earnings problem had it not been for the IMG program.

It should be stressed that IMG did not guarantee dollars for all American films shown in Germany. An American film was eligible to receive benefits only if it met criteria established by the Economic Cooperation Administration:

> The films eligible for IMG coverage include only those which present a fair and essentially accurate picture of American life, or which, regardless of subject matter, have sufficient distinction of production, design, or acting, to reflect credit on the culture of the United States.[19]

In short, IMG permitted conversion when films were deemed valuable for the message they contained. If a particular film was not approved, an American company could still distribute it in West Germany, but its earnings would remain blocked in marks. Even considering this feature, the scheme still benefitted American companies and they rapidly increased their flow of films to the German market.

During the 1948–49 rental year, only sixty-four American films were released in Germany. In the following rental year the number jumped to 145, in 1950–51 to 202, and in 1951–52 to 226. The impact of the IMG program is apparent when we recall that between V-E Day and May, 1947, only fifty American films were released in Germany. In the same way, 278 American films were released from January 1, 1950, to April 1, 1951, a sharp contrast to the 170 released between V-E Day and the end of 1949. And these pictures were not necessarily new ones, for of the 448 American films released up to April, 1951, about 20 percent had been made prior to 1940.[20] The stimulus to release came from the availability of dollars, and the availability of dollars stemmed from a need for propaganda.

The first media contract executed by IMG was signed with the MPEA in December, 1948, and covered films released from August 1 to December 31, 1948. The value of this contract was $230,000. It later was extended six months to August 1, 1949, and increased to $457,000. The MPEA proposed to distribute during this period thirty prints each of forty-four black and white features, eight color features, and a number of shorts. In the six months to the end of 1949, IMG guaranteed $636,000 for MPEA films. In 1950, contracts were signed for more than $3,000,000 and when discussions took place for the 1951 program, the American industry suggested a further increase to $4,000,000.[21]

The payment policy of IMG underwent some modification as the program functioned over the years, reflecting the amounts Congress appropriated for it and the way funds were divided among various media. The arrangement under the first motion picture contracts was for conversion of marks up to the actual direct dollar costs wholly attributable to the projects covered. Beginning in 1950, the guarantees were issued on a more liberal basis. In addition to the actual out-of-pocket costs incurred by the distributor, each approved film was eligible to have an amount equal to $25,000 in earnings from exhibition converted from marks into dollars. According to industry estimates, these out-of-pocket expenses (for raw stock and the cost of the German language version) normally ran to about $12,000 for each film. Thus, for every feature the IMG selected, it guaranteed to pay about $37,000. That the American industry benefitted financially from the IMG subsidy cannot be disputed. From the first contract, retroactive to August 1, 1948, until the expiration on February 28, 1953, of the last contract under which dollar conversion was provided, total dollar payments by IMG to American film companies amounted to more than $5,100,000.*

With the IMG program working, and with approaching favorable conversion of blocked marks into dollars, the American industry's interest in the German market drastically changed. Its policy became one of bringing into Germany as many films as it thought the market could absorb. Not only that, but the American industry thwarted the establishment of an import quota in Germany. Discussions in Washington between MPEA representatives and the State Department resulted in an order to the U.S. High Commissioner in Germany that the Department wanted no quota on the importation of American films. An official German quota never materialized.

The reluctance of American companies to send films to West Germany prior to the IMG program was a result of concern with revenue. Even the Military Government's objective, to reeducate Germany, was not sufficient incentive for the companies. The event which turned the trickle of American films into a torrent was, clearly, the initiation of guarantees by the American government. That the IMG program was lucrative to Hollywood was apparent when the House of Representatives considered an appropriation to the U.S. Information Agency in 1959. Congressman H. R. Gross attacked film industry lobbying in Washington and the IMG, declaring that through its payments the "Motion Picture Export Association has been given a pretty good ride on the informational media gravy train. . . ."[22]

While the exportation of films to Germany demonstrates one facet of industry-government relations, another area can be illuminated by an examination of the antimonopoly issue as it existed in the postwar German film industry. At the end of the war, there existed no private film business in Germany. The entire industry had been organized by the Hitler regime under the government-owned UFI, a gigantic holding company which maintained control over its subsidiary, Universum Film A. G. (UFA).

The UFI combine represented a great economic power as it in-

* Examining all media involved in the West German program, from its inception until 1955 when it became inactive, we see that the American government entered into seventy contracts and made payments of slightly more than $7,000,000. On this basis, the American film industry accounted for the greatest share of dollar conversions, about seven out of ten dollars. On a worldwide basis, from inception of IMG programs until June 30, 1966, American film companies received close to $16,000,000 under the currency conversion provisions. Thus the film program in West Germany alone represented almost a third of all government payments to American motion picture interests. See: U. S. Senate, 90th Congress, 1st Session, Committee on Foreign Relations, Hearings, U. S. Informational Media Guaranty Program (Washington: Government Printing Office, 1967).

cluded not only production, distribution, and exhibition facilities, but laboratories, music publishing, script publishing, export companies, and other interests which carried the UFI influence into broader fields. Western occupation authorities recognized the dangerous power that a reconstituted UFI could exert upon postwar German business. They believed a monopoly in the motion picture business would not be consistent with the best interests of a new, democratic Germany. In contrast to East Germany where only one large company was authorized, the Americans, British, and French agreed to place the new West German film industry on a thoroughly competitive basis. This called for the restructuring of the entire industry and the destruction of the UFI trust. The Western Powers believed that the new German industry should be composed of small independent units. The three levels of the film business—production, distribution, and exhibition—were to be separated, and within each level there was to be competition among companies.

This policy was also in broad agreement with what the American industry desired in Germany. The industry preferred to see Germany become a free market and it felt this could not be achieved if UFI were to regain the strength it had during the Hitler era. A reconstituted UFI would have offered competition, especially in view of the American industry's desire to establish its own control in the German market. The MPEA was active in pressing for the destruction of UFI and for the sale of former UFI properties. Eric Johnston transmitted his association's concern to occupation authorities on numerous occasions. As *Variety* once reported:

> With the monopoly powers of UFA under the Nazis still clearly in mind, MPEA doesn't propose to let this threat to one of its most valuable foreign markets go unchallenged. . . . In terms of dollar remittances, Germany in 1954 will deliver in excess of $13,000,000.[23]

The desires of the American companies in the UFI problem were concisely stated to this author by an American industry representative: "We would not want to see a monopoly here." In addition, American interests had expressed a wish to buy some of the UFI properties.

The policy of the western occupation authorities was put into effect as soon as the war ended, and continued during the immediate postwar years. Independent German producers were licensed in the three western zones and by 1948 more than twenty companies had been established. The UFI combine was confiscated by the Military Government which administered the properties and it appointed a German custodial committee to develop a plan for the decartelization of the industry.

Action to dissolve the UFI trust was not taken until September, 1949, when the American and British Military Governments issued Law 24, the "UFI Law," which was supplemented by Ordinance 236 from the French Military Government. The objective of Law 24, as stated in its preamble, was to

> . . . dispose of such [motion picture] property in a manner best calculated to foster a sound, democratic and privately owned motion picture industry in Germany, organized so as to preclude excessive concentration of economic power. . . .[24]

It authorized the establishment of a Liquidation Committee to have title to UFI properties and the right to sell them, subject to certain conditions. These required that sales be at public auctions and that buyers could not be government agencies, officials of political parties, former leading Nazis, or former high employees of UFI. In addition, non-Germans were forbidden to acquire more than a quarter control of any one of the three production studios up for sale. The Liquidation Committee was established in February, 1950, but according to one source it never functioned.[25]

By this time, however, Military Governments had ceased their operation, and authority was vested in the Allied High Commission and in a reconstituted West German federal government. As the status of the former Military Government's UFI Law was now ambiguous, the West German government requested clarification. In June, 1950, it asked the High Commission to replace Law 24 with a governmental decree designed to carry out the same idea. The Commission responded by repealing Law 24 and French Ordinance 236 but replacing them with High Commission Law 32. This new law dissolved the Liquidation Committee established under Military Government and set up in its place a Deconcentration Committee with power to dispose of UFI properties. Simultaneously, the High Commission declared it would repeal its own Law 32 as soon as the West German government passed legislation on film industry deconcentration.

To this point, then, three committees had had the power to split the UFI trust. There was the Custodial Committee which had been replaced by the Liquidation Committee which, in turn, had been replaced by the Deconcentration Committee. Yet by the middle of 1950 no action had been taken to destroy the UFI combine or, at minimum, to sell some of its appendages.

While the West German government was drafting its own film industry law, the High Commission went ahead with its plans to auction UFI properties. The first step began in November, 1950, and subsequent attempts did not prove fruitful. The official report from the American High Commissioner for Germany declared:

> Extensive but unsuccessful negotiations have been held with various groups who expressed interest in buying these properties. The major obstacle to selling them has been the lack of liquid capital in Germany. Banks have been unwilling to lend money to finance the purchase since very high rates of interest can be obtained in making industrial loans with less inherent risk than in the motion picture industry.[26]

High Commission efforts to sell parts of the UFI combine drew criticism from the German press and the German government. One segment of the press believed the current "financial difficulties of the motion picture business" offered a greater danger to further development of the film industry "than another motion picture monopoly in the hands of a few big companies."[27] The government contended that the High Commission ought to wait until it had formulated its own law for the disposition of UFI properties. Officials within the government were critical of the Commission's policy. Dr. Rudolf Vogel, chairman of the parliament's committee for press, film, and broadcasting, asserted that forced deconcentration of UFI was "an act of mistrust." He declared that even though there were giant production companies with diversified interests in the United States and Great Britain, the High Commission was trying to dissolve a similar one in Germany. Dr. Vogel insisted that the problem

> has nothing to do with security. Today the question is whether— five years after the capitulation—it is still possible to squander German property without the participation of the Germans.[28]

Karl Brunner of the Social Democratic party contended that UFI already had been broken because more than half of its property was in the Soviet occupation zone and inaccessible to the UFI organization in the western zones. He charged that the aim of the Commission's plan was to eliminate competition from German films.[29] Similar sentiment was expressed by Dr. Hermann Puender of the Christian Democratic party and president of the German Economic Administration. He felt the destruction of the German film monopoly was purely "for the one-sided benefit of foreign interests."[30]

At the same time, there were hints that British and American officials had disagreed about the method of disposing of UFI properties. These difficulties eventually were resolved when, late in 1951, the High Commission announced it would make no further attempts to dismantle UFI and that action would depend upon the German parliament developing a program for this purpose. In the months which followed, pieces of the UFI combine gradually were handed over to the West German government by the High Commission. The last transaction occurred in December, 1953, and at that time the fate of UFI passed into the hands of the Bonn government and German industrialists and financiers.

Meanwhile, facilities of the UFI combine had been leased and rented to independent film companies which had been established either under the Military Government licensing procedure or under subsequent arrangements. Thus, when the German government inherited control of UFI, it was an operating entity and in a structure similar to that of the Hitler days.

One writer has observed that by 1953 the "deconcentration of the UFA-UFI properties into economically viable and competitive units [had] not yet been accomplished." He noted that experience with coal, iron, and steel industries had demonstrated that "deconcentration is a very long drawn out matter." In discussing the film industry's structure in relation to other media of mass communication, the author stated:

> The German democratic press has a good chance of survival. The German radio shows a heartening consciousness of its public service functions coupled with a determination to maintain its gains. But in the film industry, it is perhaps too much to expect that future developments will be along the lines desired by [the Allied High Commission for Germany].[31]

The eventual control of much of the UFI properties passed in 1956 into the hands of a holding company in which a number of major German economic and banking interests had an investment.

As a result, the UFI combine was not broken into economically independent and viable units as the Military Government and the High Commission had planned. The UFI organization in the western zone remained virtually intact, although its ownership was no longer

in government hands. One person in the film industry in West
Germany. He writes that despite Allied efforts to deconcentrate and
the UFI properties would have aggravated the film industry crisis.
The government, according to this source, wanted "a strong pillar"
around which the entire industry would revolve, and decided this
should be the old UFI properties.

This is supported by John Dornberg in his book *Schizophrenic
Germany.* He writes that despite Allied efforts to deconcentrate and
decartelize German industry, "most of the big industrialists have made
a grand-scale recovery" and "are virtually all back at the throttle
today."[32] Dornberg adds:

> It would be unfair to say that the Germans or the Allies have tried
> to forget the plans to decentralize large industries which played a
> major role in supporting the National Socialist regime.
> But there is also no question, understandably, that the Germans
> affected by the orders and laws have dragged their feet. Most of the
> firms involved are vital to Germany's economic recovery and, con-
> sidering the change in attitudes and the turn of events for Ger-
> many, many officials and many Germans in private life cannot
> understand why there is still the demand to decentralize and
> deconcentrate the industries which will strengthen the country
> economically.[33]

In the case of motion picture deconcentration, both the American
government and the American film industry believed the destruction
of the former Reich film monopoly would serve useful purposes. The
government felt that monopoly had to be replaced by competitive and
independent companies on the assumption that only this could contribute to a democratic and economically strong Germany under *laissez-faire* principles.[34] The American film industry wanted to see the
end of the UFI monopoly because this would have removed an
obstacle in the path of the American industry's own desire to control
the West German market.

This joint industry-government policy came to nought, however.
Only the government could actively initiate dismemberment of UFI,
even though the American industry could support such a move. In the
years following 1945, there were no serious attempts by the Military
Government to dissolve UFI, and when the High Commission finally
began the job in the early 1950's, it met with strong opposition from
the West German government. In the five years after the end of
hostilities, German government officials and industrialists had begun

to wield some measure of political and economic power, and this obstructed the High Commission's attempts to break UFI. In addition, it is quite probable that German film industrialists, bankers, and other investors, had access to German government circles and strongly demanded that the film industry not be restructured in small, independent, competitive units. Considered in these terms, the deconcentration issue became a battle between American and West German industrial interests through their respective governments. The American government, of course, was not particularly attracted to the wishes of the American industry to have its own control of the German market. In contrast, the German government was interested in building a stronger Germany and recognized that this might be possible for the film industry if it were not dismantled.

Ludwig Erhard, when the Minister of Economic Affairs, discussed the "German economic miracle" and attributed economic growth to what he termed a "social market economy." He has written:

> My use of the term "social" is not intended to refurbish tacitly continued capitalistic methods, but to indicate a definite departure from the old liberalism which, as is generally known, cast the state in the role of night-watchman in the nation's economy.
>
> What "Social Market Economy" implies is that the state is given not merely the function, but in fact a *real responsibility for imposing on the economy certain politically desirable maxims and employing the broad range of instruments of economic policy* in such a manner that the free decisions of men of all categories in the course of their economic activities will nevertheless lead to the desired result. The "Social Market Economy" is based on the principles of freedom and order which, if harmony is to reign, must in my view constitute an indivisible whole; for where there is freedom without a firmly established order there is the danger of it degenerating to chaos, and where there is order without freedom, it all too easily results in brutal coercion.[35] (Italics mine)

It would seem that the policy of the Bonn government called for giving the German film industry its freedom through private ownership and for instituting "firmly established order" through the maintenance of the UFI combine.

The ultimate outcome of the deconcentration program was not a complete victory for the American film industry, because UFI was never dissolved. However, to parallel UFI's business, independent German companies were established and these have functioned with various degrees of success. On the other hand, through governmental and industrial cooperation in Germany, the film industry was permitted to remain more or less intact with anticipated benefits falling to German business and to the German economy in general. In spite of this policy, the West German film industry never has managed to get on its feet. The strong pillar, Universum Film, around which the new industry was to be rebuilt, went through years of re-organization, diversification, and economic shakiness, culminating in its bankruptcy in 1962 and its purchase by a West German publishing house two years later.

Following the deconcentration program through to the end, and for all industries, could have weakened the West German economic structure, and this result would have been inconsistent with Allied efforts to increase economic stability and well-being as a bulwark to Communism. Thus, original intentions had to be annulled due to political considerations and events of the time.

Over the years, relations, cooperation, and negotiation between the American industry and the American government have depended upon the availability of channels for interaction. For the industry, contact with government on the highest levels has assumed an important place in its overall business policies. The death in August, 1963, of Eric Johnston, president of the Motion Picture Association of America, left a vacuum in the industry's administration. In the search for a successor, one film industry executive frankly acknowledged that "our selection must be a man of stature who has entry to the White House [and] respect in international diplomatic channels. . . ."[36] Perhaps these requirements have been fulfilled by the new MPAA president, Jack Valenti, a personal friend and former influential aide to President Lyndon Johnson.

8: Financial Assistance to European Film Production

A basic characteristic of film production industries in Europe is the direct involvement of national governments which are aiding them financially. The extent of assistance is such that without it film production in Europe would hardly be solvent and the various industries would lead a most precarious existence.

Unlike most industrial enterprises, film production involves a mixture of business and art. The business dimension exists inasmuch as films are a commodity which can be manufactured, publicized, and sold for profit. In the artistic dimension, films are vehicles for creative expression, permitting the producer to give audiences his impressions of the world and its life. But the continued existence of film as a medium of expression depends upon the financial resources available for production. In turn, the availability of production funds depends upon the willingness of people to invest. Their decisions to invest can be based upon the past successes of a film maker or star and on their belief that the planned production is likely to be sufficiently successful for the original investment to be returned with an adequate profit.

The power of a film to attract revenue is related to the size of the market available to it and the market's revenue potential. By virtue of elements inherent in production styles, film scripts, acting ability, and technical craftmanship—and the tastes and wants of audiences—films can have limitations built into them which restrict the market in which they are likely to be successful. In fact, some films are consciously made with specific audiences in mind, and are geared to exploitation over a limited geographic area. In economic terms, the ability of a film to recoup its investment and to yield a profit depends upon its acceptance by audiences with sufficient money at their disposal to make production solvent. When acceptance falls, due either to qualities inherent in the films themselves or to external forces restricting the circulation of films, then subsequent production is likely to be revised commensurate with revenue. The external forces can include the availability of competitive entertainment media, business policies and the output of foreign motion picture producers, and certain economic patterns within countries which manifest themselves in box office receipts.

If films were considered solely within a business framework, then simple demand would be enough to dictate how many and what type should be produced and made available to what people. Generally, this is the rule which governs film production in the United States. When film is viewed as a medium of expression, then the context for judging its purpose changes from one of profit to one of communication, which should be encouraged for its expressive potentials. Considered in broad terms, film is a conveyor of a society's values and beliefs. It is a medium through which artists, allied with their culture and their own perception, can provide the public with views of life and its problems.

As history shows us, the arts have drifted away from being the objects of royal patronage, to become susceptible to the whims of the populace and the market place; and the support and perpetuation of them have become linked with other commodities in the economic dimension of modern life. Their continued existence, then, has come to depend upon their attractiveness to the multitude and to their ability to pay their own way. In relation to film and its development as a twentieth century expressive medium, one finds that in capitalist oriented societies the vehicle immediately found its way into the industrial complex because of its possibilities for commercial exploitation, its technological nature, and the scientific contributions which preceded its birth. Once in this complex, its purpose for existing became predominantly profit, and secondarily expressiveness. If in generating profit the film also could expand the dimensions of human feeling and intellect, then so much the better.

That a government is or is not involved financially in film is a reflection of the basic assumptions underlying that government's existence. In the United States, among the main assumptions forming the foundations of government is the belief that the government's powers should be few and the individual retain a maximum amount of freedom. These tenets are manifest in the separation which exists between government on the one hand and industry and art on the other. Government involvement or lack of involvement in the film industry also reflects the attitudes of the industry and the solvency of production. When governmental assistance does not exist (as has been the case) and there is no prevailing feeling within the industry that it is needed, then it can be assumed that production is economically healthy or that the industry has turned to private sources during periods of business difficulty.

In Europe, the relationships between government, industry, and art have been guided by different assumptions about the role of the state. There has been the belief which holds the state responsible for the maintenance and perpetuation of national heritage and culture. The authority of the state gives it the mission to preserve and encourage art and culture, for it is the only institution representative of its people and their traditions. In execution of this obligation, the state is empowered to assist morally and financially all types of art for their qualities of national expression and creativity.

Running parallel is another doctrine declaring that the state has a mandate to oversee and direct policies in the economic sphere. The principle assumes that industry can function for the common welfare only if coordinated with national objectives and programs as a whole. Robert Heilbroner, in discussing the growth in Europe "of public control over and intervention into private economic life," writes that this "is the metamorphosis of a system of *laissez-faire* into one of mild national economic collectivism."[1] He states that the development of intervention and planning "must be understood as constituting a protective device for capitalism" by which this capitalism has "sought to guard against its growing vulnerability to economic crisis."[2]

The obligation of the state to preserve and encourage art, and the growth of public control over economic matters, have provided the rationale enabling European governments to become involved in their domestic film industries.[3] Moral and financial assistance is justified and necessary because film is a medium for expression and a commodity produced by business enterprises. If left to follow their own interests, these enterprises might deem film production largely unprofitable and this channel for creative potentialities might be obstructed and unable to function in the best interests of sociey.[4]

In the film industry, production has been the segment upon which financial assitance has been most concentrated. There are, however, some cases of aid to distribution and exhibition. In France there is an automatic subsidy equal to one percent of the gross receipts given to companies which distribute a short film of distinctive quality on the same program with a long film. This short film can come from any member of the Common Market. Aid to exhibition is best typified by Italy. According to the 1965 film law, exhibitors can receive a percentage rebate from the entertainment tax for showing certain types of films. A rebate of 2 percent is given for showing newsreels, 50 percent for feature films produced especially for youth, and 50 percent for programs composed entirely of short films. Similar rebates are available for exhibition of quality films.

Nevertheless, the overwhelming weight of assistance has fallen to producers, for it is with them that films originate and are then fed through distributors to theatres. Stability and solvency in production, it is believed, eventually will spread to other levels of the industry. Financial aid made available to European film production by governments, or government-approved agencies, includes prizes, loans, and subsidies—each unique in purpose and extent.

A government or public commission can reward and encourage quality through the granting of prizes to outstanding pictures. These awards are not made automatically but depend upon the decision of special juries which judge films on the basis of artistic criteria and confer financial prizes according to the extent films meet them. There is no uniform pattern in Europe concerning when the prizes are awarded or, indeed, the exact size of the prize.

The Swedish Film Institute is authorized to grant prizes to quality feature and short films. The fund for this purpose, derived from a 10 percent levy on theatre tickets, varies with admissions in any given year. When the program started in 1963, the Institute anticipated more than $400,000 being available annually for feature film prizes. The awards are made after films are reviewed by a special seven-member jury. The intent of the system is to avoid making grants to projects which *might* seem worthwhile on paper, based on names and subject matter. Instead, the jury takes into account only the finished product. To qualify for a financial prize, a film must receive a minimum number of points from the jury. The awards fund is then divided among all films receiving at least this minimum, in proportion to each eligible film's total points. According to the Institute, it is entirely possible for an excellent film to have at least half of its production costs returned through the quality prize.

A different system has existed in Norway. There, the government has aided production when films have been deemed artistic, cultural, or as fulfilling a special interest. To qualify for assistance, a film producer must submit his plans to the Ministry of Church and Education before production is started. These plans include the complete script, a talent list, an estimated budget, and information about sources of production money for the film. If the project is judged meritorious, the Ministry can make an outright gift of money to the producer. The advantage of this system, of course, is that it provides financing which permits production to start. In this way, it would be possible to shoot a film for which sufficient commercial capital is not available.

The question of awards before or after production has been resolved in Denmark. A special commission may judge a film's artistic and cultural value before production is started or after the film is completed. If the commission decides favorably, a percentage of the film's gross box office receipts can be paid to the producer. Other prizes are available for actors, directors, and technical personnel.

The amounts of money available for prizes vary considerably from country to country. In Italy, a quality feature film can receive a maximum of about $64,000, with twenty films each year being so entitled.[5] Prizes for short films range from almost $9,000 to about $16,000. A portion of Italian funds available for quality prizes to short films has been earmarked for films of the Common Market countries. In West Germany, the 1967 budget of the Ministry of the Interior set aside some $175,000 as prizes for German films, about $165,000 for cultural films, and approximately $350,000 as quality bonuses for feature-length films and scenarios.

For the producer, the prize can be an effective means of assistance because it does not have to be repaid. On the other hand, the prize system has a basic drawback in that not all films are eligible for receipt of this gift. The method cannot fulfil a mission of stabilizing production because some films, due to their quality, content, or treatment, may not be judged worthwhile to receive a grant. While the pursuit of excellence is commendable, the prize system encourages production only of films which meet certain criteria, whatever these happen to be. In this case, the integrity of the jury is crucial.

A second method through which the state can assist film production concentrates on loans and credits. The plan generally involves the establishment by the government of a film bank which makes capital available to producers. The basic idea of the film bank, however, has been modified according to the needs of various European countries. The value of a film bank, nonetheless, is that it lends money specifically for motion pictures. Commercial banks, on the other hand, may reject loan applications from producers, believing their investments have a better chance of being repaid in other industrial activities.

The film bank of Great Britain, the National Film Finance Corporation (NFFC), is a public agency similar to the British Broadcasting Corporation. The NFFC is technically under government control because it was established by Parliament and its directors are appointed by the Board of Trade, but in practice it acts with as much autonomy as the BBC. The NFFC operates with a commercial mandate and is not necessarily in business to support or encourage the production of artistic or quality pictures. If in carrying out its obligation to assist the financial backing of British films it also can facilitate production of artistic pictures, then a double purpose is served.

The function of the NFFC, and the general idea of film banks, can be clarified by first understanding how motion pictures usually are financed. The total investment in a production is considered in two parts: front money and end money. Front money, the largest portion of the total backing, is generally around 70 percent and normally is guaranteed or advanced by the distributor to the producer on the basis of the producer's plans, script, stars, etc. The distributor agrees to supply the front money in exchange for distribution rights of the film. The remaining 30 percent, the end money, must be found by the producer. In Great Britain, he might turn to the NFFC which could agree to finance all or part of the 30 percent after reviewing the producer's plans. Normally, the NFFC would supply 25 percent of the total investment, with the final five percent coming from the producer's own resources or from other arrangements he had made.

The distinction between front money and end money also is apparent in the way these loans are repaid. The front money is repaid out of the initial earnings of the film. Once this loan is cancelled, then the producer can begin repaying the end money, most of which is due to the NFFC. The loan from the NFFC "is not normally guaranteed and therefore depends for recovery on the commercial results of the film, except to the extent that the producer may be able to offer other assets (e.g., the profits from other films) as collateral security."[6] Thus the NFFC stands to lose money if the film cannot recoup all its costs.

Between 1950 and 1967, the NFFC advanced $70,000,000 to 694 feature films and 164 short films of which only $43,300,000 was repaid.[7] In October, 1966, the lending function of the Corporation was halted because, owing to "prevailing economic circumstances," it was unable to borrow from nongovernment sources more than

$2,100,000 of the $5,600,000 authorized under law. Ten months later, the NFFC resumed making production loans but on "an extremely selective basis."[8] The problem the Corporation faces was described in its 1963 annual report:

> . . . the Corporation has since its inception been permitted to lend only to persons who in its judgment have reasonable expectations of being able to arrange for the production or distribution of cinematograph films on a commercially successful basis. Thus the Corporation is statutorily obliged to refuse to lend where it considers that the film in question is likely to prove a commercial failure.
>
> The Corporation has found this mandate extremely difficult to apply to individual projects because no reliable estimate of the public's reaction to a particular film can be made before the public sees it, still less before production has begun.[9]

Over the years, the NFFC has played an important role in financing British films. In 1952, the high point, it assisted seven out of every ten British quota films shown on the major theatre circuits. Throughout the 1950's, the Corporation, on the average, assisted more than half of the quota films so shown. During the 1960's however, a different trend set in, with its most marked manifestation in 1965 when the NFFC backed only seventeen percent of the British first and cofeatures exhibited on the two major circuits. The Corporation officially recognized this matter in its 1965 annual report.

> Over the past few years there has emerged a new pattern of film financing which has also had an effect on the Corporation's policy. Talented film-makers are now increasingly able to obtain the finance they need from a single investor, usually the United Kingdom subsidiary of a major U. S. distributor. Though welcome within limits, this growing involvement in the financing of British films by the U. S. distributors, if allowed to expand unchecked, represents a threat to the continuance of a truly British film production industry.[10]

The role American companies play in financing British production has reached an impressive magnitude. While the Corporation backed 24 percent of British first and cofeatures shown on the major circuits in 1966, American companies financed 71 percent. In fact, for the years 1962 to 1966 inclusive, American companies financed almost two and a half times as many British films as the National Film Finance Corporation.[11]

Does this mean the NFFC has outlived its usefulness? The Corporation argues that a British industry relying upon American financing hardly could be termed independent and that the maintenance of a *British* film industry, reflecting British culture, is in the national interest. The Corporation has noted, in addition, that American financing of British production results in some loss of money to Britain due to the distribution commission and finance charge payable to the American distributor. When international markets are concerned, it "follows that a high price in terms of export earnings has to be paid whenever a U.S. distributor is involved in the financing of a British film." The Corporation feels reliance upon American finance might lull the British industry into a false sense of security which could be painfully shattered were American film production "to return to Hollywood, or to go elsewhere."[12]

The future role of the NFFC will be one of the major points considered when the government reviews film legislation upon its expiration. The Film Production Association of Great Britain (a merger of the British Film Producers Association and the Federation of British Film Makers) has recommended the continuation of the NFFC. In the same way, the Corporation itself states that a reorganized and re-funded NFFC is essential for providing "financial backing for British film production independent of external sources. . . ." It sees its future task as being that of encouraging "groups of talented film-makers to form the nucleus of a viable independent British film production industry."[13] It would seem that such a valuable *national* source of aid to production should not be restricted. Its maintenance appears even more pressing due to the extensive American hold on British production.

Modifications of the film bank plan are found in other European countries. In Spain, under the 1965 film law, a producer may receive a government loan of up to 50 percent of the anticipated Spanish share of a film's cost. In special cases, the loan may be as high as 70 percent. In addition, the National Cinematography Institute can make advances of about $17,000 to a producer, repayable over a three year period without interest.

The production of feature films in the Netherlands has been assisted by a special fund set up in 1956 under the aegis of the Nederlandsche Bioscoop-Bond. It is fed by a sum withheld from dues paid to the organization and by a state grant from the Ministry of Education. An advance, averaging about $28,000, can be allotted to a producer of a Dutch film on condition that it be repaid out of the film's profits. The fund, renewable each year, has about $250,000 in it.

No unified system of guarantees exists in West Germany due to the states' autonomy in cultural affairs. However, the states of Bavaria, Hamburg, and Lower Saxony, along with West Berlin, have inaugurated plans of their own. In these cases, local governments can underwrite bank loans to producers varying between 20 and 50 percent of the production costs. In West Berlin, the guarantee has extended to 85 percent of the total budget, and films produced there are eligible for a special subsidy of about $12,500.

A similar guarantee system has operated in Norway. There, the government has guaranteed regular bank loans made to films deemed to be of artistic, cultural, or special interest. The maximum guarantee is about $40,000. The government collects no fee for offering its guarantee but stands to lose money if the production is not profitable.

In Italy, two types of loans have been available to production. The first, ordinary credit, has been available up to 60 percent of the total production cost. The fund has been fed principally by the state, but about a third of its resources have come from a state-sanctioned bank. The second type of loan, special credit, has been available for long term uses at an interest rate of 4 percent. The special credit fund has been fed by a tax formerly applied to films brought into Italy and dubbed into Italian. It will be recalled from an earlier chapter that the Andreotti Act initiated a system of dubbing certificates. A distributor of a film dubbed into Italian had to deposit with the Banca Nazionale del Lavoro a sum of lire which went into the special fund. After ten years, according to the original plan, the distributor could redeem his dubbing certificate and receive the amount he deposited with the Banca but without interest. As it actually happened however, American companies redeemed their certificates before the ten-year period expired, and instead of the original value of the certificates, they received approximately 17 percent through redemption of one lot and 25 percent through redemption of a second lot.[14]

Under the 1965 Italian film law, the production credit fund of the Banca Nazionale del Lavoro is augmented by state contributions totalling more than $1,000,000 over a three-year period. Producers can borrow from the fund up to 30 percent of the cost of production with repayment at 3 percent interest. In addition, the endowment of the Cinema Credit Section of the Banca has been enlarged from slightly more than half a million dollars to almost $5,500,000, the increase coming over a three-year period.[15] State-approved credit in

Italy has assumed an important place in film financing. From 1960 through 1965, more than four hundred films benefitted from assistance totalling more than $146,000,000. This represents about a third of Italian films made (including coproductions) and about a third of production costs.

It should be kept in mind that the film bank method of assistance is little more than a government, or government-guaranteed, *loan* to film production. When a loan is under consideration by the responsible authority, there obviously is attention given to the film's commercial possibilities because continuous failure, due either to films' content or producers' ineptness, would soon drain treasuries and negate the purpose of film banks. While state agencies may be more willing to take chances than commercial banks, they cannot make loans freely to all applicants regardless of their ability or chances of success. But the film bank can absorb losses which might otherwise destroy commercial lenders. One could say that the state has been willing to move into an economic area from which business has moved out.

A third type of assistance available to production is the subsidy. Of the three methods of encouraging production, the subsidy is perhaps the most efficient. Although its exact size and mode of operation vary from country to country, its general purpose is the same. Essentially, money equal to a certain proportion of the box office receipts or of the tax paid on the price of admission is returned to the producer by a state or public agency. In effect, this increases the producer's share of the receipts without reducing the share going to the exhibitor.

The subsidy extends beyond the scope of prizes and film banks. The prize can be awarded to certain films but the subsidy is directed to all national productions even though some may not meet quality criteria. Loans from film banks, while making production funds available, have to be repaid but the subsidy does not, and films receive it even though they may have limited commercial potential. The accomplishment of the subsidy is that it treats all national films equally, regardless of their point of view, content, or chances of success. Even the cost of production is not a factor because a very popular low-budget film can have a rebate equal to or greater than that of a mediocre high-budget film. The marketplace decides the actual magnitude of the subsidy. Considered in these terms, this form of assistance may be the fairest, as its application does not depend upon the decision of a viewing commission or upon the educated guess of an authority charged with advancing production money.[16]

The subsidy does have drawbacks, though. It does not necessarily stimulate production of artistic or cultural films, because it rewards most those producers who have made pictures which are big box office attractions. Furthermore, the subsidy has been charged with introducing false economies into the film business by encouraging producers to think in terms of an increment of revenue not directly derived from admissions. It is also said that the subsidy has generated a number of "fictive coproductions" designed solely to tap subsidy funds of two nations rather than one. Some observers feel the subsidy is "lost money" in contrast to prizes which encourage quality, and loans which have a chance of repayment. Finally, in more impassioned terms, the subsidy creates "irresistible outside pressures" and can "wither the freedom of individual thought."[17] But this charge also can be levelled at bank financing, production codes, and censorship, as well as at the marketplace itself. Strange, but the most progressive, avant-garde, and original artistic work in the postwar cinema has come, not from subsidy-free Hollywood, but from the subsidized industries of France, Italy, Britain, and Sweden!

Before discussing the operation of the subsidy system in the more important film-producing countries of Europe, one ought to examine this form of assistance as it has functioned in a smaller market.

The text of the 1963 Belgian film aid law is presented in Appendix A because it indicates in clear and concise terms the basic elements of the system. For our purposes, its most important part is that dealing with the subsidization of feature films. The Minister of Economic Affairs is authorized to distribute to the producer of a Belgian film a rebate of 70, 75, or 80 percent of the tax paid on admissions for the picture, the exact percentage being determined by a thirteen-member Film Commission. The Belgian subsidy also works in conjunction with film quality, a novel feature not found in legislation of other countries. The admission tax in Belgium is about 18 percent of the ticket price and a subsidy figured on 80 percent of this tax corresponds to approximately 14.4 percent of the gross receipts. On the low end of the scale, a 70 percent subsidy would be equal to about 12.6 percent of the gross receipts. This is quite congruent with the 13 percent subsidy in Italy and France, other Common Market countries with assisted film production.

A "Belgian" film is defined as one in which at least half of the salaries and costs of the picture are paid to Belgian nationals. The film also must have been produced by Belgians, or a Belgian company not under the control of a foreign company. A foreigner who has the status of an official Belgian resident can receive a subsidy, providing reciprocity exists between Belgium and the foreigner's country of origin. (Films made under an international coproduction agreement also qualify for Belgian nationality.) The law decrees that the film must be shot in Belgium, although exceptions are made for exteriors required by the plot and those made necessary due to climatic reasons (Belgium is rather wet). The film must be processed in Belgian laboratories, but an exemption is provided for those processes which cannot be accomplished in the country's labs.

In the case of Belgium, the national market is extremely small, and little foreign investment has been made in its film production industry. A foreign producer who makes a film there and has it recognized as "Belgian" can recover only as much as 80 percent of the admission tax for his film. With approximately one thousand theatres in the country and an average seat price of about $.45, the economic incentive is not very great for a foreign producer. Moreover, the box office power of a Belgian film outside the country is limited. Thus, few financial advantages are to be gained by an American producer who shoots a film in Belgium (or a similar small country) with local talent and technicians. These factors, the magnitude of the subsidy and the size of the market, become increasingly clear as production in the larger markets is surveyed.

Assistance to the British industry is a function of the British Film Production Fund, popularly known as the "Eady levy" after Sir Wilfred Eady, who generally is given credit for formulating the plan. According to the British Film Producers Association, "the film production industry in [Britain] is not subsidised by the Government" and the "levy is not a subsidy."[18] This opinion is grounded on the fact that funds available for assisting production do not come from the state treasury but originate in the money audiences pay to see films. On the other hand, one could point to the government legislation which was necessary for the Production Fund to begin operating, and to the fact that the British Film Fund Agency, which administers the Production Fund, was organized by the Board of Trade through powers conferred upon it by Parliament. Essentially, one is faced with a public agency operating independently of the government but carrying out government policy. Whether a payment from the Production Fund constitutes a subsidy is a moot question which will not be debated here. However, in this discussion of the British industry, payments will be referred to as subsidies, because they constitute an additional increment of revenue available to producers, are made automatically regardless of a film's artistic or cultural value, and do not have to be repaid by producers.

The Production Fund operates in the following way. According to the price of each ticket, the exhibitor sets aside a portion of the entrance fee and turns it over to the Film Fund Agency which puts the revenues into the Production Fund. The maker of a British film then applies to the Agency for a payment from the Fund based upon the distributor's gross of his film. (The distributor's gross is that portion of the box office receipts remaining after deductions are made for entertainment tax [when it was in force] and the exhibitor's share. The distributor's gross includes his own and the producer's share of the film's earnings.) The Fund is fed from admissions paid for all films but payments are made only to makers of "British" pictures.

The Production Fund, started as a one-year and voluntary measure in September, 1950, was part of a larger plan which included adjustment of the entertainment tax and the raising of certain admission prices. It was voluntary to the extent that exhibitors were not penalized if they did not join the scheme. The following year, it was recognized that "although the first Eady plan went a long way towards solving the industry's financial problems it did not close the gap between the producers' costs and their receipts. . . ."[19] It was believed the effectiveness of the subsidy could be felt only over a long period. As a result, the Production Fund was extended first until 1954 and subsequently until 1957.

One study of the British film industry has observed

> . . . that the only means of survival for a British production
> — industry might be through permanent Government support. There
> can be no denying that however indirect it may be the [1951 to
> 1954] Fund is a form of subvention, but it is not permanent.
> Nevertheless it does offer producers a security which they lacked
> previously. . . .[20]

Responding to demands from the film industry, the government made the Production Fund statutory in 1957 and thereby officially recognized the industry's need for a compulsory and long-term form of assistance. The act made it public policy to subsidize production of "British" films on a continuous basis.

The eligibility of films to receive payment has been a problem raised numerous times within the British industry because subsidiaries of American companies produce films legally defined as "British," therefore qualifying for the subsidy. In 1956 for example, John Davis, then president of the British Film Producers Association, commented on this problem.

> The British Film Production Fund was established in 1950 on the initiative of the Government for the purpose of providing British producers with a supplementary revenue over and above receipts from cinema box-offices in this country. Although it was agreed at the time that the distribution of the Fund should, generally speaking, be for the benefit of British quota films, it is obvious that the scheme would not have been put forward by the Government or accepted by the industry on the ground that the levy recoverable from the box office takings was required to support films made in this country by American subsidiaries.[21]

At the center of this issue is the definition of a "British" film. The 1960 Films Act states which criteria must be met for declaring a film to be "British quota" because only films so labelled can receive the subsidy. According to the Act, a film can be declared "British" providing

> (a) that the maker of the film was, throughout the time during which the film was being made, either a British subject or a citizen of the Republic of Ireland, or a company to which this paragraph applies; and
>
> (b) that the studio, if any, used in making the film was in a Commonwealth country or the Republic of Ireland; and
>
> (c) that not less than the requisite amount of labour costs represents payments paid or payable in respect of the labour or services of British subjects or citizens of the Republic of Ireland or persons ordinarily resident in a Commonwealth country or the Republic of Ireland
>
> Paragraph (a) . . . of this section applies to a company if, and only if,—
>
> (a) it is incorporated under the laws of any Commonwealth country or of the Republic of Ireland; and
>
> (b) its directors, or the majority of its directors, are British subjects or citizens of the Republic of Ireland.[22]

"The maker of the film" is construed as meaning the company which handles arrangements for the production of the picture, and does not refer to the company which actually does the shooting, although the two often are identical. The 1965 coproduction agreement between the United Kingdom and France stipulates that films made in accordance with its terms also are eligible for "British" nationality.

The actual average rate of subsidy in Great Britain is somewhat higher than in Belgium, France, or Italy. A claim for payment is made on the total distributor's earnings of the film. An amount based on a percentage of these earnings is then paid as the subsidy. This percentage has fluctuated between a low of 39.6 percent (year ending October, 1963) and a high of 51.0 percent (year ending October, 1966). During the first nine years of the statutory Fund, the *average* payment has been 44.3 percent of the distributor's share of the film's earnings.

For the purpose of computation, if one takes as a guide that the distributor's share is about 37 percent of the gross,[23] then 44.3 percent of the distributor's share is equivalent to slightly more than 16 percent of the gross receipts of the film. This compares with 13 percent of the gross in France and Italy and about 12 to 14 percent in Belgium. This 16 percent subsidy (based on the gross) is only an average over a nine-year period, however, and is somewhat lower than the actual current rate. The Fund paid at the rate of 51.0 percent of the distributor's share in the year ending October, 1966. Again, assuming the distributor's share as 37 percent of the gross (rather low for extravagant films), then it appears that the present average subsidy rate is more on the order of almost 19 percent of the gross receipts for a picture. Considered on this basis, it is not surprising that "at almost any given time of the year, British studios are dominated by American-sponsored production."[24] The subsidy in Great Britain means that for every dollar paid to see a "British" film, the Production Fund pays the producer about $.19 over and above the producer's normal share of the admission price.[25]

Aside from the large share of the subsidy taken by American companies (as the next chapter will reveal), the Production Fund has provided over the years much-needed support for film production in Britain. In its nine years of statutory operation to October, 1966, the Fund paid more than $97,000,000 in subsidies to British film production. As an authoritative source in Great Britain told this author, "film production here would collapse without the Fund."

The manner of assisting French film production is somewhat different from that in Great Britain. The subsidy (French producers do not argue against the use of this word) is paid directly by a government agency to a producer toward the cost of his *next* film, thus encouraging further production (over-production, some say). The subsidy comes from a fund fed by a tax on the admission price (yielding from $13,000,000 to $14,000,000 annually) and a release tax calculated on the length of a film sent into distribution (yielding about $1,000,000 annually).

To be eligible to generate a subsidy (payable for the next film), a picture must be declared "French" by the Centre National de la Cinématographie under criteria in Articles 13 and 14 of Law 59–1512 (as amended) of December, 1959, or be "produced in international co-production conforming to dispositions of a governmental co-production agreement." "French" films must meet these criteria:

Article 13

. . .

1. Be made by French producers in an original version recorded in the French language using French authors, technicians, production personnel, as well as principal actors.

   Concerning the application of these conditions, foreigners having the quality of resident or privileged resident can be considered as French citizens;

2. Considering paragraph 1 above, be made with labor corresponding to conditions cited in the decree of April 23, 1933 fixing the proportion of foreign workers able to be employed by entertainment establishments;

3. Be shot in recognized studios situated in metropolitan France or in overseas departments and territories, or in places not necessitating set construction;

4. Be developed, edited, and printed in recognized laboratories situated in metropolitan France or in overseas departments and territories.

   The criteria which films of international co-production must meet are fixed by the governmental agreements concluded to this effect. . . .

Article 14

Authorized production companies of French nationality benefit from financial support. The presidents, general directors, directors, and managers as well as the majority of administrators must be of French nationality.

Foreigners satisfying the quality of resident or privileged resident and practicing the cinematographic profession in France for more than five years can be considered as French citizens for the application of the present article.[26]

Several modifications have been made in the French subsidy plan, the more recent ones being of primary interest.[27] In 1963, the scheme was changed and based entirely on earnings in metropolitan France and in French overseas territories. The producer was awarded a sum equal to 14 percent of the film's gross receipts. A subsequent modification provided for a 13 percent payment for all films shown publicly for the first time after July 1, 1964. The present system is an automatic subsidy to production calculated at the rate of 13 percent of the gross receipts earned during five years from exhibitions in metropolitan France and in French overseas territories.[28]

Perhaps the rationale for modification of the French subsidy program existed in the drive for consistency among those members of the European Economic Community which subsidized production at that time. Paralleling French changes, Italy revised its own scheme from a flat 16 percent of a film's earnings to 14 percent. More recently, the 1965 Italian film law reduced this to 13 percent. Currently, Italian production subsidies are automatic and are paid at the rate of 13 percent of the gross receipts made in Italy during a period of five years. The standardization of the French and Italian programs mean, then, that payments are based only on receipts accruing to films in their home markets and are computed by the same percentage.

At least brief reference should be made to details of the Italian subsidy which, unlike those in Britain and France, is part of the state budget and not susceptible to box office fluctuations. The subsidy is granted only to films declared "Italian" and to official Italian coproductions. The film law of November, 1965, established criteria for Italian nationality. The film, either fiction or documentary, must be at least 1,600 meters long, and at least 70 percent of the interior scenes must be shot in Italian studios with sound recorded at the time of shooting. Among other criteria which must be met are those noted in Title II, Article 4 of the film law:

> Declared national are long films produced in original Italian version which have been produced predominantly in Italy by companies belonging to Italian citizens, or by companies having a legal office in Italy, with Italian administrators who carry on in Italy the greatest part of their activity, and which fulfil the following conditions:
> a) that the scenario comes from an Italian author or is revised or adapted by an Italian author;
> b) that the director, and the majority of script writers, must be Italian;
> c) that at least two-thirds of the principal roles, and at least three-fourths of the secondary roles must be given to Italian actors. Foreign actors can be admitted in a greater percentage than is

authorized if they have official Italian residence for more than three years and in cases where they are required for special roles;

d) that at least three-quarters of the following must be Italian: musicians, set designer, costume designer, director of photography, cameraman, editor, sound engineer, production assistant, production director, production supervisor, production secretary, and make-up man;

e) that all remaining technical, executive, and production personnel must be Italian.[29]

The 1965 film law slightly revised the definition of an "Italian" film and this is pertinent to American investment in Italian production, covered in the following chapter.

Of the Common Market countries, only Luxemburg produces no films. The Netherlands, with little feature film production, has no formal subsidization system, although Dutch films do benefit from indirect measures. Belgium, also a small producer of features, does have a subsidization program, similar to those of France and Italy. But what of West Germany with its economically faltering and artistically thin film industry? And equally important, has the Bonn government financially assisted production in keeping with the general mandate to manage the national economy and to encourage and perpetuate artistic media?

January 1, 1968, may well become the turning point for the postwar German film industry, for on that date a subsidization plan went into effect. After more than a decade of government resistance, coupled with deadly antagonism between producers and exhibitors, a film aid law finally was approved in December, 1967. Its significance can be estimated on a number of scales, not the least of which is that each major film-producing nation in the Common Market now has a subsidization plan.

The new program (its effectiveness still to be evaluated) will allocate about $37,000 to each German film grossing over $125,000 in Germany, measured over a two-year period. The sum must be reinvested by the producer in his next film. In exceptional cases, the producer can be allowed to use the subsidy to pay for the cost of the original film if it loses money at the box office. Moreover, and this is a novel feature, the producer of an assisted film must sell its television rights for five years to the Film Aid Institute for about $25,000, whether or not the Institute uses these rights.[30] Similarly, this sum must be reinvested by the producer within a two-year period. Films eligible for the subsidy include "German" national films and those made under international coproduction agreements, with at least a 40 percent German participation. Furthermore, the assisted film has to be rented to threatres for a "normal" fee, and its exhibition cannot be restricted.

The law established the Film Aid Institute, whose missions are developing the quality of German films, supporting coproduction, assisting the economic status of the entire film industry, reviewing cooperation between the industry and television, publicizing German films at home and abroad, and, significantly, advising the federal government on the *harmonization of aid systems* within the European Economic Community.

The aid fund is fed from a portion of the admission price, about three cents per ticket, paid for performances comprising at least one feature film. It is expected to be worth about $6,250,000 annually, compared to about three times that figure for the French aid fund. Money will be dispensed to production and exhibition on a ratio of two to one. The right of an exhibitor to financial assistance depends upon his business turnover; the greater it is, the smaller his aid.

Ultimate passage of the aid law was delayed for years because of industry in-fighting. Exhibitors demanded better competitive conditions with television (notably reservation of television rights to new films), no aid to production without aid to theatres, the fixing of rental terms for subsidized films, and the subsidization of "good entertainment films" as the basis for government intervention in the film industry. The West German government, it is said, was inclined to defer passage of film legislation until the industry settled its own internal difficulties.

Another factor which hindered passage was the distribution of legislative power within West Germany. The federal constitution relegated cultural matters to state governments, each one having complete autonomy over such affairs within its domain. This worked against inauguration of any unified system of production aid in Germany. Significantly, the federal film aid law was approved under the title of *economic* action, by-passing and implicitly ignoring film as a cultural entity.[31]

Certainly, additional pressure against a subsidy in West Germany came from the federal government's adherence to the free enterprise philosophy and the belief that business could be run through competition and private incentive. It is no secret, of course, that these tenets are carry-overs from the occupation days and result from the direction in which the West German economy was pushed by the High Commission. The change of policy is somewhat embarrassing, for it is an implicit admission that free enterprise has not been able to achieve the goal of a healthy economy operating in the general welfare. If the lack of subsidization seemed out of tune with the "Social Market Economy" enunciated by Ludwig Erhard, then one has to conclude that the government had closed its eyes to film industry problems or that it was laboring under the illusion that German film production would right itself after painful growing years. Sources in West Germany have been frank in admitting that film production there is a sick industry and not likely to recover without some form of continuous, effective aid.

West Germany's position was even more striking when considered within the framework of the Common Market. Its objective, to unify and standardize economic matters—and implicitly to develop a uniform attitude toward film production aid—thus bore greatly on the policies adopted by France, Italy, and West Germany. France and Italy already were subsidizing film production and both had modified their programs to make them identical. On the other hand, to repeat, West Germany had had no subsidy.

It would be an understatement to say that this was a major discussion topic whenever European film industry authorities met to consider how the various industries could be matched, let alone integrated. (Efforts to standardize film industry matters actually preceded by several years the official beginning of the Common Market itself.) France and Italy consistently took the position that subsidization was the rock stabilizing their film industries, and urged West Germany to build on the same foundation. Before France and Italy had identical systems their position against West Germany was not as strong. There were always hints, for example, that one of the two would stop subsidization and join West Germany's position. However, with the matching of the French and Italian aid schemes, the policy of subsidization was reaffirmed. The governments acknowledged that production subsidies are indispensable and they waited for the Bonn government to come to the same realization. Now this has happened.

In terms of the EEC's mechanisms, subsidization of film production has posed a problem and has had to be reconciled with provisions of the Treaty of Rome condemning subsidization which distorts competition. The European Commission has observed that members' film industries, like maritime construction, are worthy of special consideration because they are "important industries going through structural

difficulties."[32] In addition, the European Community film industries
are faced competitively by an American industry which not only
controls distribution on a worldwide basis but has dominant positions
in non-Community markets and a strong position within the Community itself. This has put EEC films at a disadvantage. When coupled
with the cultural aspects of film, it has been recognized that some
form of aid must exist if film industries are to remain solvent. The
crucial question now facing the Community is not whether to subsidize production, but what form the subsidization will take.

The solution can be seen in two phases. The first is harmonization
of national subsidy systems, apparent in the similarity of the French
and Italian plans. The Belgian program, although operating on somewhat different criteria, yields about the same results. West Germany's
scheme has some identity with the others but does not involve a
percentage payment. Harmonization would mean, of course, as many
plans as there are members subsidizing production. They would be
administered domestically by each country after the basic concepts
were approved by the European Commission. This is essentially the
approach being taken now within the Community. For example, in
1964 the French government notified the European Commission of
the reduction of the subsidy rate from 14 to 13 percent. When the
Italian film law was considered in 1965, the Commission also was
notified, and examined a draft version. In both cases, the Commission
raised no objections to the final form of the legislation; thus an implicit
opinion became obvious that the plans were justified and did not give
one industry an advantage over others. In this connection, it is important to note that in January, 1965, the first meeting under Community
auspices was held to study the framework for film aid within the
EEC. This meeting in Brussels produced the opinion that the first
step should be alignment of existing national legislation on financial
assistance. Moreover, it was recognized that maintaining film production on a sound basis in the Community was in the common interest.

The second step, admittedly in the future, is a *Community* system
of subsidization which would treat the six member nations as *one
domestic market* for the computation of the subsidy payment. As
national subsidy legislation becomes similar, the various plans could
be merged under the aegis of the EEC with one organization adminis-
tering payment from one central fund. Precedents for integration of
film industries and standardization of policy already exist in the First
and Second Directives (and the proposed Third Directive) pertaining
to film matters of the EEC Council. Significantly, the First Directive

defines a "Community" film—without, however, calling it that in so many words.[33] The French and Italian definitions for their national films parallel the Community definition, while that of a "German" film is identical with it. In this respect, harmonization of subsidy legislation can be the first step toward complete integration of financial aid.

Automatic subsidization of production is economically important and, in many ways, necessary for European film industries. While prizes and loans do perform essential functions of rewarding excellence and making production financing available,[34] only the subsidy provides a consistent increment of revenue above normal box office receipts. Almost all European countries have adopted the subsidy to make film production economically feasible and artistically and culturally possible.[35]

Progress is being made toward resolving the subsidization problem in the Community, especially in view of West Germany's recent action. Moreover, two prospective Community members, Spain and the United Kingdom, have subsidized production. The current work of aligning various financial schemes proceeds as the lessons of experience unfold. But while this matter seems to be more or less in hand, another one is becoming increasingly important—that of third party (American) investment in Community film production.

9: Trends in the European Film Industry: American Investment in European Film Production

One of the most impressive developments in the last twenty years is the phenomenal rise in American financial interest in British, Italian, and, to a smaller degree, French film production. The causes of this can be found here and abroad.

When the American market was able to support film making in Hollywood, the industry gave relatively little attention to Europe. But in the decade after World War II, the situation changed with the lessening of demand for films in the United States, the growth of competitive entertainment and diversion, and the consent decrees which restructured the industry. At the same time, production costs were increasing, due to general economic inflation and to the nature of films being produced.

While these profound changes were occurring in the domestic market, the American industry was being influenced by events abroad. Because of an aggressive American export campaign, foreign markets slowly increased in importance until they were contributing slightly more theatrical revenue to the American industry than was the United States. The economic policies of foreign countries also affected Hollywood. The balance of payments problem forced most European nations to freeze American film companies' earnings. With the exchange into dollars of pounds, francs, and lire prohibited, companies found themselves with large accounts of foreign revenue. As these earnings could not be taken out of Europe in dollars, the companies felt they could be taken out in the form of goods—motion pictures. The availability of unremittable funds drove companies to shooting abroad, and films were made, partially or entirely, in Europe.[1]

This initial desertion of the Hollywood lots for the studios and countrysides of Britain, Italy, France, Spain, and other nations was a direct result of blocked earnings and company desires to spend them. True, some films produced in this way were of little merit, hardly more noteworthy than the grade B pictures made in this country. Their claims to fame, it seems, were in unmotivated pans of landscapes and towns, contrived scenes taking place in "native" cafes, and local actors in secondary roles saying a few words (but not too many) in their own languages to add color. Films of this era occasionally are available today for viewing on television.

In producing in Europe, American companies quickly learned that a given film could be made less expensively and often with fewer union problems than in the United States. Moreover, the companies had to keep in mind that revenues and corporate solvency were depending more and more upon foreign audiences. Thus, the American film industry was thinking not only in terms of Denver and Boston but was considering the reaction of audiences in other parts of the world.

The initial wave of runaway production acquainted American companies more thoroughly with European methods of film making. It demonstrated that Hollywood was not the only place in the world where films could be produced, and that foreign studios, technicians, and actors were competent and experienced. In one sense, it proved that multimillion dollar plants and multimillion dollar payrolls were not necessarily the prerequisites for financial success or artistic excellence, nor necessarily the causes of trite plots and make-believe worlds. The new closeness to European production also showed American companies that some American-made films shot on location with foreign actors could have box office appeal in the United States.

Familiarity with European production did not lessen when blocked earnings were spent and remittances liberalized. The original relationships were cemented when American producers and film companies realized that by rearranging their corporate structures and by forming new ones they too could benefit from production subsidies available in Europe. Having introduced themselves to shooting films abroad, American companies saw the next logical step as having these films declared "national" by European countries so they could have access to subsidization. The turning point was around 1950, the year in

which a subsidy was initiated in Britain and two years after inauguration of subsidization in France and Italy.

While blocked earnings were responsible for the first wave of
runaway production, the availability of subsidization was the cause of
its perpetuation and development into a second wave which cannot be
attributed to unremittable revenues. One could argue that lower labor
costs are the sole cause. While they certainly cannot be dismissed, a
moment's reflection will reveal that the subsidy, as a variable, is of
greater importance.

The vast majority of American overseas financial participation is
centered in the United Kingdom, Italy, and France, in that order.
Each has a subsidy program. Certainly production costs in England
are not less than they are in West Germany, which until 1968 had no
subsidization and drew little American investment. Nor are production costs in the three countries less than they are in Spain which had
no subsidy plan until 1965. Although production costs are rising in
Spain, the availability of a subsidy has begun to attract American
producers. But even though Spain is still cheaper than Italy, there
certainly is more American money in Italian than in Spanish production.

The size of the market and the existence of adequate production
facilities also must be considered. Sweden has a subsidy plan and
production facilities, the latter not on the same scale as Britain, Italy,
or France. Yet Sweden has attracted little American investment, presumably due, among other points, to the smallness of the home market
(less than eight million population) and the equally small rebates
obtainable. Belgium, with a production subsidy plan equal to that of
France and Italy, has drawn no American investment. The lack of
extensive studios there and the smallness of the home market constitute barriers, although the wage scale is comparable to that of France.
The Netherlands, with no subsidization, without substantial production facilities, and in spite of low wage rates, likewise has drawn no
American money.

Considered in these terms, low labor costs may make Europe an
attractive place for American production, but the availability of subsidies and sufficiently large markets dictates the countries in which most
of the American investment will be made. Certainly production costs
are even lower in other parts of the world. Yet American investment
gravitates to a handful of western European countries—all with subsidized film production.

It is not surprising that American companies have restructured themselves and added new appendages. As production subsidies are not offered in the United States, it is natural that these companies should want to avail themselves of this extra revenue. By designing new corporate bodies they act in their own self-interest, for to neglect acquiring additional income would hardly make sense in business terms.

Perhaps the situation in Great Britain indicates the simplest form of an American production subsidiary.[2] There, an American company which wholly owns a British subsidiary can produce pictures which meet the legal criteria for being designated "British," and therefore have access to the British Film Production Fund. This is accomplished by subscribing to conditions for the maker of a "British" film as established in the Films Act. According to it, "the maker of the film" must be "either a British subject . . . or a company [which is] encorporated under the laws of any Commonwealth country [and whose] directors, or the majority of its directors, are British subjects. . . ." The law says nothing about the nationalities of stockholders or where overall control of the company is exercised, nor does it set criteria for the source of production money. In organizing a subsidiary, an American parent can incorporate the company under British laws and appoint a majority of British subjects to the board of directors. This yields a British company whose affairs are conducted by directors predominantly British, but which is owned by, and its overall policies determined by, the American parent. The membership lists of the Federation of British Film Makers and the British Film Producers Association (prior to their merger) included such subsidiaries as Columbia (British) Productions Ltd., Paramount British Pictures Ltd., M.G.M. British Studios Ltd., Twentieth Century-Fox Productions Ltd., United Artists Corporation Ltd., Walt Disney Productions Ltd., and Warner Brothers Productions Ltd.

American majors have not been the only ones active in this field, for independent producers and directors have also established British companies. Carl Foreman, an advocate of a production subsidy in the United States, has been the managing director of Open Road Films Ltd., a British producing company. Open Road, a member of the Federation of British Film Makers, was the producing company for *The Key, The Mouse That Roared, Guns of Navarone,* and *Born Free.* In the same way, Sam Spiegel is director of Horizon Pictures (G.B.) Ltd., a company responsible for making *Lawrence of Arabia* and a number of other films. Horizon was a member of the British Film Producers Association. Stanley Kubrick's Hawk Films Ltd. and

Martin Ritt's Salem Films Ltd., both FBFM members, are British companies. The former produced *Dr. Strangelove,* and the latter *The Spy Who Came in From the Cold.* Between 1958 and 1961, Hecht-Hill-Lancaster Films Ltd. was a member of the FBFM and produced *The Devil's Disciple* and *Season of Passion.* Because these British companies are normally private, details of their capitalization and stock ownership do not have to be reported publicly. As a result, there could well be a number of such producing companies held by Americans which go undetected.

One can ask whether there have been serious efforts to stop American subsidiaries from receiving the subsidy. The answer is illuminated by an event in April, 1959, when the House of Lords was considering problems involving payments from the British Film Production Fund. To clarify the position of films made in Commonwealth nations to the Fund, an amendment was introduced which would have excluded such films from drawing subsidies. The amendment would have limited eligibility to pictures

> the maker of which was throughout the time the film was being made, a person ordinarily resident in, or a company registered in, and the *central management and control* of whose business was exercised in, the United Kingdom.[3] (Italics mine)

The implication of this amendment extended beyond Commonwealth films and hit precisely at American subsidiaries which were making "British" pictures. Lord Archibald, president of the FBFM, asked for clarification of the amendment, for he believed it would implicitly endanger the status of "British" films made by such companies as Paramount, Twentieth Century-Fox, or M.G.M. He noted that the phrase "central management and control" could be construed as meaning that British Metro, for example, was a subsidiary of an American company and that management and control were exercised in the United States rather than in the United Kingdom. In answer to Lord Archibald's question, the Minister speaking for the government gave formal assurance

> that the position of U. K. resident companies which are subsidiaries of American or other companies was not endangered by the amendment. This assurance was repeated when the Draft Regulations came before the House of Commons.[4]

It is understandable from this vignette that the British government is quite aware of the production activities of American subsidiaries and that their films can qualify for subsidies. That this condition has been permitted to continue and grow is explainable in that American production is a source of employment for British actors and technicians and that American investment is a stimulant to the production industry. Even the National Film Finance Corporation has observed:

> The financial support of the US companies to film production in Britain is to be welcomed. Without it indeed there would scarcely be a film production industry here. The Corporation believes that nothing should be done to discourage the continuance of US investment.[5]

The production subsidy in Britain can be seen as an exchange—employment of British workers and use of British studios in trade for an increment of revenue above that coming from the normal receipts of a picture. That the employment aspect is real can be judged from comments made by Walter Wanger, producer of *Cleopatra*. The original planning for that film called for it to be made in such a way as to be declared "British" and be eligible for subsidization. In describing the preproduction phase of *Cleopatra*, Mr. Wanger noted in November, 1959:

> [Buddy] Adler [Twentieth Century-Fox studio head] talking about taking advantage of the Eady Plan for *Cleopatra*, which confirms London as headquarters [for the production].
>
> Under the Eady Plan, it is possible for an American company to get financial aid from the British government [sic] if a certain percentage of cast and crew are British. The idea is to give more employment to British workers.[6]

By July, 1960, plans for the film had undergone several changes. Mr. Wanger was opposed to shooting in England and preferred to have the whole film done in Italy. He felt that even though a subsidy was involved, shooting interiors in England and exteriors in Italy would not be practical because

> . . . the budget arrived at was 5,200,000 dollars. Consequently, anybody could have figured out, by coming to England where they were shooting a five-day week instead of a six-day week, it must mount up to more. Also, we would be in two location operations—London and Rome—rather than just in Rome, which again would run up expenses, *especially under the Eady Plan, where we would have to take a lot of English staff wherever we went.*[7] (Italics mine)

Cleopatra was started in England, but the work done there was scrapped and the picture never materialized as a "British" film eligible for a subsidy. This is a rather clear case of a film which would have been an American project but, at the same time, legally "British." The financing for the film was American, the production policy was set by the Fox corporation in the United States, yet it would have received a subsidy in Great Britain (and perhaps have gone on to be hailed as still another example of the rebirth of the British cinema).

A more recent case, and on the other end of the cost scale, is *Dutchman,* the film version of an off-Broadway play about race relations in New York City. The script has been described as "indigenously American" but the film as "technically British."[8] The main shooting was in Twickenham Studios in England and took only six days (reportedly, three cameras were used). Production costs were about $70,000. Its American producer, Gene Persson, established a British company, Kaitlin Productions, to be the maker of the picture. It was directed by Anthony Harvey, who is British, and was registered as a "British" film with the Board of Trade in January, 1968. It will receive payments from the Production Fund.

Given that American subsidiaries do produce "British" pictures, do they draw substantial sums from the Fund? Unfortunately, there are no official public data available revealing the amounts any producer receives from the Fund. The evidence which is obtainable, however, indicates that American subsidiaries have discovered the Eady Plan to be quite lucrative.

According to a report on the Production Fund's second year of operation from September, 1951, to August, 1952, (before it became statutory), American subsidiaries drew about $154,000 in payments. During the fourth year of operation, 1953 to 1954, American companies drew almost $500,000 from it.[9] The substantial rise in payments between the two periods reflects the increase in the number of "British" films made by American companies. But that was some fifteen years ago when runaway production was only beginning, when rental terms had not yet soared to the heights of the 1960's, and the era of the big budget picture had hardly started.

One recent estimate is that American subsidiaries in Great Britain now receive as much as 80 percent of the subsidy from the Fund.[10] For the operating year up to October, 1965, the Fund made total payments of $12,400,000. If the 80 percent estimate is accurate, then in 1965 American companies received close to $10,000,000, a twentyfold increase from the 1953–1954 period before the Fund became statutory. The $10,000,000 estimate does not seem unreasonable as it is reported that *Goldfinger, Tom Jones,* and *Guns of Navarone* (all involving American participation) collected among them about $3,500,000 in subsidy payments.[11] The lucrative aspect of producing in Britain has led to a situation in which, according to one British film producer, "We have a thriving film production industry in this country which is virtually owned, lock stock and barrel, by Hollywood."[12]

The extent of American investment in British production can be illustrated in other ways. The British Film Producers Association conducted a survey during the 1965–1966 year which revealed that about half of all films made by its members were supported by American investment and that in terms of money the proportion was even greater.[13] The National Film Finance Corporation has determined, for 1962 to 1966 inclusive, that 57 percent of British first and cofeatures exhibited on the two main theatre circuits were financed wholly or partially by American companies. A trend during those five years was clearly present, as the proportion of American-financed pictures increased steadily from 43 percent in 1962 to 71 percent in 1966. Concerning the magnitude of finance, American sources provided almost 75 percent of the production money for British films in 1965 and 1966. The NFFC predicted that the "corresponding proportions for 1967 and 1968 may exceed 90 percent."[14]

It seems there are two major reasons British film makers are willing to accept American backing. First, American companies, in many instances, agree to finance 100 percent of the production cost as opposed to British companies which might finance, say, 70 percent of it. Connected to this is the often-heard comment that British finance today is drier and tighter than in the past.[15] In this respect, American money might not only be easier to obtain, but obtainable in larger amounts.

Second, the American industry has the only integrated worldwide film distribution system. Administratively at least, it is easier to deal with such a system. Moreover, access to the wealthy American market is virtually guaranteed if an American company is involved financially in the production. A British producer would obviously give preference to American finance in order to achieve this sort of circulation for his film.

The adage about control of distribution giving one control of the industry bears on the nature of films produced with money from

American sources. The British Monopolies Commission noted in its 1966 report on the film industry:

> . . . for most producers the very fact that they rely on distributors for finance inevitably means that they cannot be wholly independent of them, since clearly distributors cannot decide to finance a project or to guarantee it without some assessment of its commercial prospects. Generally therefore the producer is not in a position to determine wholly independently what kind of film shall be made.[16]

The financier obviously has veto power over a film. This can be exercised in the broadest way by approval or disapproval of the entire project, or in more specific terms by modification of the script, actors, locale, etc.

Nevertheless, there is a considerable body of opinion in the United Kingdom which is not disturbed about American companies' control of British film production. The basis for this exists in the financial success many American-financed "British" pictures have had. In business terms, the large American investment has been seen as a panacea for the ailments of the British industry. One recent study, which believed the British industry should be judged on "its commercial performance," rejected the "chauvinism that distrusts American investment in British films."[17] By the same token, the Monopolies Commission felt that "even where there are signs of American influence in a film, . . . we would not consider this to be a matter affecting the public interest. . . ."[18] The Federation of British Film Makers, declaring that the recent successes of British pictures "owe more to American than to British finance," has asserted that American involvement has meant "an enhanced status for British films throughout the world" and that this cooperation "must be welcomed and encouraged."[19]

The British production industry, if one can argue that a substantial *national* one really does exist today, is little more than a branch of Hollywood, dependent upon American companies for both finance and distribution. In economic terms, and in the short run, there is no question that American finance has been a needed elixir for the British film industry. Most producers and industry experts approve the current state of affairs, for the industry is economically healthier now than in the past. Yet, one is forced to wonder whether the British industry has not lost something in the trade; if it has not exchanged autonomy and the chance to manifest its own culture for the appetizing glory of financial success with many of what are often called mid-

Atlantic productions. Indeed, it seems strange that the British industry, which for years pressed for a screen quota, a film production bank, and a subsidy plan to protect itself from extinction at the hands of the American industry and its films, has now become part of the organism it sought to hold at arm's length—and willingly accepts this position. This certainly has been an extraordinary turning of tables. The screen quota assures American-financed "British" films a place in British theatres at the expense of foreign films; most of the production subsidy now goes to American subsidiaries; and the film bank wonders whether it will be rendered sterile by American largesse. If Britain should become a member of the Common Market, the American film industry will not have to worry about trade obstacles for it is already firmly entrenched.

A survey of American interests in European films must consider Italy and France, the only continental nations which have drawn substantial sums of American money. Together, they attract a conservatively estimated $40,000,000 annually. Perhaps the most interesting and significant development in these countries regarding finance is the modification of those portions of film laws which bear on nationality, and thus implicitly determine which films are eligible for subsidization. In the case of the United Kingdom, its law established no criteria for the ownership of the producing company—that is, who might capitalize it. The film laws of both France and Italy have changed on this point, and in the direction of liberalizing the definition of a national picture. (Perhaps they are competing with Britain for American production dollars?)

In France, the film law of December, 1959, established criteria for the conferral of "French" nationality. In addition to the usual standards relating to actors, technicians, writers, place of shooting, etc., the law dealt with production companies and required that the "capital for these companies must be held in the majority by French citizens."[20] A wholly American-owned subsidiary could not have made a "French" film eligible for subsidy due to the origin of the company's capital—American. However, this did not prove to be a barrier to American investment. An American party wishing to make a "French" film could establish a legal French company with nominal assets held, in the majority, by French citizens or foreigners with resident quality. The rest of the capital for the company could be supplied directly from American sources. In this way, a paper company could be formed which would be the producer of a film.

Current French film legislation, the amended December, 1959,

law, removes the requirement on the producing company's capital being French in majority and makes it possible for a wholly American-
owned subsidiary to produce "French" films. But as in Great Britain,
the French film law set no requirements on the source of capital for
the production. As before, an American investor could provide a
French company (wholly-owned by French citizens) with funds for
the making of a film. The consequence of the change is simply that a
French paper company no longer need be established.

In Italy, the same modification has been made. Under legislation of
July, 1956, one criteria for an "Italian" film was that the capital of the
producing company had to be predominantly Italian.[21] The November, 1965, law does not refer to the capitalization of the producing
company. The change removed a small barrier which had never really
prevented American investment; American interests still could have
been involved in Italian films (as they were and are) by providing
capital *for any individual production.*

Another change in the Italian film law pertinent to nationality and
American investment concerns directors of films and the method of
sound recording. The current law declares that the director must be
Italian and the sound must be recorded at the time of shooting. The
1956 legislation however, did not refer explicitly to the manner of
sound recording. The old law decreed that a film could be declared
"Italian" if it were "produced in an original Italian version, or if in
several versions, one of which is Italian. . . ." In addition, the director
had to be Italian, "at least in the original Italian version."[22] The law
said nothing about the nationality of the person credited with directing other language versions of the same film.

The consequence of this requires a brief explanation of a "straw
director" and how some films have been shot in Italy. In industry
terms, a straw director is someone given credit for directing a picture
even though another person did the work. In practice, an American
may have directed an "Italian" film, but on the print released in Italy,
an Italian is cited as the director. This straw director, in fact, may
have been only an assistant. When the film is presented to the board
which confers nationality, the credits list an Italian national as director, and the film, therefore, is eligible for being designated "Italian."
When the picture leaves Italy, it no longer need carry the name of the
straw director. Because of this, it is not surprising to discover in the
1961 Unitalia catalog of Italian productions that *El Cid* was directed
by Giovanni Paolucci. Elsewhere, Anthony Mann is given credit for
it. The catalog also lists Sergio Leone as director of *Sodom and*

Gomorrah, although Robert Aldrich is cited in other sources as the director.

Many Italian films have been shot without the direct sound recording used by Hollywood. Instead, only a guidance dialogue track is recorded. This is particularly true when multi-lingual casts are involved and eliminates the difficulty of having an American, German, or French actor trying to speak his lines in Italian. This track guides the dubbers, who later substitute Italian voices for those of the film's actors. Essentially, the film is shot almost as a silent, with dialogue and effects put in after it is completed. The reference to sound recording in the 1965 film law points to a tighter definition of an "Italian" film.[23]

According to sources in Italy, officials are aware that some exceptions to the law exist. Nonetheless, authorities believe the stimulating effect of foreign investment and foreign companies' use of Italian production facilities far outweigh the possible dangers to Italian films in a cultural sense. If regulations become too stringent, foreign capital and foreign productions could be chased away and this would have an unpleasant economic impact. In many ways, the reaction to American investment has been similar in Italy and Great Britain, and to a lesser extent in France. The choice has been between American money ensuring relative economic health, on the one hand, and no American money and probable economic sickness on the other.

American investment in Europe has not only been tacitly accepted but openly encouraged. As early as the 1948 film agreement between France and the United States, American companies were permitted to spend their blocked earnings by coproducing films with French companies and by purchasing distribution rights of films made in France. More recently, Franco-American cooperation has yielded such "French" films as *The Train, Viva Maria,* and *Is Paris Burning?.* The last involved a reported investment by Paramount of more than $6,000,000. Artistically at least, it represents a step downward from René Clément's less expensive but more impressive *La Bataille du Rail,* produced twenty years earlier.

In Italy, film agreements between the MPEA and ANICA have permitted blocked American earnings to be invested in Italian production. The 1956–1959 pact stipulated that unremittable revenues of American companies could be used for the financing of Italian production companies, purchase of rights to Italian films for foreign distribution, payment of minimum guarantees for the distribution of Italian films in Italy, and participation in films of Italian nationality.[24] The 1959–1962 agreement extended the spending of blocked funds to coproductions with third countries, provided the films involved were predominantly Italian.[25] While Italian legislation established criteria to be met by producers of "Italian" pictures, the MPEA-ANICA pacts allowed American money to finance them. Indeed, Eitel Monaco, president of ANICA, recently remarked that between 1957 and 1967 American companies spent about $350,000,000 to acquire and to participate in Italian films and to make their own pictures in Italy.[26]

The approaches to financing in Great Britain, France, and Italy are brought together in Figure 1 which follows, showing the possibilities for an American company, Magnus Films. While this name is fictional, the opportunities are real, for they represent the methods several American companies have used to produce "national" films in Europe. Through a combination of wholly-owned and partially-owned subsidiaries, paper companies, and production financing, Magnus can have financial interests in "British," "French," "Italian," and coproduced films (and their subsidies). Magnus, of course, would be in a position to distribute these pictures in the United States and other markets.

Recognizing the degree of foreign participation in European films raises the interesting question of their ability to transmit local cultural values. It is questionable whether they do, in fact, reflect domestic themes when the investment in them cuts across national boundaries and when they are made with international audiences in mind. Considered in these terms, the assignment of nationality to a film indicates the fallacy of believing that a given picture represents entirely the characteristics of any one country. Moreover, as these nominally national films circulate around the world, their nationalities change.[27]

Certainly the most important factor working for internationalization is the American presence in Europe. It cannot be denied that the relationships between American and European producers have resulted in significant changes in the output of European studios. It could not have been otherwise, for the amalgamation of diverse cultural interests generally has a "melting pot" effect.

If one claims that British or Italian films are Americanized, then the reverse also must be acknowledged—that American films are Anglicized and Italianized. Europe is pulling production money from the United States and causing it to be invested in films which are not native American. In contrast to twenty years ago, American companies now find themselves with heavy investments in foreign-made films. The connections established between the two industries are yielding hybrid films, not typical of either the United States or of any Euro-

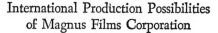

FIGURE I

International Production Possibilities
of Magnus Films Corporation

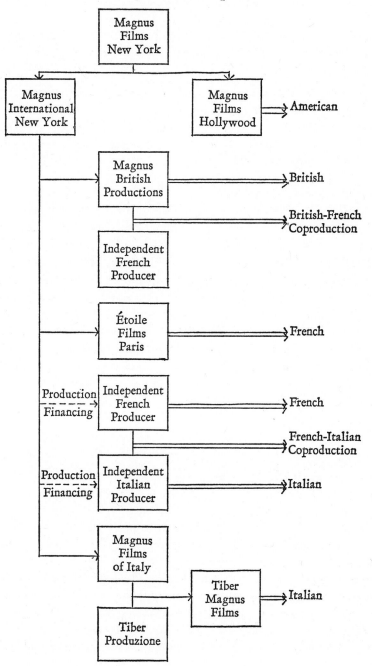

pean country. Indeed, American presence in Europe has modified European production, but foreign films in which there is an American interest represent a significant change in American production policy.

Siegfried Kracauer has contended that the films of a nation reflect that nation's mentality for two reasons. First,

> films are never the product of an individual. . . . Since any film production unit embodies a mixture of heterogeneous interests and inclinations, teamwork in this field tends to exclude arbitrary handling of screen material, suppressing individual peculiarities in favor of traits common to many people.
> Second, films address themselves, and appeal, to the anonymous multitude. Popular films . . . can therefore be supposed to satisfy existing mass desires.[28]

To extend this, one could contend that when a film is the product of peoples of different lands it will reflect their different traits and characteristics and be an homogenization of the ingredients brought to the production. The finished product will reflect universal idioms at the expense of national ones. These social and artistic features are further enhanced by the economic imperatives connected with the production. What is happening is the extension, on an international scale, of industrial production applied to culture. While this can yield products which are technically slick, the range of differences among them is reduced considerably—as among loaves of commercial white bread.

Anthony Asquith, British film director and president of the Association of Cinematograph, Television and Allied Technicians, once observed:

> We are neither anti-American nor anti-European, but we have always contended that British films should express our own attitudes and our own beliefs. Mid-Atlantic or mid-Channel productions are no substitute. To take an example from another country, I offer no prize for the answer to the question, which is the better or more typical Italian film—"Bicycle Thieves" [sic] or "Sodom and Gomorrah?"[29]

In the artistic sense of "better," *Bicycle Thief* would be the correct answer. But as far as which film is "more typical," one has to conclude that both are typical—typical Italian products resulting from different ways of organizing and financing film production in Italy.

One possible, but hopelessly inadequate, solution to the problem of

American investment entails some form of balance between it and local autonomy. The matter really becomes one of how to accept, within limits, foreign capital without falling into the power of the giver—a dilemma many nations have had to face in considering American foreign aid. Many Europeans would reject a film industry which was European in name only, a mere facade for American runaway production and runaway investment. Yet American money has not been refused, for in many ways it has stimulated domestic film making.

Certainly the problem can be approached in another way by creating healthy film industries through development of long-range programs and policies *within* countries or *within* the framework of the Economic Community. This includes maintenance of import and screen quotas, continuation of production subsidies, as well as initiation of an effective national or supra-national plan providing production financing in greater amounts. More specifically, in conjunction with a redefinition of a national film to include only those produced with national or Community capital, the state could take steps to provide enlarged production financing (100 percent, if necessary) and to create an organization for the international distribution of Community-made pictures.

This would come to grips with the two principal reasons for foreign producer reliance upon American companies. First, a sufficient *national* source of finance would be available, either from individual countries or an EEC agency. Second, an integrated worldwide distribution system would exist to handle these films. The chain could be a publicly-owned Community corporation or a consortium privately-owned by existing European film distribution companies, with encouragement and, if necessary, financial assistance from the state. It would provide a much needed alternative throughout the world, and inaugurate competition in international distribution.

The redefinition of a national or Community film would mean that financial and trade benefits flowing from nationality would accrue only to Community films made with Community capital (private or public), in contrast to the present system in which national films made with American money are eligible. Of course, this would not bar American investment in foreign-made films, but it would make such films ineligible for subsidization and other advantages.

This could be the basis for solving the problem of third-party (American) investment in EEC production. If the United Kingdom can be cited, the lack of a worldwide British distribution system, the inability of the NFFC to provide for majority or complete film financing, and the tightness of private sources have been prime factors in American domination of production. This has been spurred on (if not caused) by the lucrative subsidies for American-financed "British" films.

The consequences of this plan can be viewed best from the perspective of Canada's Association Professionnelle des Cinéastes. One need but substitute Britain, France, or Italy in the text:

> The most perplexing dilemma with which Canada is faced is the increasing foreign ownership and control of the Canadian economy. It has become apparent that there is a need for a new understanding between the public and private sectors of the economy, as well as some emboldening of government initiative. Private enterprise alone is no longer able to fulfil its obligation toward society's needs. The State must intervene, and this intervention cannot be seen as an indication that the State is dabbling in totalitarianism. For the actions that government takes are not intended to replace those of private investment but rather to open new fields of action and to increase its efficiency.[30]

The EEC has recognized that film making cannot be treated in the same way as other industries. For western Europe, film is not only a culture carrier but a commodity faced with local and international competition from the American industry. There is no argument that European film production should be permitted to continue. Moreover, it is agreed that its continuation can be only as a protected industry. To shield it so that it can become an appendage of a foreign country's industry could hardly be the aim of the EEC members or the EEC itself.

The solution must protect cultural integrity and enhance economic viability of film production. Limited loans and subsidization, as valuable as they have been, are no longer sufficient. Means now must be provided for substantial public financing of films and for international distribution of them.

Governments, the EEC itself, and film industry authorities have been studying the problem of American investment. The response to it will not be painless to develop and put into action for it requires vision and experimentation. At the time of this writing, it would be no exaggeration to say that this is the crucial problem facing the European film industry. Its resolution will have a decided impact on the future of that industry's development.

10 : Trends in the European Film Industry: Coproduction

Cooperation between American and European film makers is but one trend that developed in the last twenty years. An equally important trend toward internationalization is coproduction among European nations. This brings together financial, artistic, and technical contributions from two or more countries under criteria established by formal bilateral governmental agreements, or with the expressed approval of the governments involved.[1]

Coproduction is important to European film makers for a number of reasons. While broadening the base of financial investment in a picture, it assures a film two (or more) home markets where no import quotas are applied to it and where it is recognized as a "national" film for the mandatory screen quota. Another advantage is the dual base for calculation of the subsidy. If the coproducing countries have such a scheme, the film, by virtue of being "national" in each, is eligible to collect two production subsidies.

Last, coproducing permits the inclusion of a greater range of stars and other artistic and technical personnel without endangering the nationality of a film. That is, a coproduction has access to personnel of each partner country, while a purely "national" picture generally must confine its cast and technicians predominantly to domestic talent. And over-employment of foreigners can result in loss of nationality.

The 1966 coproduction agreement between France and Italy is presented in Appendix B. It establishes the legal and economic mechanics of the coproduction system and sets criteria films must meet. Treaties such as this have been the basis for close to eight hundred French-Italian films.

The coproduction trend, which started in the postwar period, gained momentum during the 1950's and now has become an integral part of European film making. Table 1 shows the growth and importance of coproduction in France, Italy, Spain, and West Germany, the four continental nations which are the chief film producers. During the 1960's, approximately 67 percent of French, 52 percent of Italian, 40 percent of Spanish, and 36 percent of German films were coproduced. By 1966, the purely national film had been eclipsed by the coproduction in each of these nations.

The rationale for coproducing asserts that all possible means must be used to make quality films. As such pictures often demand high budgets, it is imperative that their cost be absorbed by more than one producer. The collaboration of production teams and resources from two (or more) countries fulfills this need.[2] It also could be said that coventures are an attempt to compete with the American presence in Europe through the making of high quality, high budget films with international appeal.

The availability of more capital for a given film increases the likelihood of greater attention to production details, use of color and scope processes, lavish production methods, as well as more well-known (and more highly paid) international stars. Considered on this basis, coproduction may not only be a result of rising costs in general, but their cause, for certain films. Moreover, in instances to be pointed out presently, coproductions must not cost less than prescribed amounts.

Data from France indicate a relationship between coventures and more elaborate production methods. Using 1961 and 1966 as examples (even a five-year spread demonstrates the point), Table 2 reveals that French coproductions have twice as often as national films been in color and in a scope process. The use of these cinematic devices obviously results in higher production costs, especially for color where special attention must be given to sets, costumes, lighting, and matching in editing. In Spain, between 1950 and 1966, 60 percent of the coproductions were in color, but this was true for only 32 percent of the national films.

It also is possible that the higher the budget for a film, the more attention can be paid to details of its making and the more care can be taken in shooting it. A reciprocal relationship might be at work. The more money available, the more opportunity to reshoot a scene until something more than just adequate results are obtained. On the other

TABLE 1

Feature Film Production and Coproduction in France, Italy, Spain, and West Germany

	1950	1951	1952	1953	1954	1955	1956	1957	1958	1959	1960	1961	1962	1963	1964	1965	1966	TOTAL
FRANCE																		
Total production			109	112	98	110	129	142	126	139	158	178	150	161	161	151	130	2054
Percent coproduced			19.3	40.2	45.9	30.9	30.2	43.0	40.5	51.1	50.0	61.2	70.0	77.0	72.0	77.5	65.4	53.7
ITALY																		
Total production	100	107	163	148	201	133	105	129	135	167	168	213	241	239	313	182	148	2892
Percent coproduced	12.0	12.1	12.9	25.7	21.4	24.8	47.6	71.3	47.4	44.3	51.8	45.5	46.5	55.6	45.7	75.3	50.7	42.3
SPAIN																		
Total production	49	41	41	43	69	56	75	72	75	67	68	78	86	94	109	133	160	1316
Percent coproduced	4.0	7.3	12.2	16.3	18.8	12.5	29.3	30.6	32.0	25.4	14.7	21.8	24.4	37.2	39.4	54.1	57.5	31.3
WEST GERMANY																		
Total production	82	60	82	104	109	128	122	107	115	106	94	80	61	66	77	69	60	1522
Percent coproduced	11.0	5.0	4.9	14.4	13.8	6.3	6.6	10.3	14.8	19.8	11.7	13.8	29.5	33.3	54.5	63.8	55.0	19.2

Sources: Centre National de la Cinématographie, Associazione Nazionale Industrie Cinematografiche ed Affini and Unitalia, Uniespana, and Spitzenorganisation der Filmwirtschaft

hand, an obsession with details in the production, and extensive reshooting can force up the cost.

The only relevant and obtainable data come from Great Britain's National Film Finance Corporation.[3] Although they pertain only to films assisted by the Corporation and only to British "national" pictures, they suggest a relationship between cost and care of production which seems applicable to coproductions. Taking films started and finished between March 31, 1966, and March 31, 1967, the figures consider three cost ranges: $56,000 to $210,000; $210,000 to $350,000; and over $490,000. (There were no films between $350,000 and $490,000.) For films in the first, and cheapest, category, average screen time was 77 minutes and the average amount of this shot per camera day was 3 minutes and 51 seconds. Films in the second group had an average running time of 95 minutes with the

TABLE 2

Use of Color and Scope Processes[1] in French Film Production

| | | 1961 | | | 1966 | |
	Number	Color	Scope	Number	Color	Scope
French national	69	15.9%	21.7%	45	57.8%	37.8%
French coproductions	98	43.9%	45.9%	85	91.8%	67.1%

[1] Includes 70mm films.
Source: Based upon data from Centre National de la Cinématographie

average amount of screen time per camera day of 3 minutes and 10 seconds. Films in the third, and most expensive, group had an average screen time of 103 minutes while the average amount of this shot per camera day was only 1 minute and 58 seconds. Thus, a typical high-cost film is not only longer in actual running time, but a proportionately smaller share of it is shot per camera day. If this is true for coproductions, which generally are more expensive than national films, then it tends to support the point that coproductions are related to greater care in production and more attention to detail.

That the typical coproduction consistently has been more expensive than a national film is substantiated by data from France. From 1952 through 1966, the mean cost of a coproduction has exceeded that of an entirely French film. Table 3 indicates the magnitude of difference in the form of an annual ratio, with the base of 100.0 being used for the average cost of a French national film. The cost of a coproduction is from about one and one-half to at least three times as great as that of

TABLE 3

Ratio of Cost
French Coproductions Compared to French National Films[1]

1952	248.9	*1957*	179.1	*1962*	324.0
1953	226.3	*1958*	216.8	*1963*	234.3
1954	205.3	*1959*	226.1	*1964*	169.9
1955	246.7	*1960*	242.6	*1965*[2]	164.1
1956	224.7	*1961*	220.4	*1966*	174.9

[1] Average cost of a French national film for each year equals 100.0.
[2] Excludes one completely French film with an exceptional budget.
Source: Based upon data from Centre National de la Cinématographie

a national film. With only four years as exceptions, the average coproduction has cost more than twice as much as an all-French film. The year of greatest difference was 1962 when the cost of an average French film was $196,000 while that of a French coproduction was about $635,000. In 1965 (the year of least difference and the year in which costs of pure French films hit a peak), the cost of the average coproduction was almost $476,000, while that of a national film was about $290,000. The latter figure excludes one unnamed, entirely French, film with an exceptional budget (presumably *Is Paris Burning?*).

Another way of illustrating this is to examine the actual budgets of coproduced and French national films. Data from the Centre National de la Cinématographie indicate that, compared to entirely French films, a greater proportion of coproductions have high budgets. Table 4 presents these two groups of pictures broken down by budgets for 1956 and 1966. Although the cost categories are not precisely comparable, they are sufficiently similar to support the point. In 1956, 3 percent of the national films had budgets over $570,000 while almost 36 percent of the coproductions exceeded that figure. In 1966, 13 percent of the French national films had budgets greater than $612,000 while the figure for coproductions was 43 percent.

Table 4 also points out that a smaller proportion of films with low budgets are being made now than a decade ago. In 1956, almost 76 percent of the national films had budgets less than $285,000, as opposed to the 36 percent which had budgets under $204,000 in 1966. The same is also true for coproductions, although the degree of change is not as great.

Data presented so far disclose that the frequency of coproduction

TABLE 4

Production Budgets of French Coproductions and French National Films

1956

	Coproductions	National
Less than $285,000	12.8%	75.6%
$285,000 to $570,000	51.3	21.1
Over $570,000	35.9	3.3
Total Films	39	90

1966

	Coproductions	National
Less than $204,000	4.8%	35.6%
$204,000 to $408,000	22.4	33.3
$408,000 to $612,000	29.4	17.8
Over $612,000	43.4	13.3
Total Films	85	45

Source: Based upon data from Centre National de la Cinématographie

has increased in magnitude over the last fifteen years and that, at least for France, the cost of coproducing is rising, since substantial proportions of these films are high budget productions. However, one must ask whether the increase in cost of the typical coproduction has been at a rate comparable to that for national pictures.

Table 5 reveals that the yearly average production cost for national films has increased somewhat faster than that for coproductions. In only one year (1962) was the relative cost of the average coproduction higher than that of the average national film. While costs have risen for both types, the cost of making a French national film has increased the most sharply, presumably because there was more room for expansion into higher budgets from the relatively small ones in the early 1950's. In addition, it could very likely be that cheap productions have been forced out by competition and that there is a smaller market for them today. Thus by 1966 the mean cost of a national picture was four times what it was in 1952, while that of a coproduction was only about three times more.

Investment in coproductions also must be considered, and Table 6 indicates significant growth in this area. In 1952, for every 100 francs in French national pictures, there were only 29 invested as the French share in coproductions. The turning point was 1959 when 109 francs were channeled into coproduced films for every 100 put into national films. The peak was 1963 when 342 francs went into coproductions for every 100 into national pictures. Since then, the difference has diminished somewhat even though the share of French films which

TABLE 5

Average Production Cost Index[1]
for French Coproductions and French National Films

	Coproductions	*National*
1952	100.0	100.0
1953	110.3	121.3
1954	133.3	161.7
1955	158.1	159.6
1956	155.6	172.3
1957	131.6	183.0
1958	176.1	202.1
1959	177.8	195.7
1960	209.4	214.9
1961	258.1	291.5
1962	265.8	204.3
1963	216.2	229.8
1964	197.4	289.4
1965	199.1	302.1[2]
1966	297.4	423.2

[1] Dollar value of 1952 base is $239,000 for coproductions and $96,000 for national films.
[2] Excludes one film with an exceptional budget.
Source: Based upon data from Centre National de la Cinématographie

TABLE 6

Ratio of French Investment in
French Coproductions to Investment
in French National Films[1]

1952	29.3	*1957*	77.1	*1962*	286.3
1953	87.3	*1958*	67.6	*1963*	342.7
1954	90.0	*1959*	109.5	*1964*	177.2
1955	56.1	*1960*	112.8	*1965*	145.1
1956	53.4	*1961*	145.5	*1966*	167.3

[1] Value of French investment in French national films for each year equals 100.0.
Source: Based upon data from Centre National de la Cinématographie

are coproduced has increased. This is due, in one respect, to the rise of the tripart coproduction which splits the cost three ways instead of two.

Considering the magnitude of capital channeled into films, Table 7 reveals there was 12 times more French money invested in coproductions in 1966 than in 1952. But for national films, 1966 showed only a two-fold increase over 1952. This suggests that even the costs of national films have climbed, although their number has declined.

TABLE 7

French Investment in
French Coproductions and National Films
($000,000)

| | Coproductions | | National | |
	Amount	Number	Amount	Number
1952	$ 2.5	21	$ 8.4	88
1953	6.9	45	8.0	67
1954	7.3	45	8.2	53
1955	6.5	34	11.6	76
1956	8.0	39	14.9	90
1957	11.0	61	14.3	81
1958	9.8	51	14.5	75
1959	14.0	71	12.8	68
1960	18.4	79	16.3	79
1961	28.2	109	19.4	69
1962	24.1	105	8.4	45
1963	27.4	124	8.0	37
1964	22.1	116	12.5	45
1965	25.1	117	17.3	34
1966	30.6	85	18.3	45

Source: Based upon data from Centre National de la Cinématographie

With the French data as background, the matter of which countries coproduce with what other countries can be surveyed. Some noteworthy trends are apparent which bear on cost, investment, and international policy.

The first coproduction agreement was signed by Italy and France in October, 1949, and over the years they have been each other's most frequent partners. Seventy percent of French coproductions have been with Italy. Second in importance to France are tripart films, accounting for about 14 percent, followed by those made with West Germany and with Spain.

Table 8 also indicates that of all Italian coventures made from 1950 through 1965, some 66 percent were produced solely with France. The peak occurred in 1961 when eighty-eight films were made in this way. More recently, Italian data[4] reveal that in 1965 only forty-seven Italian-French films were produced, and information from the Centre National de la Cinématographie indicates that only forty-three were made in 1966.

Meanwhile, Spanish producers are becoming increasingly important as partners to the Italians. Table 8, while indicating that about 16 percent of Italy's coproductions have been solely with Spain, obscures the strong recent trend in this direction. For example, 60 percent of

TABLE 8

Coproduction Partners of
Italy, France, and West Germany[1]

ITALY	1950–1965		FRANCE	1949–1966		WEST GERMANY	1950–1966	
Partner	Films	Percent	Partner	Films	Percent	Partner	Films	Percent
France	764	66.5	Italy	792	70.5	Tripart	101	34.6
Spain	190	16.5	Tripart	157	14.0	Austria	50	17.1
Tripart	141	12.3	West Germany	73	6.5	Italy	46	15.7
West Germany	46	4.0	Spain	46	4.1	France	38	13.0
Other	8	.7	Belgium	6	.5	Spain	18	6.2
Total	1149	100.0	Other	50	4.4	Belgium	2	.7
			Total	1124	100.0	Other	37	12.7
						Total	292	100.0

[1] Discrepancies between figures exist in the original data from these countries.

Sources: Associazione Nazionale Industrie Cinematografiche ed Affini, Centre National de la Cinématographie, and Spitzenorganisation der Filmwirtschaft

the 190 Italian-Spanish films were produced between 1962 and 1965. The Unitalia catalogue lists forty such films for 1966, and the Uniespana catalogue mentions forty-eight for 1967.

Third in importance for Italy are tripart films. These involve Italy in partnership with, generally, France and Spain, and to a smaller extent with France and West Germany, and with Spain and West Germany. Tripart Italian films increased sharply after 1962, with 80 percent of them having been made since then. Production with West Germany alone represents only 4 percent of Italian coventures, although there is a slight trend toward an increase of this type.

Considering West Germany, a different picture emerges. Ranking first in importance for it are tripart productions, representing a third of all German coproductions. These are German partnerships predominantly with France and Italy, and to a smaller degree with Spain and Italy, although West Germany has been involved in tripart films with Yugoslavia and France, and with Spain and France. The data reveal that Austria is an important partner for West Germany, accounting for 17 percent of German coventures. Ranking third and fourth in importance are Italy and France, representing 16 and 13 percent, respectively, of German coproduction activity.

Based upon these figures, it is apparent that the three countries considered have coproduced some 254 films with Spain (excluding tripart productions). The total number of Spanish coventures between 1950 and 1966 has been 412. On this basis, about two-thirds of all Spanish coproductions have been with these three countries. If tripart films were included, then the share would approach at least 80 percent.

Looking at Table 8 from a different perspective, it is evident that members of the European Economic Community are their own most important partners for film production. About 90 percent of French coventures have involved other EEC members. For Italy the share is about 70 percent, while that for West Germany is about 60 percent. This relates to a point to be made later in this chapter.

Another facet of the coproduction phenomenon concerns the amount of domestic film capital channeled into activity *with various nationalities*. Data from Italy in Table 9 illuminate this aspect. About 76 percent of Italian money invested in coproduction has been put into Italian-French films whose *total cost* accounted for almost 72 percent of the expenses of all Italian coventures. However, only 67 percent of Italian coproductions have had France as the sole partner.

TABLE 9

Italian Coproductions, 1950–1965

Partner	Coproduced Films		Italian Share		Total Cost		Average Cost Per Film	Percent of Total Cost Supplied by Italy	Average Italian Share per Film
	Number	Percent	Amount (millions)	Percent	Amount (millions)	Percent			
France	764	66.5	$193.1	76.2	$370.6	71.9	$485,000	52.1	$253,000
Spain	190	16.5	26.4	10.4	52.7	10.2	278,000	50.0	139,000
Tripart	141	12.3	25.4	10.0	73.5	14.3	521,000	34.6	180,000
West Germany	46	4.0	7.0	2.8	15.9	3.1	346,000	44.0	152,000
Other	8	.7	1.5	.6	2.7	.5	338,000	55.6	189,000
TOTAL	1149	100.0	$253.4	100.0	$515.4	100.0	$449,000	49.2	$220,000

Source: Based upon data from Associazione Nazionale Industrie Cinematografiche ed Affini

This means that Italian-French pictures are more expensive than those made by Italy in partnership with other nations.

For 1950 through 1965, the average cost of an Italian-French film has been $485,000, substantially more than the average for any other bipart production. The data further indicate that Italy has supplied 52 percent of the investment for Italian-French films. Not apparent in the table is the recent increase in cost to make these pictures. Prior to 1961, the mean cost was $461,000. But for 1962 through 1965, it rose to almost $530,000 per film.[5]

Considering Italian-Spanish productions, these 190 films represent 10 percent of Italian investment in all coventures but 16 percent of all coproduced pictures. The average cost has been around $278,000 per picture, with a slight increase to $289,000 in the 1962–1965 period.

Figures for tripart production point out that while these pictures accounted for 12 percent of all coproductions, Italy's investment in them represented only 10 percent of its financial share in all coventures. The average cost of Italian tripart films has been $521,000, an amount higher than that for Italian-French pictures and substantially greater than other types. However, Italy contributed but 35 percent of the total costs of these 141 films, about $180,000 per picture. This is much less than the Italian share in Italian-French films and just a shade more than its contribution to Italian-German films.

In view of this, it is not surprising that Italian bipart production with France is declining, while tripart and Italian-Spanish production is increasing. France may be pricing itself out as a coproducer, especially because of the more attractive lower wage scales in Spain. In 1966, Italy and Spain were joined in 50 bipart and tripart films while in 1967 the figure was seventy.[6]

In any case, the tripart film is a superb demonstration of the value of coproduction. By pooling resources, a more elaborate picture with bigger stars can be made than if only one country were financing it. This also explains why tripart production has increased within the last five years. While lavish production techniques, color, scope processes, and big stars are not necessarily prerequisities for good films, they do perform the vital functions of attracting audiences in several nations and competing on more or less even terms with the costly productions from other countries, notably the United States. Thus, bipart and tripart films may be considered as bargains in cost terms, in that producers in two or three countries receive revenue (and subsidies) from a bigger film than any could afford to produce separately.

Coproduction takes place within the framework of bilateral treaties among partner countries. The treaty's value is that it establishes the context for such activity while formalizing the responsibilities of the commercial partners and the states involved. It is essential for setting requirements on a long-term basis for such things as the minimum financial participation of partners, minimum budgets, the employment of artistic and technical personnel, and the permissible places of shooting and laboratory work.

A brief survey of a few recent Italian coproduction agreements illustrates some of these requirements.[7] These establish three broad classes of bipart films: normal coproductions; coproductions of artistic value; and coproductions of exceptional entertainment value.[8]

According to the 1966 Italian-French agreement, films in the first class must have a budget no less than $285,000, and the minority financial contribution must be at least 30 percent of the cost. In addition, the minority party must supply at least a writer, an assistant director, an actor in a main role, and one in a secondary role. The Italian-West German agreement of 1966 has almost the same requirements except that the minimum budget can be $274,000, while the minority partner must supply one technician in place of the assistant director. The 1966 Italian-Spanish agreement established the minimum budget at $240,000 (increased to $250,000 in 1967) and further specified the personnel each party must contribute to the picture.

The second class, films of artistic value, provides exemption from the minimum cost requirement and lowers the minority party's financial participation to 20 percent of the production cost. In addition, the Italian agreements with France and West Germany provide for waiving of requirements for technical and artistic personnel.

Considering the third class, Italian-French productions must have a minimum budget of about $509,000, although the investment of one of the partners can be as low as 20 percent. The minimum technical and artistic personnel requirements also are relaxed. The agreement between Italy and West Germany is similar, except that the budget can be as low as $499,000. The Italian-Spanish treaty provides for a minimum budget of $400,000 with at least 20 percent of it coming from the minority partner. The technical and artistic obligations conform to those for normal Italian-Spanish pictures.

Now these standards are in force when Italy produces a film with only one partner. They become baroque when the responsibilities and obligations of three parties are involved. As an example, consider a tripart production in which Italy has the majority investment. If the film is made with France and either Germany or Spain, the minimum budget must be $530,000. If France does not participate, and the other partners are Germany and Spain, then the budget must be at least $480,000. When France is involved, the major partner's share of the cost can be no less than 40 percent and the minority share can be 20 percent. The minimum artistic and technical contribution is an actor in a major role, or a qualified technician, or a writer. Similar requirements exist for Italian tripart pictures when the majority partner is France, Germany, or Spain.

Criteria also exist for quadpart Italian productions, films produced by Italy and three partners. Admittedly, pictures of this type are now rare. However, twenty years ago even coproduction was unusual, and only ten years ago the tripart film was a novel experiment. In a quadpart Italian picture with, say, France as the majority partner, the budget cannot be less than $710,000. The majority partner's financial participation must be no smaller than 30 percent while the least a minority partner can contribute is 20 percent. The minimum technical and artistic contribution is an actor in a principal role, or a qualified technician, or a writer. Regulations of a similar kind cover quadpart films when the majority party is Italy, Germany, or Spain.

These elaborate and complex rules are essential, in one way at least, for the granting of nationality, because this implicitly decides which films can be eligible for subsidization and other benefits.

The nature of coproduction has resulted in a labyrinth of overlapping bilateral treaties among film making nations. The meaning of this becomes clearer if only the major producing nations of the European Economic Community are considered.

France began coproduction in 1949 after signing its first treaty with Italy. Since then, ten other nations have enacted agreements with France, the most significant recent one being the French-British pact of 1965, renewed in May, 1967. (Interestingly, the first film to be completed under this agreement was *The Night of the Generals*, produced by Sam Spiegel and distributed by Columbia Pictures.) Italy has nine agreements in force and has been discussing coproduction arrangements with Canada, Bulgaria, and the Soviet Union. West Germany counts seven pacts, and five others are in the discussion stage with the United Kingdom, Sweden, Denmark, Brazil, and Greece.

Eliminating double counting, these three nations have twenty-four bilateral production treaties among themselves and with third countries. (This does not take into consideration bilateral film *trade* agreements such as France has with the Soviet Union and Mexico, or Italy has with Poland, Japan, and East Germany.) Included in this total are the six agreements governing coproduction among only four members of the Common Market (France, Italy, West Germany, and Belgium), the fourteen additional treaties between France, Italy, West Germany and seven other European nations (Spain, Yugoslavia, Austria, Great Britain, Sweden, Rumania, and Switzerland), and the four treaties they have with western hemisphere nations (Argentina, Brazil, and Canada).

Even a superficial reading of these agreements discloses that while they are essentially the same in purpose, language, and structure, therefore largely duplicating each other, they occasionally differ on details. This was apparent in the Italian agreements cited earlier. While this condition in the late 1960's for international film production may seem unique, it is identical to situations existing more than one hundred years ago for other media of communication—international postal service and international telegraph service.

George A. Codding, Jr., has pointed out that by the middle of the nineteenth century, a European nation's *normal* postal relations required at least a dozen treaties.[9] As late as 1873, Germany had seventeen bilateral postal agreements regulating its international mail service with its neighbors and other nations. France was signatory to sixteen bilateral agreements, Belgium to fifteen, and Great Britain to a dozen. Even the United States had at least nine agreements to expedite mail. Just as is true now for coproduction agreements, all these postal treaties served the same purpose—the international transport of mail and parcels. Yet their bilateral nature produced a veritable jungle of weights, rates, letter sizes, and routes.[10]

International telegraph service also began in a maze of bilateral treaties.[11] Prussia and Austria concluded an agreement in 1849. By 1850, two other Germanic states had been bound by bilateral treaties and in the same year the four formed the Austro-German Telegraph Union. Five other states joined this Union in the years up to 1854.

Meanwhile, France had signed bilateral telegraph treaties with four other states who, in 1855, formed the West European Telegraph Union. Relations between it and the Austro-German Union were formalized in 1858 with a convention regulating service between them. In spite of this, a telegram sent from, say, France to Prussia, was subject to rules from three conventions—the West European Telegraph Union, the Austro-German Telegraph Union, and a third applying to relations between the Unions.

This confusion was ended in 1865 when the International Telegraph Union was formed, embodying *one* convention to which all states became signatories. In addition to eliminating bilateral and multilateral treaties, it established rates and service standards while simplifying and clarifying responsibilities of members toward each other. The Union, known today as the International Telecommunications Union, embraces telegraph, telephone, and radio communication.

The founding of the ITU and what it did for electrical communication provided impetus for the creation in 1874 of what is known today as the Universal Postal Union. To quote Codding:

> . . . a treaty was drafted and signed that transformed the territories of 21 nations into a single unit for the exchange of postal correspondence, standardized and simplified postal rates and procedures, and created the second oldest international organization.[12]

Virtually all nations of the world are members today.

The experience of the ITU, the UPU, and much later the Benelux Union, the Coal and Steel Community, Euratom, and, indeed, the Economic Community itself, can be the framework in which the numerous bilateral coproduction treaties can be merged into a single convention, perhaps under the aegis of the EEC. Just as there is a movement among EEC members to standardize subsidy schemes, thought also is being given to unifying bilateral production agreements. Because the EEC nations are each other's most frequent partners in film making, it would seem that benefits could be derived from the ultimate merging of these numerous agreements.

While the first step toward greater uniformity among them is already under way, it is apparent that a Community Coproduction Convention might be a possibility. One such treaty could eliminate the present bilateral agreements among France, Italy, West Germany, and Belgium, while standardizing the responsibilities among them. It also would simplify the relationship between non-EEC members in Europe (such as Spain, Austria, Yugoslavia, and Great Britain) and Community members, for the adherence of Spain, say, to the convention would automatically establish coproduction links with all Community members on an equal basis.

Of course, numerous problems seem to block the path to such unification. Not the least of them are labor matters and differences in living standards, which manifest themselves in, for instance, the cost of film making. The convention also would have to consider the problem of American investment in EEC films. While Community members have welcomed American finance, there is a general fear of American domination of the kind present in the United Kingdom, for economic dependence usually leads to cultural colonialism.

Another difficulty is that film industries are privately-owned as opposed to the publicly-owned postal and telecommunications services. However, that increasing harmony is being achieved in subsidy programs dispels the pessimism which declares that coproduction agreements cannot be merged. In one way, the very fact that an agreement can exist between France and Yugoslavia, with different living standards and, indeed, different governmental and economic systems, suggests that barriers are not too great for one agreement among EEC members. If postal and telecommunications services, as well as even broader economic relations, provide a model, then the merging of coproduction agreements (subsidy plans and production financing schemes, too) is inevitable.

11: Conclusions

In the two decades covered by this study, the film industries in the United States and Europe have become internationalized, not only in economic and political areas, but culturally as well.

Film is following the path of other industrial activities in searching out the largest markets. The growth in technology and costs work against serving small and selective markets. These can be satisfied only if they are wealthy enough to support the work of craftsmen, or if production resources can be organized so as to reduce costs to make serving them worthwhile.

For years, British industrial manufacturers have been exhorted to export or die. The same warning is increasingly in order for motion pictures. Only the cheapest films will be able to survive without export earnings. Just as the United States is no longer the sole market for American pictures, Britain is no longer the only market for the British film industry, and France and Italy are no longer the only markets for their own films.

Successful exportation, however, implies getting other people to "like" the product, and this often leads to homogenization, blurring the differences which are the sharp edges of distinct cultures. With film, this growing similarity—apparent in what many observers refer to as "mass culture"—is taking a leap onto an international plateau where local idioms are erased or played down in favor of broader ones. In the United States, television has already blurred sectional achievements and differences.

Indeed, international financing, international settings, international stars and production teams, and dependence upon world markets, breed international films appealing to most people in most places.

True, many films not made under these conditions have become universal favorites. As examples, consider the Chaplin films or those in the Italian neo-realist tradition. They were international, but in a much different sense.

They were able to convey a *human* message in terms understandable to people everywhere. While the neo-realist films were grounded in conditions and times of a particular country, they spoke to diverse cultures because they struck a chord of human sensitivity. But so many of the new international films border on dehumanization by brutalizing sensitivity, often deflecting attention from reality. They count on developing audience response with synthetic, machine-made images. Their shallowness and cardboard characters are camouflaged with dazzling colors, wide screens, and directorial slickness. Of course, undistinguished pictures always have been made, but now the context in which they are produced and marketed is substantially different. Films of this genre are not a form of cultural exchange. In reality, they are anti-culture, the antithesis of human culture.

Perhaps the crucial distinction is that many of the makers of today's pictures are playing consciously to *international consumers*. The "human" films found their way around the world because of qualities intrinsic to them and for what their makers had to say, not because finance dictated it.

Complete internationalization has not been reached, and probably never will be. The craft aspect of film making in Europe is too firmly rooted to be completely obliterated, and a few European nations will manage, somehow, to keep some form of national production alive on an identifiable cultural basis. There always will be room for a local film which can talk to people in their own language. That some film industries in small countries thrive on this is not surprising. This does not mean, of course, that all such films are great works of art.

The American presence in Europe is leading to internationalization as nothing else has. With it comes another culture's perspective on the world, intertwined with production money and international distribution possibilities. Inevitably, this leads to thoughts of universal markets, because investments must pay. Films produced in this atmosphere reflect these underlying currents. They are no longer considered as films made for the French, or for the Italians, or for the British—but as films made for consumers everywhere.

On a more obvious level, the American presence in Europe has been assisted by the American government. Our diplomatic corps and our trade specialists lend their help to the film industry in dealing with import restrictions, negotiations for film agreements, and in alleviating currency problems. Our government recognizes that film is not only a commodity which brings dollars to the United States, but that it is useful in a propaganda sense. It tells our story (often with deadly accuracy!). Furthermore, the shift of personnel between industry and government cannot be overlooked. This is true not only on the level of Eric Johnston and Jack Valenti, but in the lower echelons as well. At times, it is difficult to determine where loyalties lie. True, governments everywhere maintain contact with their film industries, but almost exclusively in internal and national terms. None surpass in extent the assistance given by our government to our film industry internationally.

American overseas expansion is not confined only to film. Leo Model, writing in *Foreign Affairs,* observed:

> The role of U. S. direct investment in the world economy is staggering. According to the U. S. Council of the International Chamber of Commerce, the gross value of production by American companies abroad is well in excess of $100 billion a year. That is to say, on the basis of the gross value of their output, U. S. enterprises abroad in the aggregate comprise the third largest economy . . . in the world—with a gross product greater than that of any country except the United States and the Soviet Union.[1]

He noted that three American companies dominate the foreign automobile industry, and that in western Europe, American companies have almost a monopoly in producing complex business machines. One also could point to the growth of American advertising agencies in western Europe, setting up offices there, buying out European agencies, or merging with them. It seems American expansion in Europe has been mainly in the consumer-oriented industries, and obviously film is one of them.

In motion pictures, American control is increasing quietly but at a frightening pace. The British industry is that in name only, having lost its independence in the last decade. The Italian film industry has become so tied to American investment and American companies that its autonomy can be questioned. In these two countries, it is no longer merely the case that American film imports capture the market. The problem now is that native production industries have been absorbed by a foreign interest. France and Spain are approaching the danger point. The matter becomes more significant because in the trend toward internationalization these industries are compelled to channel their films through American distributors who are in a position to determine implicitly the nature of films to be made. Important directors do have some measure of autonomy, but they are few in number.

In one way, Europeans have themselves to thank or blame for this state of affairs, because their film industries and governments encouraged American investment. Aside from the immediate benefits of employed workers and capital for production, this open arms policy was one way in which these industries could live with their chief competitor. In a sense, it meant a reduction of competition, because the warring groups combined for their own welfare. European countries received American capital, distribution facilities, and access to the United States market. American companies, meanwhile, benefitted from foreign wage scales and subsidies. In this way, film is analogous to other industrial activity in which "competitors" fix prices, divide the world into exclusive markets, or consolidate to cultivate all markets without fear of competition.

The alarm was sounded occasionally in the 1940's and 1950's as concerned Europeans noted the rising tide of American control. Especially in Great Britain, tenacity and adamancy in some quarters of the cinema industry yielded statements such as this:

> American companies have established subsidiaries in this country which are legally British companies and enjoy all the advantages which have been devised by Parliament and otherwise chiefly in order to enable British producers to survive notwithstanding the fierce competition in their home market from American imports. American subsidiaries . . . not only have the benefit of Exhibitors' Quota but receive payments from the Production Fund on precisely the same terms as British producers. They also claim British export licenses for foreign countries. . . .
>
> At the present time American production in England is greatly increasing and it is this increase which is so disturbing to British picture makers. . . .
>
> I am confident that it will not be in the best interest of this country or of British film production to leave things as they are at the present time—an equitable solution to the problem must and can be found.[2]

It was. It entailed greater American involvement in the British industry. Now the insecurity of the either-or question is irrelevant. Most film people there seem to be satisfied because production money and international distribution are available. Moreover, "British" films have demonstrated a remarkable degree of financial success around the world, chiefly in the American market. What economic state of affairs could be better for the British film maker? Now he has a steady job.

International relations in the film industry today are vastly different from those in the 1920's and 1930's. Certainly some American companies did produce features abroad; many French and German film makers were brought to Hollywood; and some European companies tried desperately to copy American films. But in those days, the autonomy of European film production was not at stake. Today it is.

In relation to this, two old myths must be laid to rest. One claimed that because the United States was such a large market, American films could be offered in Europe at prices lower than new local productions. This is not the case today, nor has it been for the last twenty years. Rather than trying to undersell competitors, American companies have been instrumental in raising rental terms to support their increasingly expensive style of film making. The second myth asserted that the great number of American films on the European market drew a reaction based on protectionism. This is no longer accurate. American films have declined numerically and they are not now seen as a threat, such as they were in the late 1940's and throughout the 1950's. European chauvinism today has its roots in the fear of American control of production and distribution through investment.

Twenty or even fifteen years ago, Europeans undoubtedly did not realize the consequences of their open arms policy. They saw foreign involvement as an aid—but were slow to recognize it as a danger. American interests found fertile ground and grew rapidly. Indeed, people on the continent may discover in the not too distant future that many of their film industries are not really theirs, but overseas branches of Hollywood which merely hire the locals.

If economic independence and cultural integrity are to prevail, then European industries and governments must respond to the two thrusts of the American industry—production financing and the international distribution system. Government programs to this time have placed European film industries on a moderately healthy basis and have saved them from total destruction. But these schemes are not geared to industries of the 1970's which are faced with threats unknown two decades ago. If European production is to remain in European hands, the public sector must accept the responsibility which the private sector has not been able to manage.

Independence does not necessarily mean "better" films in an artistic or financial sense, any more than internationalization means "better" films. But autonomy can increase the chances for diversity and different points of view. Because film is an art which portrays man's interpretation of life, it is imperative that contrasting perspectives be given the opportunity to exist and develop. The movement toward oligopoly and monopoly in American industry in general is now spreading elsewhere, paralleling American expansion. While this might spell efficiency in economic terms through elimination of duplication, with fewer producers serving larger markets, it is to be avoided in the field of culture. It would be a pity to have but one control over all the printing presses in a nation—or in the world. The same can be said for film production and distribution. Yet this is coming about in the world of the West.

Appendixes

APPENDIX A

Royal Decree for the Aid of the Belgian Film Industry[1]

Baudouin, King of the Belgians, To all present and to come, greetings. In view of Article 29 of the Constitution; In view of the law of February 15, 1963, containing the budget of the Ministry of Economic Affairs for the year 1963, notably Article 24–3; In view of the advice of the Council of State; In view of the agreement of the Minister of Finance, dated July 29, 1963; On the proposal of our Minister of Economic Affairs and the advice of our Ministers who have deliberated in Council, We have decreed and decree:

Article 1

Within budgetary limits, a subsidy to production is granted by the Minister of Economic Affairs to producers of Belgian films in respect of the following conditions.

Not to be recipients of the subsidy:

    1st: Advertising films, that is to say, those which have as objective publicity in favor of a product, a service, a brand, or a commercial or industrial firm;

    2nd: Films commissioned by the State, the provinces, the communities or organizations endorsed by Article 1 of the law of March 16, 1954, with the exception of films for which the commercial distribution is left to the producer.

The Minister of Economic Affairs may, on the advice of the Film Commission cited in Article 8, refuse a subsidy to films which do not possess the required qualities.

Article 2

Producers are eligible for subsidy benefits with the following conditions:

1. Producers must present to the Minister of Economic Affairs a declaration concerning the film for which a subsidy is requested showing the type of film (for example: fiction, documentary, newsreel, etc.), its anticipated length, its plot, a cost estimate of the film as well as the date for the start of production. This declaration must be presented to the Minister before the start of shooting. After production, the producer is responsible for furnishing the actual detailed cost of his film.

2. The film must have been recognized as Belgian. The title of recognition is delivered to producers by the Minister of Economic Affairs following the advice of the Film Commission cited in Article 8.

When a newsreel is concerned, the title is valid only for those editions produced during the current half of the year. It is renewable upon request of the producer.

3. The film must have a minimum length of 300 meters, except for cartoons and animated films when the minimum is 115 meters, or 275 meters for newsreels. In the last case, the length considered is the average length of editions calculated on the basis of all black and white editions exhibited during the half year, a meter of newsreel in color counting as three meters. It must contain scenes of life in Belgium accounting for at least one-third of the total meterage for the half year.

Lengths are applicable to the 35 millimeter format. For other sizes, lengths are reduced proportionately to the format used.

Article 3

Films which meet the following conditions are recognized as Belgian films under the terms of Article 2, 2:

1. For all films, with the exception of newsreels:

a) The films must be produced by persons or organizations that are of Belgian nationality and whose technical and commercial activity is carried on principally in Belgium.

The producing person or organization mentioned in the preceding paragraph must not be dependent upon or under the control of a foreign company.

However, foreigners meeting the requirements of Belgian residents and practicing the profession of film producers are eligible to benefit from Belgian film aid, the right of reciprocity being reserved.

b) The film must be shot in Belgium. However, exteriors can be shot outside the country in cases required by the plot, or for reasons of climate. All studio and laboratory work must be done in Belgium, except for those technical processes which are not possible.

c) All workers and all persons contributing to the production must be of Belgian nationality or possess a work permit in Belgium.

In duly justified cases, exemptions from points b) and c) can be requested prior to shooting outside the country.

d) At least 50 percent of the salaries and costs due to all persons engaged in intellectual, artistic, or technical collaboration for the production of the film must be paid to Belgians.

Included in films recognized as Belgian are those films conforming to coproduction agreements concluded between Belgium and foreign countries or between Belgian producers and foreign producers.

The inclusion is obtainable only after prior approval of the coproduction terms by the Minister of Economic Affairs.

2. For newsreels:

a) They must be produced and distributed by a person or organization of Belgian nationality whose technical and commercial activity is carried on principally in Belgium; the administrative agency and management as well as editing and technical production personnel must be of Belgian nationality.

The actual or responsible producing person or organization noted in the preceding paragraph must not be dependent upon or under the control of a foreign company.

This person or organization cannot be dependent either as a subsidiary carrying the trade name of a foreign firm and formed as a company under Belgian rights, or as an editor of foreign newsreels.

b) They must be edited, titled and have sound tracks added in Belgian laboratories.

Article 4

The subsidy must not surpass, in any case, the cost of the film. If the Minister of Economic Affairs judges the cost of the film to be excessive, he can, by a decision taken at the time of the granting of Belgian recognition, fix the maximum amount of the subsidy at a reduced level.

Article 5

The subsidy is distributed in the form of premiums. The exhibition of a film which is part of a program for which an admission tax is collected gives the right to a premium.

The premium is fixed:

1st: For long films, that is, films of 1,800 meters or more, with the exception of those cited in 3rd and 4th below, at 70, 75, or 80 percent of the amount of the admission tax. The Minister of Economic Affairs fixes the percentage according to the quality of the film, following the advice of the Film Commission.

2nd: For short films, that is, films less than 1,800 meters, with the exception of those cited in 3rd and 4th below, at 18, 21 or 25 percent of the amount of the admission tax. The Minister of Economic Affairs fixes the percentage according to the quality of the film, following the advice of the Film Commission.

Concerning the supporting program, it must be shown at least 100 days within the period of one year from the date of its first commercial exhibition in order to be eligible for premiums.

3rd: For newsreels, at 5 percent of the amount of the admission tax.

4th: For films commissioned by public bodies, but for which the commercial distribution is left to the producer, at 5 percent of the amount of the admission tax.

Only those taxes due from exhibition after the date of submission of the request for recognition of the film as Belgian are taken into consideration for the calculation of the premium.

Those exhibitions more than three years after the first exhibition of the film in commercial distribution for the supporting program, and more than five years after this date for long films, cease to be eligible for collection of premiums.

In cases where the estimated percentages above would be greater than the allotted budgetary credits, the Minister of Economic Affairs can reduce these percentages in proportion necessary to avoid a deficit.

Article 6

At the risk of being unacceptable, requests for premiums must be submitted quarterly during the year within the three months following the quarter in question.

This requirement is applicable to films of the supporting program even though they have not as yet fulfilled the condition imposed by Article 5, 2nd, paragraph 2.

The request for premium, in four copies, must indicate the places and dates of exhibition and be accompanied by written proof of the amount of admission tax.

All fraudulent declarations nullify the premium request for the film in question, without, however, prejudicing the rendering of penalties.

Article 7

Advances may be granted on the basis of quarterly estimates.

The final allocation of premiums takes place at the end of the budget year.

Article 8

Within the Ministry of Economic Affairs is a Film Commission composed of a President and twelve members, four members representing film interests, two members chosen for their technical and artistic competence, and six members, representing public interests, nominated by the Minister of Economic Affairs for a term of two years. The Minister of Economic Affairs nominates a deputy for each of these members.

The Minister of Foreign Affairs and Foreign Commerce and the Minister of National Education and Culture each propose two members and two deputies. The President and the two other members as well as their deputies are designated from among officials of the Department of Economic Affairs.

The Commission is composed in such a way as to insure a just balance between the two language communities.

The Secretariat of the Commission is provided by the administrative service designated by the Minister of Economic Affairs within his department.

The Commission gives its advice to the Minister in cases cited in Articles 1, 2, and 5.

The Commission establishes its internal rules of order and submits them for approval to the Minister of Economic Affairs.

Article 9

The Film Commission delivers to the producer of a Belgian film a letter of identification indicating the title and the registry number of the film.

This title or a duplicate of it must accompany all copies of the film.

Article 10

The Minister of Economic Affairs, by decision, can withhold future subsidy benefits from a producer who makes false or incomplete declarations or who has not observed the measures prescribed in Articles 5 and 9.

Before taking the decision, the Minister notifies the concerned party of the facts which may justify withholding the subsidy.

Within fifteen days from the date of this notification, the concerned party can submit a statement to the Minister.

Article 11

Representatives of the General Economic Inspection have the right to verify the declarations submitted by film producers.

For this purpose, they can demand all papers, documents, or books and examine all information relevant to their assigned task concerning film producers.

Article 12

The present decree is applicable to films on which production has started after its entry into force.

Films started before this date remain under regulations of the Royal Decree of July 25, 1957.

Article 13

The present decree becomes law on the day of its publication in the *Moniteur Belge.*

Article 14

The Minister of Economic Affairs is charged with the execution of the present decree.

Enacted at Brussels, October 23, 1963.

APPENDIX B

French-Italian Film Agreement of August 1, 1966[1]

The French and Italian authorities announce with satisfaction the general results of the motion picture policy followed by the two countries.

They decide to continue this policy, endeavoring to expand it within the framework of the present agreement.

The responsible authorities have the conviction that the union of effort and means of the Italian and French film industries, by trade and coproduction, will continue to contribute effectively to expansion of the national cultures and the civilization to which the two countries are related, and will favor their economic expansion.

The authorities of the two countries declare that films able to reflect credit on the cinematic reputation of Italy and France, on the one hand through their technical quality and on the other hand by their artistic or entertainment value, can be admitted to benefits accorded by the authorities to coproductions between the two countries.

Article 1

Long films made in coproduction and admitted to benefits of the present accord are considered as national films by the authorities of the two countries.

They benefit in full right from advantages accruing to them by virtue of laws in effect or laws which could be passed in each country.

These advantages are provided to the producer only by the country which grants them.

The competent authorities from the country of the majority partner can ask the authorities of the other country to suspend financial benefits to the minority partner if he does not fulfil his financial obligations to the majority partner.

Article 2

In order to be admitted to the coproduction system, coproducers must justify in a valid way their choice of technical and artistic elements brought together to participate in the making of the film.

To assure the best functioning of coproduction, a film project can receive the benefits of coproduction only if the majority producer in charge is qualified by his professional activity and, particularly, if he has produced at least three national, or majority national, films in the preceding three years. Exceptional cases may be permitted by the authority of the majority country.

The coproducers, in addition, must give proof of finance permitting them to accomplish the project.

A producer can receive permission to make a film as a minority partner only if he has produced in the two preceding years a national film or, as a majority partner, a coproduction recognized as national.

The number of films which can be made in coproduction by a producer as a minority partner cannot exceed twice the number of national films he has made, or twice the number of coproductions he has made as a majority partner.

Foreign directors, technicians, and actors ordinarily resident in and employed in one of the two countries can, in exceptional cases, participate in the making of coproductions in the name of their country of residence.

However, French ordinarily resident in and employed in Italy, and Italians ordinarily resident in and employed in France can participate in a coproduction only in the name of their country of citizenship.

The participation of actors not having the nationality of one of the coproducing countries can be permitted in exceptional cases only, and after agreement between the authorities of the two countries, taking account of the film's requirements.

Shooting of exteriors or of natural locales in a country which does not participate in coproduction can be authorized if the plot of the film and the technical conditions of its production require it.

Article 3

All coproductions require two negatives or, in place of this, a negative and a dupe.

Each coproducer is owner of a negative or of a dupe.

Coproductions are made in a French or an Italian language version, or in a bilingual Italian-French version.

Close-ups must be shot in two versions.

There must be direct recording of sound.

Article 4

All facilities are accorded for the movement and stay of artistic and technical personnel collaborating in these films as well as for the importation or exportation in each country of material necessary for the making and exploitation of coproduced films (raw stock, technical equipment, costumes, set pieces, advertising materials).

Article 5

I The budget of a coproduction can be no less than $285,000.

II The minority participation in each film cannot be inferior to 30 percent of the cost of its production.

III 1. The contribution of the minority coproducer must include an effective technical and artistic participation and at least an assistant director, a writer, an actor in a principal role, and an actor in a secondary role.

2. Each film must include employment of an Italian director or a French director corresponding to conditions cited in Article 2.

IV Exceptions to the conditions of the preceding paragraphs can be granted by the authorities of the two countries to films of obvious artistic value or to special entertainment films.

For films in this secondary category, the production cost can be no less than $510,000.

The participation of a minority coproducer can be no less than 20 percent of the cost of the film.

Article 6

Authorities of the two countries will view favorably the coproduction of films of international quality among Italy, France, and countries to which both are joined by coproduction agreements, the conditions for admitting these films being subject to a case by case examination;

1. The Mixed Commission cited in Article 14 fixes annually the minimum total budget for films made in tripart and multipart coproduction;

2. No minority participation in these films can be less than 20 percent of the budget;

3. The minority coproducer whose participation does not exceed 20 percent of the budget can be exempt from technical and artistic contributions;

4. The contract for a tripart film must designate a deputy coproducer whose participation will not be less than 40 percent of the budget. In case participations are equal, the competent authorities of the two countries can make exceptions to the rule of minimum participation;

5. The contract for a quadpart coproduction must designate a deputy coproducer whose participation will not be less than 30 percent of the budget.

Article 7

Equality of financial, artistic, and technical contributions from the coproducing countries will be examined annually by the Mixed Commission.

The balance of financial transfers also will be established with respect to equality between the coproducing countries.

Article 8

For a film to be admitted to the benefits of the coproduction agreement, a request accompanied by necessary documents must be presented to the competent authorities thirty days before the start of shooting.

Article 9

The balance of the minority coproducer's financial participation must be paid to the majority coproducer within sixty days from the delivery date of all materials necessary for the making of the minority country version.

Nonobservance of this rule brings withdrawal of the benefits of coproduction.

Article 10

Clauses of contracts indicating the division of receipts or markets among coproducers must be approved by the competent authorities of the two countries.

Article 11

I In the case where a coproduction is exported to a country where the importation of films is under a quota, the film is charged, in principle, to the quota of the country which has the majority financial participation.

II In the case of films with equal participation from the two countries, the film is charged to the quota of the country having the best possibilities of exportation.

In case of difficulties, the film is charged to the quota of the country which has jurisdiction of the director.

III If one of the coproducing countries is accorded free entry of films by the importing country, coproduced films in this case benefit in full right, the same as national films.

Article 12

Coproduced films must be presented with the title "French-Italian Coproduction" or "Italian-French Coproduction."

This mention must be in a separate box and must be included in commercial advertising and during their presentation at artistic and cultural gatherings, notably at international film festivals.

In case of disagreement between coproducers, films are presented at international festivals by the country having the majority financial participation.

Films with equal participation are presented by the country which has jurisdiction of the director.

Article 13

The film authorities of the two countries fix, in common, the procedural regulations for coproduction.

Article 14

During the duration of the present agreement, a Mixed Commission is convened each year, alternately in Italy and in France, on the initiative of the competent administrations.

However, in case of important modification in the internal legislation of one of the two countries, a special session will be called within a period of one month.

The Italian delegation is presided over by the Directeur Général du Spectacle.

The French delegation is presided over by the Directeur Général du Centre National de la Cinématographie.

The delegations are assisted by administrators and experts qualified in this respect.

This Commission has the mission of examining and resolving difficulties of application of the present agreement, studying possible modifications of it, and proposing conditions for its renewal.

In addition to the annual session, each administration has the right to demand a special session of the Mixed Commission.

Article 15

The present agreement becomes effective on the date of its signature and replaces that of October 7, 1961.

It is in force until December 31, 1966.

It is renewed annually by tacit agreement, except for cancellation by one of the contracting parties with written notice of at least three months.

Application Procedures of the French-Italian Film Agreement

Requests for admission to the benefit of coproduction must be made to our two administrations a minimum of thirty days before the start of shooting.

Documents for admission must include the following items, prepared in the national language of each of the countries:

I a detailed prospectus,

II a document proving that the copyright for the film adaptation has been acquired legally or, in place of it, that a valid option exists,

III a coproduction contract (a signed copy and three certified copies) entered into with approval reserved by the competent authorities of the two countries.

This document must specify:

1. the title of the film,

2. the name of the author of the story or of the adapter if a story drawn from a literary work is concerned,

3. the name of the director (a safeguard clause being acceptable in case of change),

4. the total budget,

5. the total contribution of each coproducer,

6. the division of receipts and markets,

7. the responsibility of the coproducers to participate in possible deficits or to benefit from savings on the budget of the film, proportional to their respective contributions. The contribution to deficits can be limited to 30 percent of the film's budget,

8. a clause of the contract must indicate that admission to the benefits of the agreement does not obligate the competent authorities of the two countries to deliver an exhibition permit.

Another clause, accordingly, must specify the conditions of financial accounting between the contractors in case the competent authorities of one or the other country do not permit the requested admission after examination of the complete file.

A similar clause also must take into account the case where the competent authorities do not authorize exhibition of the film in one of the two countries or abroad.

A special clause also must anticipate the nature of relations between the coproducers in the case where payment of a financial contribution could not be made according to the requirements cited in Article 9 of the agreement.

9. the anticipated date for the start of shooting.

IV the financial plan,

V a list of technicians and artists, with their nationalities, and the roles given to actors,

VI the work schedule.

The competent authorities of the two countries can demand, in addition, all documents and related details deemed necessary.

The editing plan and script of films must reach these authorities, in principle, before the start of shooting.

Contract modifications, including the change of one of the coproducers, can be provided for in the first coproduction contract delivered; they must be submitted for the approval of the competent authorities of the two countries before the end of production.

The replacement of a coproducer can be permitted in exceptional cases only, and for reasons deemed valid by our two administrations.

The request for admission to benefits of the agreement can be accompanied by documents comprising:

    a) a synopsis of the story permitting evaluation of the principal roles given to actors of the two countries,

    b) the coproduction contract.

APPENDIX C

Currency Exchange Rates

The exchange rates below were used as the basis for computations in which foreign values were converted to American dollars. They are based upon data in the International Monetary Fund's *International Financial Statistics.* Unless noted, the rates are for the years 1950 through 1967.

Currency Units Per United States Dollar

Danish Krone	6.9
German Mark	4.2; 1961 to 1967, 4.0
Netherlands Guilder	3.8; 1961 to 1967, 3.6
Norwegian Krone	7.15; 1959 to 1967, 7.16

Currency Units Per United States Dollar (contd.)

Italian Lira	625; 1959 to 1962, 621; 1963, 622; 1964, 625; 1965 to 1967, 624
French Franc	350; 1957, 420; 1958 and 1959, 491; 1960 to 1967, 4.9
Spanish Peseta	60

United States Dollars Per Currency Unit

British Pound	2.80

Notes

Introduction

1. U. S. Senate, 83rd Congress, 1st Session, Committee on Foreign Relations, *Overseas Information Programs of the United States,* Part 2 (Washington: Government Printing Office, 1953), p. 235.

Chapter 1

1. Political and Economic Planning, *The British Film Industry* (London: May, 1952), p. 242.

2. Vernon Jarratt, *The Italian Cinema* (New York: The Macmillan Company, 1951), p. 30.

3. Enrico Giannelli, *Economia Cinematografica* (Rome: Reande Editore, 1956), p. 29.

4. Forsyth Hardy, *Scandinavian Film* (London: Falcon Press, 1952), p. ix.

5. In some respects, the sale of films to television has tended to offset higher production costs. For example, in 1966 the American Broadcasting Company and the Columbia Broadcasting System acquired more than 100 films for a price said to be about $92,000,000. Included in this figure is the approximately $5,000,000 which ABC reportedly paid for *Cleopatra.*

6. U. S. House of Representatives, 87th Congress, 1st and 2nd Sessions, Committee on Education and Labor, Subcommittee on the Impact of Imports and Exports on American Employment, *Impact of Imports and Exports on Employment,* Part 8 (Washington: Government Printing Office, 1962), p. 465.

7. Negative cost may be considered as the price of actually making the picture, exclusive of advertising, distribution, and similar fees.

8. U. S. Senate, 84th Congress, 2nd Session, Select Committee on Small Business, *Motion Picture Distribution Trade Practices—1956* (Washington: Government Printing Office, 1956), pp. 352–353.

9. Ibid., p. 403.

10. Ibid., p. 395.

11. Ibid., p. 356.

12. U. S. Senate, 83rd Congress, 1st Session, Committee on Foreign Relations, *Overseas Information Programs of the United States,* Part 2 (Washington: Government Printing Office, 1953), p. 273.

13. Ibid., pp. 292–293.

14. U. S. Senate, *Motion Picture Distribution,* p. 6.

15. Nicola de Pirro, "Post-War Expansion of the Italian Film Abroad," *Lo Spettacolo,* Volume 5, Number 3 (July–September 1955), p. xx.

16. Political and Economic Planning, op. cit., p. 241.

17. Ibid., p. 121.

18. British Film Producers Association, *Seventh Annual Report 1948–1949,* p. 27.

19. *Board of Trade Journal,* June 25, 1949.

20. Terence Kelly, Graham Norton, and George Perry, *A Competitive Cinema* (London: The Institute of Economic Affairs, 1966), p. 89.

21. Federation of British Film Makers, *Ninth Annual Report 1965–1966,* p. 17.

22. Siegfried Kracauer, *From Caligari to Hitler* (New York: Noonday Press, 1959), p. 5.

Chapter 2

1. Political and Economic Planning, *The British Film Industry* (London: May, 1952), p. 41.

2. U. S. Senate, 83rd Congress, 1st Session, Committee on Foreign Relations, *Overseas Information Programs of the United States,* Part 2 (Washington: Government Printing Office, 1953), p. 272.

3. The Film Centre, *The Film Industry in Six European Countries* (Paris: UNESCO, 1950), p. 21.

4. Political and Economic Planning, op. cit., p. 43.

5. Ibid., p. 99.

6. *Board of Trade Journal,* May 1, 1948.

7. Centre National de la Cinématographie, *Bulletin,* Number 6 (1948).

8. *The Film Daily Year Book of Motion Pictures, 1960,* "Trade Restrictions on U. S. Motion Pictures."

9. A person active and influential in American film industry affairs during this period told this author that Secretary Byrnes "laid it on the line and extracted" the agreement from the French representative.

10. Georges Sadoul, *French Film* (London: Falcon Press, 1953), p. 110.

11. British Film Producers Association, *Seventh Annual Report 1948–1949,* p. 28.

12. *Variety,* August 10, 1960.

13. Nicola de Pirro, "Post-War Expansion of the Italian Film Abroad," *Lo Spettacolo,* Volume 5, Number 3 (July–September 1955), p. xii.

14. The Andreotti Act is credited with providing an important economic stimulant to Italian film production. On the other hand, one writer has suggested that it simultaneously worked to kill Italian neorealism. George A. Huaco, in *The Sociology of Film Art* (Basic Books, 1965), makes his case by stating that it formalized the sources of finance under the state and provided for closer scrutiny of film scripts prior to production.

15. The Film Centre, op. cit., p. 90.

16. *Variety,* November 1, 1950.

17. *Variety,* May 30, 1951.

18. *Variety,* June 8, 1955.

19. *Variety,* May 2, 1962.

20. Early in 1963, the distribution activity in Spain of Columbia Pictures was forced to cease operation because of a restriction imposed on the company by the Spanish government. This reduced the number of American companies with regular offices in Spain authorized to distribute pictures to four: Paramount, Fox, Metro, and Warner Brothers. In effect, Columbia was not permitted to receive licenses under the baremo system for the importation of films. This ban on Columbia was lifted in January, 1966. The restriction was brought about by Columbia's participation in the production of *Behold a Pale Horse,* which allegedly portrayed a Spanish police chief in an unfavorable light.

21. *Variety,* April 26, 1961.

22. British Film Producers Association, *Sixth Annual Report 1947–1948,* pp. 15–16.

23. British Film Producers Association, *Seventh Annual Report 1948–1949,* p. 19.

24. Political and Economic Planning, op. cit., p. 78.

25. U. S. House of Representatives, 87th Congress, 1st and 2nd Sessions, Committee on Education and Labor, Subcommittee on the Impact of Imports and Exports on American Employment, *Impact of Imports and Exports on Employment,* Part 8 (Washington: Government Printing Office, 1962), p. 472.

Chapter 3

1. A step toward standardization has been taken by the Committee of European Cinema Experts. In its first meeting in Brussels in December, 1966, the Committee decided that one of its functions ought to be the assembly and maintenance of an up-to-date file of European film industry documentation. It is to be hoped that collection of statistics will lead to greater compatibility and uniformity in their presentation.

2. This figure of 30 percent should be taken as an approximation for the

entire Italian market and applicable to the films of many nationalities in it. Of course, it is obvious that certain films—notably some American features —are often rented on terms much greater than 30 percent of the gross. In practice, it can reach double that for an exceptional film in a key theatre. On this basis, the 30 percent figure applicable to American films across the board is an underestimate. What the actual average, mode, or median is for any given year depends upon those films accepted for exhibition, the localities or types of theatres and the frequencies with which these films were exhibited, the duration of exhibition contracts, and, of course, the variety of rental terms and scales which might be applicable to each of these contracts.

3. Excellent data on this matter are presented in *Résultats d'Exploitation Par Année d'Ancienneté et Par Nationalité de Films,* Centre National de la Cinématographie, Paris.

Chapter 4

1. This does not mean that sex was not used to sell films before European pictures came on the market. Quite to the contrary, indignation over "immoral" themes and advertising prompted the founding of the Production Code in the 1930's. The difference is that while many American films promised daring themes and scenes, many European films actually delivered them.

2. An interesting reversal of this preference is known to the author. In a university community in the Midwest, a theatre showed a dubbed version of an Italian film. After a number of patrons complained, the manager apologized and issued free passes permitting patrons to return the following week to see the subtitled version of the same film.

3. An excellent treatment of this legal action is provided in Michael Conant's *Antitrust in the Motion Picture Industry* (Berkeley: University of California Press, 1960).

4. *Variety,* September 29, 1954.

5. More recently, the reverse also has been the case. Outstanding performances in wholly foreign films caught attention and the names were soon found in films financed by American companies.

6. *Variety,* May 19, 1954.

7. *Variety,* March 6, 1957.

8. *Variety,* March 18, 1959.

9. *Variety,* September 23, 1959.

10. *Variety,* July 16, 1952.

11. *Variety,* August 1, 1951.

12. *Variety,* February 17, 1954; also *The New York Times,* February 16, 1954.

13. *Variety,* ibid.

14. *Variety,* June 9, 1954.

15. According to the Federal Trade Commission, several investigations were conducted between 1951 and 1957 involving the MPEA and its agreements with certain foreign governments and industries, IFE being only one of them. For example, in 1953, the FTC's New York office investigated the relationship between the MPEA and IFE. The 1953 investigation as well as the action taken on IMPDAA's 1954 complaint have been classified by the FTC as "confidential" and can be disclosed to third parties or made public only with Commission approval.

16. *Variety*, August 11, 1954.

17. *Variety*, July 7, 1954.

18. *Variety*, July 14, 1954.

19. *Variety*, August 11, 1954.

20. The American parties involved in the dispute over the arrangements with France have denied any memory of the event.

21. *Variety*, February 1, 1956.

22. *Variety*, December 26, 1956.

23. *Variety*, January 30, 1957.

24. The ways in which *Variety* dealt with the problem are noted here:

1957 — "[The tabulations do not] take in several important American productions shot in Britain and technically British, but too American to be included here."

1958 — "It is becoming increasingly difficult to distinguish between the 'pure' British films and those which, while British quota pictures, were financed by American money and, being produced by Americans, carry considerable U. S. flavor."

1959 — "For purposes of this survey, the term 'British films' includes not only those pictures made by strictly British producers, but also those films in which American majors have had substantial financial participation but which still are classified as 'quota' films by the British government."

1960 — "For purposes of this Variety estimating, any film which qualified for Britain's Eady plan [production subsidy] is considered 'British.' Thus the 1960 total would include as 'British' the earnings of two Walt Disney pictures, 'Third Man on the Mountain' and 'Kidnapped,' even though to the naked eye they would seem as American as apple pie. . . ."

1961 — ". . . it should be made clear at the outset that the swollen totals for Britain and Greece, in 1961 as opposed to 1960, reflect business done by 'British' and 'Greek' releases actually made with American money and talent." [Referring to *The Guns of Navarone, The World of Suzie Wong*, and *Swiss Family Robinson, Variety* declared:] "1961 was a bonanza year for such American-sponsored Eady product, and these three ["British"] films alone racked up domestic rentals aggregating $24,-800,000."

"The totals include rentals on those pictures either wholly or partially financed by Americans and which are either in a foreign language and/or qualify as 'local' productions under the laws of the countries in which they were made."

This definition of a foreign film also was used by *Variety* in 1962, 1963, and 1964.

25. Terence Kelly, Graham Norton, and George Perry, *A Competitive Cinema* (London: The Institute of Economic Affairs, 1966), p. 132.

26. *Variety,* December 29, 1965.

27. There seems to be no adequate definition of an "art" film although the term does conjure a distinction between, on the one hand, some films of Ingmar Bergman and Resnais' *Last Year at Marienbad,* and on the other, films starring Peter Sellers and the more recent ones of Jean-Paul Belmondo, Jeanne Moreau, and Sophia Loren.

Chapter 5

1. For example, see "Functions of the Association" in *1956 Annual Report,* Motion Picture Export Association of America, Inc.; and Jack Valenti, "The 'Foreign Service' of the Motion Picture Association of America," *The Journal of the Producers Guild of America* (March, 1968) Volume 10, Number 1.

2. *Variety,* October 10, 1956.

3. *Variety,* March 4, 1959.

4. U. S. Senate, 84th Congress, 2nd Session, Select Committee on Small Business, *Motion Picture Distribution Trade Practices—1956* (Washington: Government Printing Office, 1956), p. 408.

It is interesting to note how this view of the subsidy has changed. Today, the subsidy is one of the major causes of runaway production and runaway investment. American companies, including United Artists, have availed themselves of such assistance.

5. *Variety,* April 16, 1958.

6. *Variety,* December 23, 1959.

7. Ibid.

8. *Variety,* May 7, 1952.

9. *Variety,* September 9, 1953.

10. *Variety,* August 24, 1960.

11. A source within the American industry has revealed that a short term halt in shipments to Nigeria was initiated for the purpose of adjusting rental terms. When it was terminated, American films resumed their flow, but at higher fees.

12. UNESCO, *Developing Information Media in Africa,* Reports and Papers on Mass Communication, Number 37, 1962.

13. *Variety,* August 24, 1960.

14. Henry P. Pilgert, *Press, Radio and Film in West Germany, 1945–1953* (Historical Division of the Office of the United States High Commissioner for Germany, 1953), p. 85.

15. The MPEA had been active before this to keep West Germany an open market. As early as June, 1949, for example, Eric Johnston lodged a protest with the then Secretary of State Dean Acheson concerning a proposed import quota on American films in West Germany.

16. Department of State, *Germany 1947–1949: The Story in Documents* (Washington: Government Printing Office, 1950), p. 609.

17. *Variety,* October 25, 1950.

18. Pilgert, op. cit., p. 97.

19. *Italo-American Film Agreement, September 1, 1959 to August 31,* 1962, Appendix G.

20. Op. cit., p. 105.

21. Albert Norman, *Our German Policy: Propaganda and Culture* (New York: Vantage Press, 1951), p. 62.

Chapter 6

1. U. S. Senate, 83rd Congress, 1st Session, Committee on Foreign Relations, *Overseas Information Programs of the United States,* Part 2 (Washington: Government Printing Office, 1953), p. 235.

2. *Variety,* October 6, 1954.

3. As an example, one can point to the period during which Stanton Griffis was ambassador to Spain, from early 1951 to early 1952. From the late 1940's, American distributing companies were having difficulty in bringing American films into Spain. While Mr. Griffis was ambassador, the problem was resolved, and beginning in 1952 a greater volume of American films flowed to the country. Relaxation of restrictions on film was connected, perhaps, with American financial aid and the exporting to Spain of certain foodstuffs and materials. It should be mentioned that Mr. Griffis was on the board of directors of Paramount Pictures at this time. He resigned from Paramount in 1966.

4. *Variety,* April 25, 1956.

5. *Variety,* May 21, 1958.

6. *Variety,* August 16, 1950.

7. *Variety,* April 20, 1960.

8. *Variety,* April 15, 1959.

9. Federation of British Film Makers, *Second Annual Report 1958–1959,* p. 5.

10. Ibid., p. 4.

11. *Variety,* December 2, 1959.

12. British Film Producers Association, *Eighteenth Annual Report 1959–1960,* p. 6.

13. U. S. Senate, op. cit., p. 278.

In discussions with former officials of the MPEA, this author heard even more fantastic ways of freeing blocked currency. Unfortunately, most remain unconfirmed, without the cooperation of the film companies themselves.

14. *Variety*, July 28, 1954.

15. *Variety*, September 21, 1955.

16. See *Italo-American Film Agreement, 1956–1959*, Rome, August 8, 1956, and *Italo-American Film Agreement, September 1, 1959 to August 31, 1962*.

17. *Variety*, April 20, 1960.

18. *Memorandum of Agreement Between His Majesty's Government in the United Kingdom of Great Britain and Northern Ireland and the Motion Picture Industry of the United States of America, dated 1st October, 1950*. Cmd. 8113, His Majesty's Stationery Office, London, 1950.

19. Centre National de la Cinématographie, *Bulletin*, Number 6 (1948).

Chapter 7

1. *Congressional Record*, Proceedings and Debates of the 81st Congress, 2nd Session, Volume 96, Part 3, p. 3766.

2. *Variety*, January 7, 1953.

3. *Variety*, January 28, 1953.

4. Of course, manipulation of film content has existed for decades. While government interference with content has been resisted conscientiously by the industry, film producers have accepted nongovernmental forms of content management. These center on the specific and formal provisions of the old and new Production Codes and the general informal provisions imposed by banks which grant loans for production and thereby influence content. (See George E. Yousling, *Bank Financing of the Independent Motion Picture Producer*, The Graduate School of Banking, Rutgers University, June, 1948.) The film situation is analogous to that of broadcasting, whose content the Federal Communications Commission is legally barred from censoring; however, program content is subject to the controls of the codes of the National Association of Broadcasters and the wishes of specific sponsors. For example, see the censorship provisions which have been used by the Procter and Gamble Company (*Broadcasting*, October 2, 1961).

5. U. S. Senate, 83rd Congress, 1st Session, Committee on Foreign Relations, *Overseas Information Programs of the United States*, Part 2 (Washington: Government Printing Office, 1953), p. 236.

6. Ibid., p. 272.

7. Ibid., p. 279.

8. U. S. Senate, 84th Congress, 2nd Session, Select Committee on Small Business, *Motion Picture Distribution Trade Practices—1956* (Washington: Government Printing Office, 1956), p. 357.

9. Ibid., p. 353.

10. Ibid., p. 356.

11. Albert Norman, *Our German Policy: Propaganda and Culture* (New York: Vantage Press, 1951), p. 9.

12. U. S. Senate, *Overseas Information Programs,* p. 232.

13. Ibid., p. 285.

14. Norman, op. cit., p. 60.

15. Ibid., p. 61.

16. Ibid., p. 61.

17. Ibid., p. 64.

18. Ibid., p. 64.

19. Contracts Officer, Informational Media Guaranty Division, United States Information Agency, letter to the author, Washington, October 23, 1963.

20. Henry P. Pilgert, *Press, Radio and Film in West Germany, 1945–1953* (Historical Division of the Office of the United States High Commissioner for Germany, 1953), p. 97, and U. S. Senate, *Overseas Information Programs,* pp. 264–268.

21. Print media also were covered by the IMG program. For example, in January, 1949, The Reader's Digest Association, Inc., signed a contract for $41,000 for distribution in Germany of about 30,000 copies per issue of the monthly English language edition of *Reader's Digest.* This six-month contract went into effect in March, 1949. Similarly, Time, Inc., had a contract worth almost $17,000 for distribution in Norway of about 5,600 copies per issue of the international edition of *Life* magazine. The six-month contract began in October, 1948.

22. *Congressional Record,* Proceedings and Debates of the 86th Congress, 1st Session, Volume 105, Part 7, p. 9128.

23. *Variety,* September 22, 1954.

24. Pilgert, op. cit., p. 87.

25. Ibid., p. 87.

26. Office of the U. S. High Commissioner for Germany, *Report on Germany,* September 21, 1949 — July 31, 1952, p. 116.

27. Pilgert, op. cit., p. 89.

28. *Variety,* December 20, 1950.

29. Ibid.

30. *The New York Times,* August 12, 1949.

31. Pilgert, op. cit., p. 105.

32. John Dornberg, *Schizophrenic Germany* (New York: The Macmillan Company, 1961), p. 158.

33. Ibid., p. 168.

34. The deconcentration effort in Germany bears more than casual similarity to the antitrust program in the United States—not only in terms of objective but also in terms of results. The oftimes hollow success of antitrust action, resolved in the majority of instances by consent decrees, suggests compromise rather than enforcement. See U. S. House of Representatives, 86th Congress, 1st Session, Report of the Antitrust Subcommittee of the Committee on the Judiciary, *Consent Decree Programs of the Department of Justice,* January 30, 1959.

35. Ludwig Erhard, "A New Bond Between Economists," *The German Economic Review*, Volume 1, Number 1 (1963), pp. 3–4.

36. *Variety*, September 11, 1963.

Chapter 8

1. Robert L. Heilbroner, *The Future As History* (New York: Harper and Brothers, 1960), p. 103.

2. Ibid., p. 106.

3. This is indicated clearly in Article 1 of the Italian film law: "The State considers the cinema a means of artistic expression, a cultural form, a social communication, and recognizes its economic and industrial importance. The activity of production, distribution, and exhibition of films is deemed to be in the general interest."

4. The general governmental policy in Europe toward assistance of the arts bears some analogy, perhaps, to the American government's policy on postal rates. The Post Office Department handles second and third class mail (periodicals and advertising matter) at a considerable loss. This is rationalized by pointing to the advantages gained by having a broad dissemination of information, literature, and advertising matter. In a sense, the government, by providing low rates, is subsidizing the publishing industry and that portion of the business community which advertises by mail on the assumption that they contribute to the general welfare.

5. The quality prize is divided among those people responsible for the film in the following way: 71 percent to the producer, 10 percent to the director, 7 percent to the script author, 3 percent each to the scenario author and the director of photography, 2 percent each to the composer of the musical score, the set designer, and the film's editor.

6. National Film Finance Corporation, *Annual Report and Statement of Accounts for the Year Ended March 31, 1959*, p. 7.

7. The NFFC also has advanced funds for television films and episodes. Between 1950 and 1967, 583 received such assistance with the largest number, 403, in 1959. This large number is somewhat deceiving as almost 400 of them were five-minute episodes and accounted for only about $450,000 in loans.

8. National Film Finance Corporation, *Annual Report and Statement of Accounts for the Year Ended March 31, 1967*, p. 3.

9. Ibid., March 31, 1963, p. 4.

10. Ibid., March 31, 1965, pp. 3–4.

11. Ibid., March 31, 1967, p. 4.

12. Ibid., March 31, 1966, p. 6.

13. Ibid., March 31, 1967, pp. 4–5.

14. *Italo-American Film Agreement, 1956–1959*, Rome, August 8, 1956, and *Italo-American Film Agreement, September 1, 1959 to August 31, 1962*.

15. *Gazetta Ufficiale della Repubblica Italiana*, Volume 106, Number 282 (November 12, 1965).

16. One charge levelled against the subsidy based upon box office receipts is that films which need it least get the greatest rebates. A high-grossing film, one with considerable box office revenue, receives a larger subsidy than a not-so-popular film which is, perhaps, only breaking even at the box office. In this case, the marginally profitable film would be in greater need of a rebate. One way to avoid this inequity is by arranging the percentage rebate on a sliding scale—the higher the gross, the smaller the percentage of rebate, with grosses over a certain figure receiving no subsidy at all.

17. Irving Allen, "Subsidy Creates Mediocrity," *The Journal of the Producers Guild of America,* Volume 9, Number 2 (June 1967), p. 19.

18. British Film Producers Association, *A Guide to British Film Production* (London, 1962), pp. 15–16.

19. Political and Economic Planning, *The British Film Industry* (London, May 1952) p. 128.

20. Ibid., p. 131.

21. British Film Producers Association, *Fourteenth Annual Report 1955–1956,* p. 7.

22. *Films Act, 1960,* 8 and 9 Elizabeth II, Ch. 57.

The phrase "requisite amount of labour costs" is defined in the Films Act by a rather complicated formula. In practice, about 75 percent of labor costs must be paid to British subjects if the film has one foreign star. If there are two foreign stars, then the figure becomes 80 percent.

23. The Monopolies Commission report (*Films, A Report on the Supply of Films for Exhibition in Cinemas,* London, Her Majesty's Stationery Office, 1966) gives on page eight the terms of an exhibition contract. The rental fees, on a sliding scale, range from 25 to 50 percent. The midpoint, 37 percent, was selected for the computations.

24. *Variety,* January 26, 1966.

25. For films with labor costs of less than $56,000, the distributor's share (for purposes of payment from the Fund) is reckoned at two-and-a-half times the actual amount.

26. Décret No. 59–1512 du 30 décembre 1959, Portant Application des Dispositions du Décret Modifié du 16 juin 1959 Relatif au Soutien Financier de l'Etat à l'Industrie Cinématographique, *Textes du Cinéma Français,* Centre National de la Cinématographie, Volume 2, Title 4, Chapter 1.

27. A synopsis of twenty years of financial assistance to the French film industry is presented in *Le Cinéma Français,* a study prepared by Claude Degand and Dominique Corbet (Notes et Études Documentaires, November 29, 1966, Number 3341, La Documentation Française, Secrétariat Général du Gouvernement, Paris).

28. See Arrêté du 30 décembre 1959, Fixant les Taux de Calcul des Subventions Allouées aux Producteurs de Films de Long Métrage, modifié

par Arrêté du 8 novembre 1962, and Arrêté du 10 septembre 1963, Fixant les Taux de Calcul des Subventions Allouées aux Producteurs de Films de Long Métrage, modifié par Arrêtés du 29 avril 1964 et 23 juillet 1965, *Textes du Cinéma Français*, Centre National de la Cinématographie, Volume 2, Title 4, Chapter 1.

29. *Gazetta Ufficiale della Repubblica Italiana*, op cit.

30. The principle of restricting television's access to new films also was embodied in the Film Industry Defence Organisation which formerly existed in Great Britain. There, exhibitors among themselves contributed to a pool under FIDO which bought television rights to films. If a producer refused to sell such rights, theatres could threaten a boycott against his pictures.

31. State autonomy in the area of culture also proved a handicap in television. To remove the danger of a centralized broadcasting system under government control being used for propaganda purposes, the allied occupation authorities segmented the structure of German radio and gave the parts to the various states, excluding the federal goverment from possession of any station. When television service was inaugurated, it was realized that its high cost necessitated the sharing of programs among the stations. The First Network was started on the basis of program swopping, which proved rather cumbersome and difficult to administer. Plans for a central Second Network were worked out by the Bonn government but the supreme court decided that it would be unconstitutional. To resolve the dilemma, and to institute a centrally-operated network, the German states delegated their control rights for a Second Network to a newly created state agency in Mainz which would administer and program it. This network began transmitting in 1963.

32. *Les Industries Cinématographiques de l'Europe des Six et le Marché Commun*, Notes et Etudes Documentaires, March 10, 1966, Number 3271, La Documentation Française, Secrétariat Général du Gouvernement, Paris, p. 22.

33. Ibid., Annex 4, "Directives de la C.E.E. en Matière de Cinéma." The terminology used is "the nationality of a member State."

34. In March, 1967, after much study and research, a Canadian Film Development Corporation was established with a capital of $10,000,000 payable from the general revenue fund. The CFDC is empowered to invest in Canadian feature films in exchange for a share of the revenue, to make interest-bearing loans to Canadian producers, and to award prizes for outstanding achievements in Canadian feature production. Thus, the measure provides two of the three possible forms of state support for film production. See *An Act to Provide for the Establishment of a Canadian Film Development Corporation*, 14–15–16 Elizabeth II, Ch. 78 (1967).

35. There is growing interest in some form of subsidy for American films. As early as 1963, Carl Foreman, an American producer and director,

advocated a production subsidy in the United States because of the film's "contribution on the cultural level and to the economic community." According to *Variety* (October 16, 1963), Mr. Foreman believed the subsidy was the "means to producer and exhibitor survival." Apparently he speaks with some authority as he has been involved in the production of "British" films which have qualified for subsidy there. More recently, *The Journal of the Producers Guild of America* devoted its June, 1967, issue to a discussion of subsidies and their application to production in Hollywood.

Chapter 9

1. A similar situation occurred in Canada more than twenty years ago. Presumably to augment tourist trade and to solve currency problems, the Canadian government developed a Canadian Cooperation Project with the Motion Picture Association of America. American film distributors in Canada were permitted to export their revenues providing that the MPAA encouraged its members to make American films in Canada and to mention the country in Hollywood scenarios. According to l'Association Professionnelle des Cinéastes (*Twenty-Two Reasons Why the Canadian Government Should Encourage the Establishment of a Feature Film Industry in Canada*, Montreal, February 1964):

> During the '40s a number of films conceived in the United States were produced by American artists and technicians in Canada. Canadian scenery was shown while the human dimension was overlooked. This was a short-sighted policy (even from the viewpoint of the tourist trade), for though it sometimes acquainted the foreigner with an aspect of our geography, we in fact exported our natural scenery as raw material just like iron ore or pulpwood.

2. Portions of the discussion of the British industry originally appeared in: Thomas H. Guback, "American Interests in the British Film Industry," *The Quarterly Review of Economics and Business*, Volume 7, Number 2 (Summer 1967), pp. 7–21.

3. *Variety*, April 15, 1959.

4. Federation of British Film Makers, *Second Annual Report 1958–1959*, p. 9.

5. National Film Finance Corporation, *Annual Report and Statement of Accounts for the Year Ended March 31, 1967*, p. 4.

6. Walter Wanger and Joe Hyams, *My Life With Cleopatra* (New York: Bantam Books, 1963), p. 19.

7. Ibid., p. 31.

8. *The New York Times*, January 24, 1967.

9. *Variety*, December 3, 1952, and December 29, 1954.

10. *Variety*, January 26, 1966.

11. Ibid.

12. *Variety,* May 4, 1966.

13. British Film Producers Association, *Twenty-Fourth Annual Report 1965–1966,* pp. 5–6.

14. National Film Finance Corporation, op. cit., p. 4.

15. It will be recalled that the NFFC suspended lending activity for a ten-month period in 1966 and 1967 because of its inability to borrow from commercial sources.

16. The Monopolies Commission, *Films, A Report on the Supply of Films for Exhibition in Cinemas* (London: Her Majesty's Stationery Office, 1966), pp. 6–7.

17. Terence Kelly, Graham Norton, and George Perry, *A Competitive Cinema* (London: Institute of Economic Affairs, 1966), p. xi and p. xiv.

18. The Monopolies Commission, op. cit., p. 74.

19. Federation of British Film Makers, *Ninth Annual Report 1965–1966,* p. 8.

20. Décret No. 59–1512 du 30 décembre 1959, Portant Application des Dispositions du Décret du 16 juin 1959 Relatif au Soutien Financier de l'État à l'Industrie Cinématographique, *Textes Réglementaires du Cinéma Français,* Centre National de la Cinématographie, Volume 2, Title 4, Chapter 1.

21. Associazione Nazionale Industrie Cinematografiche ed Affini, *Ordinamento Legislativo della Cinematografia,* Rome, 1962.

22. Ibid.

23. *Variety* (January 31, 1968) reported that fourteen Italian directors issued a manifesto urging implementation of direct sound recording in the film industry. This suggests that provisions of the 1965 law were not being followed and that interpretation of them was quite elastic.

24. *Italo-American Film Agreement, 1956–1959,* Rome, August 8, 1956.

25. *Italo-American Film Agreement, September 1, 1959 to August 31, 1962.*

26. Quoted in Centre National de la Cinématographie, *Bulletin d'Information,* Number 108 (December 1967), p. 233.

27. In an unpublished study conducted by this author in 1963, a number of films were selected from those listed in Unitalia catalogues of Italian production. At least in Italy, all these pictures were "Italian." Official agencies in West Germany, Norway, France, and Great Britain were asked to reveal the nationalities under which these selected films were registered when they entered these countries. Some interesting points were uncovered which indicate that the nationality often reflects neither the producing country nor the source of production financing. A few examples are in order:

Sodom and Gomorrah, "a film by Robert Aldrich, directed by Sergio Leone," was produced by Titanus and starred Stewart Granger, Stanley Baker, and Anna Maria Pierangeli. In Germany, the film was "Italian-

French"; in Norway, "British"; in France, "French coproduction"; in Britain, "Italian."

El Cid, backed by American and British money, was "a film for Anthony Mann, directed by Giovanni Paolucci." It was produced by Samuel Bronston Productions (Madrid) and Dear Film (Rome) and starred Charlton Heston and Sophia Loren. Although "Italian" in Italy, the picture was "American" in Germany, Norway, and France, but "Dutch" in Britain. Further investigation of the "Dutch" registration indicated, according to the Board of Trade, that the maker of the film was listed as Bronston Distributors, N.V., Netherlands Antilles.

The Fair Bride, directed by Nunnally Johnson and produced by Titanus, starred Dirk Bogarde, Joseph Cotten, Ava Gardner, and Vittorio De Sica. Although the film was registered "Italian" in each country surveyed, its financing came from an American company.

Barabbas, directed by Richard Fleischer and produced by Dino DeLaurentiis Cinematografica, starred Anthony Quinn, Silvana Mangano, Jack Palance, and Vittorio Gassman. In West Germany and Great Britain, the film was "Italian" but in Norway and France it was "American."

Considering these fluctuating identities, it is apparent that data concerning nationalities of films imported, and their earnings, must be viewed with a degree of caution.

28. Siegfried Kracauer, *From Caligari to Hitler* (New York, Noonday Press, 1959), p. 5.

29. Presidential address to the Thirtieth Annual Conference of the Association of Cinematograph, Television and Allied Technicians, London, March 23, 1963.

30. Association Professionnelle des Cinéastes, *Measures Recommended by l'Association Professionnelle des Cinéastes to the Government of Canada in Order to Encourage the Development of a Feature Film Industry Compatible with the Country's Economic and Cultural Aspirations,* Montreal, March 1964.

Chapter 10

1. Some coproductions have reached levels of excellence: *I Vitelloni, Il Bidone, Notti di Cabiria, La Dolce Vita, Generale della Rovere, La Notte, L'Avventura, Casanova '70, Boccaccio '70, Marriage Italian Style, Moment of Truth, Last Year at Marienbad, Gervaise, Masculin Feminin,* and *La Guerre est Finie.* Of course, not all coproductions are of this calibre. The list must be balanced with such films as these: *Terror in Space, Two Against Al Capone, The Sheriff Doesn't Shoot, A Gunman Called Nebraska, Monkey Woman,* and *Sexy al Neon (Neon Nightlife).*

2. See Article 1 of the French-Italian coproduction agreement of October 19, 1949, and "La Coproduction des Films en Europe," speech by

Claude Degand to the Second Congress of the International Secretariat of Entertainment Trade Unions, London, September 25–29, 1967.

3. National Film Finance Corporation, *Annual Report and Statement of Accounts for the Year Ended March 31, 1967*, p. 11.

4. Associazione Nazionale Industrie Cinematografiche ed Affini, *L'Industria Cinematografica*, Rome, 1966, Appendix 2, p. 7.

5. Limited data are available for comparison on production costs in other countries. Figures from Britain's National Film Finance Corporation indicate that the thirty-six films it financially assisted and which started into production between April, 1962, and March, 1963, had an average cost of $346,000. The figures for the years following are: 1963–1964, eleven films averaging $255,000; 1964–1965, fifteen films averaging $374,000; 1965–1966, fourteen films averaging $520,000; 1966–1967, eleven films averaging $779,000. It should be noted that these figures exclude films costing less than $56,000 and films which received no financial backing from the NFFC. In the latter group would be many films financed by American interests which did not have to rely upon the Corporation.

6. Figures for 1966 from Unitalia catalogue; 1967 figures from Uniespana catalogue.

7. Associazione Nazionale Industrie Cinematografiche ed Affini, *La Coproduzione Cinematografica*, Rome, 1966.

8. The name of the third group of films is somewhat difficult to translate into English. The original Italian is "coproduzioni bipartite di valore spettacolare." In French, the term is: "un film de caractère spectaculaire."

9. See George A. Codding, Jr., *The Universal Postal Union* (New York: New York University Press, 1964).

10. While the United States and Great Britain calculated weight by the ounce, France, Belgium, and Italy used the gram. Germany, Austria, and other states used the zolloth or loth, which even differed from region to region. Postal rates, different in each country, became a nightmare as international letters passed from country of origin, through other countries, to country of destination. Rates were a function of distance, either weight or number of sheets in a letter, and the route the letter was to follow. Thus, a letter from Germany to Rome could travel by any one of three routes, each with a different rate.

11. See George A. Codding, Jr., *The International Telecommunication Union* (Leiden: E. J. Brill, 1952).

12. Codding, *The Universal Postal Union*, op. cit., p. 25.

Chapter 11

1. Leo Model, "The Politics of Private Foreign Investment," *Foreign Affairs*, Volume 45, Number 4 (July 1967), pp. 640–641.

2. Presidential address by John Davis, British Film Producers Association, *Fourteenth Annual Report 1955–1956*, pp. 6–7.

Appendix A

1. Translated by the author from *Annuaire du Film Belge 1964*, Cinémathèque Royale de Belgique, Bruxelles.

Appendix B

1. Translated by the author from *Textes du Cinéma Français*, Centre National de la Cinématographie, Volume 2, Title 5, Chapter 6.

Selected Bibliography

A. BOOKS, MONOGRAPHS, PAMPHLETS

Associazione Nazionale Industrie Cinematografiche ed Affini, *La Copro-duzione Cinematografica*, Rome, 1966.

Associazione Nazionale Industrie Cinematografiche ed Affini, *Coprodu-zioni di Film*, *1950–1960*, Rome, no date.

Associazione Nazionale Industrie Cinematografiche ed Affini, *Coprodu-zioni di Film*, *1961*, Rome, no date.

Associazione Nazionale Industrie Cinematografiche ed Affini, *L'Industria Cinematografica Negli Anni 1960 e 1961*, Rome, 1962.

Associazione Nazionale Industrie Cinematografiche ed Affini, *L'Industria Cinematografica Negli Anni 1964 e 1965*, Rome, 1966.

Associazione Nazionale Industrie Cinematografiche ed Affini, *La Nuova Legge del Cinema*, Rome, 1965.

Balcon, Michael, Ernest Lindgren, Forsyth Hardy, and Roger Manvell, *Twenty Years of British Films*, *1925–1945*, London, Falcon Press, 1947.

Bardèche, Maurice and Robert Brasillach, *Histoire du Cinéma*, Paris, Les Sept Couleurs, 1964.

Batz, Jean-Claude, *A Propos de la Crise de l'Industrie du Cinéma*, Institut de Sociologie, l'Université Libre de Bruxelles, 1963.

Bernstein, Irving, *Hollywood at the Crossroads: An Economic Study of the Motion Picture Industry*, Hollywood, A. F. of L. Film Council, 1957.

British Film Producers Association, *A Guide to British Film Production*, London, 1965.

Conant, Michael, *Antitrust in the Motion Picture Industry*, Berkeley, University of California Press, 1960.

Film Centre, *The Film Industry in Six European Countries*, Paris, UNESCO, 1950.

Giannelli, Enrico, *Economia Cinematografica*, Rome, Reanda Editore, 1956.

Hardy, Forsyth, *Scandinavian Film*, London, Falcon Press, 1952.

Huaco, George A., *The Sociology of Film Art,* New York, Basic Books, 1965.

Jarratt, Vernon, *The Italian Cinema,* New York, Macmillan Company, 1951.

Kelly, Terence, Graham Norton, and George Perry, *A Competitive Cinema,* London, The Institute of Economic Affairs, 1966.

Kracauer, Siegfried, *From Caligari to Hitler,* New York, Noonday Press, 1959.

Mayer, Michael F., *Foreign Films on American Screens,* New York, Arco, 1965.

Mercillon, Henri, *Cinéma et Monopoles,* Paris, Armand Colin, 1953.

Norman, Albert, *Our German Policy: Propaganda and Culture,* New York, Vantage Press, 1951.

Pilgert, Henry P., *The History of the Development of Information Services Through Information Centers and Documentary Films,* Historical Division of the Office of the U. S. High Commissioner for Germany, 1951.

Pilgert, Henry P., *Press, Radio and Film in West Germany, 1945–1953,* Historical Division of the Office of the U. S. High Commissioner for Germany, 1953.

Plischke, Elmer, *History of the Allied High Commission for Germany,* Research Project 107, Historical Division of the Office of the U. S. High Commissioner for Germany, 1951.

Political and Economic Planning, *The British Film Industry,* London, 1952.

Political and Economic Planning, *The British Film Industry 1958,* London, 1958.

Sadoul, Georges, *French Film,* London, Falcon Press, 1953.

Schmidt, Georg, Werner Schmalenbach, and Peter Bachlin, *The Film: Its Economic, Social, and Artistic Problems,* London, Falcon Press, 1948.

Sieklucka, Catherine, *Les Aides à l'Industrie Cinématographique,* Paris, Presses Universitaires de France, 1967.

Spraos, John, *The Decline of the Cinema,* London, George Allen and Unwin, 1962.

Svenska Filminstitutet/The Swedish Film Institute, untitled and undated pamphlet.

Wanger, Walter, and Joe Hyams, *My Life with Cleopatra,* New York, Bantam Books, 1963.

Wollenberg, H. H., *Fifty Years of German Film,* London, Falcon Press, 1948.

B. DOCUMENTS AND REPORTS

An Act to Provide for the Establishment of a Canadian Film Development Corporation, 14-15-16 Elizabeth II, Ottawa, Queen's Printer and Controller of Stationery, 1967.

Annuaire du Film Belge, Brussels, Cinémathèque de Belgique.

Annual Reports, Association of Cinematograph, Television and Allied Technicians.

Annual Reports, British Film Fund Agency.

Annual Reports, British Film Producers Association.

Annual Reports, Federation of British Film Makers.

Annual Reports, National Film Finance Corporation.

Annual Reports, Nederlandsche Bioscoop-Bond.

Association Professionnelle des Cinéastes, *Measures Recommended by L'Association Professionnelle des Cinéastes to the Government of Canada in Order to Encourage the Development of a Feature Film Industry Compatible with the Country's Economic and Cultural Aspirations,* Montreal, March, 1964.

Association Professionnelle des Cinéastes, *Twenty-Two Reasons Why the Canadian Government Should Encourage the Establishment of a Feature Film Industry in Canada,* Montreal, February, 1964.

Associazione Nazionale Industrie Cinematografiche ed Affini, *Ordinamento Legislativo della Cinematografia,* Rome, 1962.

Batz, Jean-Claude, *Action Syndicale et Politique Européenne du Film,* Institut de Sociologie, l'Université Libre de Bruxelles, mimeo, no date.

Batz, Jean-Claude, *Le Problème de la Production de Films en Belgique,* Rapport sur le sous-développement de la production de films en Belgique et l'assistance financière et administrative de l'état, Institut de Sociologie, l'Université Libre de Bruxelles, mimeo, no date.

Bilan de l'Activité Cinématographique Française, Paris, Centre National de la Cinématographie.

Bulletin d'Information, Paris, Centre National de la Cinématographie.

Le Cinéma Français, Notes et Études Documentaires, November 29, 1966, No. 3341, La Documentation Française, Secrétariat Général du Gouvernement, Paris.

Colloque Sur le Problème de la Production de Films en Belgique, Compte Rendu des Travaux, 2 au 6 décembre 1963, Institut de Sociologie, l'Université Libre de Bruxelles, mimeo, no date.

Des Mesures Institutionnelles Destinées à Promouvoir la Production et la Diffusion du Film Belge, Texte presenté à la session plénière de la commission chargée d'examiner les mesures institutionnelles destinées à promouvoir la production du film en Belgique (Sessions plénières des 19 et 20 mars 1964), Institut de Sociologie, l'Université Libre de Bruxelles, mimeo, no date.

Developing Information Media in Africa—Press, Radio, Film, Television, Reports and Papers on Mass Communications, No. 37, Paris, UNESCO, 1962.

Die Deutschen Filme, Wiesbaden, Spitzenorganisation der Filmwirtschaft.

Film og Kino Arbok, Oslo, Kommunale Kinematografers Landsforbund.

Films Act, 1960, 8 & 9 Elizabeth II, Ch. 57, London, Her Majesty's Stationery Office.

The Film Co-Production Agreement (France), Order 1965, No. 1856, London, Her Majesty's Stationery Office, 1965.

Films—A Report on the Supply of Films for Exhibition in Cinemas, The Monopolies Commission, London, Her Majesty's Stationery Office, 1966.

Filmstatistisches Taschenbuch, Wiesbaden, Spitzenorganisation der Filmwirtschaft.

Gazzetta Ufficiale della Repubblica Italiana, Rome.

Germany—Unfinished Business, Office of Public Affairs, Department of State, mimeo, February, 1946.

Germany 1947–49: The Story in Documents, Department of State Publication, No. 3556, Washington, Government Printing Office, March, 1950.

Impact of Imports and Exports on Employment, Part 8, Subcommittee on the Impact of Imports and Exports on American Employment, Committee on Education and Labor, House of Representatives, 87th Congress, 1st and 2nd Sessions, Washington, Government Printing Office, 1962.

Les Industries Cinématographiques de l'Europe des Six et le Marché Commun, Notes et Études Documentaries, March 10, 1966, No. 3271, La Documentation Française, Secrétariat Général du Gouvernement, Paris.

Italian Film Production, Rome, Unitalia.

Memorandum of Agreement Between His Majesty's Government in the United Kingdom of Great Britain and Northern Ireland and the Motion Picture Industry of the United States of America, dated 1st October 1950, Cmd. 8113, London, His Majesty's Stationery Office, 1950.

Motion Picture Distribution Trade Practices, Select Committee on Small Business, United States Senate, 83rd Congress, 1st Session, Washington, Government Printing Office, 1953.

Motion Picture Distribution Trade Practices—1956, Select Committee on Small Business, United States Senate, 84th Congress, 2nd Session, Washington, Government Printing Office, 1956.

Overseas Information Programs of the United States, Part 2, Committee on Foreign Relations, United States Senate, 83rd Congress, 1st Session, Washington, Government Printing Office, 1953.

Problems of Independent Motion Picture Exhibitors, Report of the Select Committee on Small Business, United States Senate, August 3, 1953, Washington, Government Printing Office, 1953.

Report on Germany, 1949–1952, Office of the U. S. High Commissioner for Germany, Washington, Government Printing Office.

The Spanish Cinema, Madrid, Uniespana.

Textes du Cinéma Français, Paris, Centre National de la Cinématographie.

Textes Réglementaires du Cinéma Français, Paris, Centre National de la Cinématographie.

Thiel, Reinold E., "Lebenslauf eines Ungeborenen—Eine Chronologie des Martin-Plans," *Filmreport*, Munich, mimeo, no date.

United States Foreign Policy, Compilation of Studies Prepared Under the Direction of the Committee on Foreign Relations, United States Senate, 87th Congress, 1st Session, Washington, Government Printing Office, 1961.

United States Information Service in Europe, Report of the Committee on Foreign Relations, United States Senate, 80th Congress, 2nd Session, Washington, Government Printing Office, 1948.

C. PERIODICAL LITERATURE

Breccia, Gastone, "Forms of State Intervention in the Cinema Business in Several Producing Countries," *Lo Spettacolo*, Vol. 5, No. 1, January–March, 1955, pp. xii–xvii.

"Les Capitaux Américains et l'Industrie Française," *Enterprise* (special edition), August 11–18, 1962.

"Le Cinéma Espagnol Face au Marché Commun," *Revue du Marché Commun*, Vol. 7, No. 69, May, 1964, pp. 307–309.

"Colloques sur le Cinéma Européen," *Revue du Marché Commun*, Vol. 7, No. 73, October, 1964, pp. 465–467.

"Conférence Européenne du Cinéma et de la Télévision," *Revue du Marché Commun*, Vol. 4, No. 32, January, 1961, pp. 11–12.

Dawson, Anthony H., "Motion Picture Economics," *The Quarterly of Film, Radio and Television*, Vol. 3, No. 3, Spring, 1948, pp. 217–240.

Degand, Claude, "Le Cinéma dans le Marché Commun," *Revue du Marché Commun*, Vol. 6, No. 55, February, 1963, pp. 76–83.

Degand, Claude, "Le Cinéma et les Problèmes du Marché Commun," *Revue du Marché Commun*, Vol. 2, No. 10, January, 1959, pp. 33–39.

Degand, Claude, "La Crise de l'Industrie du Cinéma et Son Financement à l'Echelle Européenne," *Revue du Marché Commun*, Vol. 7, No. 72, September, 1964, pp. 381–389.

Degand, Claude, "L'Industrie Cinématographique Prépare Son Insertion dans la C. E. E.," *Revue du Marché Commun*, Vol. 3, No. 26, June, 1960, pp. 226–232.

Degand, Claude, "Le Marché Commun du Cinéma," *Revue du Marché Commun*, Vol. 9, No. 94, September, 1966, pp. 686–695.

Frenay, Henri, "Shall We Have a European Film Market?" *Lo Spettacolo*, Vol. 6, No. 1, January–March, 1956, pp. vii–xiii.

Guback, Thomas, "American Interests in the British Film Industry," *The Quarterly Review of Economics and Business*, Vol. 7, No. 2, Summer, 1967, pp. 7–21.

Joesten, Joachim, "The German Film Industry, 1945–1948," *New Germany Reports*, No. 3, May, 1948.

Jones, Dorothy B., "Hollywood's International Relations," *The Quarterly of Film, Radio and Television*, Vol. 11, No. 4, Summer, 1957, pp. 362–374.

Lawrence, Eric, "The Motion Picture Industry in Sweden," *The Quarterly of Film, Radio and Television*, Vol. 5, No. 2, Winter, 1950, pp. 182–188.

Montero, R. Romero, "Aspects of the Spanish Cinema Market," *Lo Spettacolo*, Vol. 7, No. 1, January–March, 1957, pp. viii–xii.

Neergaard, Ebbe, "The Rise, the Fall, and the Rise of Danish Films," *Hollywood Quarterly*, Vol. 4, No. 3, Spring, 1950, pp. 217–232.

de Pirro, Nicola, "Post-War Expansion of the Italian Film Abroad," *Lo Spettacolo*, Vol. 5, No. 3, July–September, 1955, pp. xii–xxxiv.

de Pirro, Nicola, "Italian Cooperation with France, Germany and Spain in the Production of Cinema Films from 1949 to 1958," *Lo Spettacolo*, Vol. 9, No. 2, April–June, 1959, pp. x–xiii.

Puente, Antonio Cuevas, "The Present Status of the Spanish Cinema," *Lo Spettacolo*, Vol. 6, No. 3, July–September, 1956, pp. x–xiv.

Sadoul, Georges, "The Postwar French Cinema," *The Quarterly of Film, Radio and Television*, Vol. 4, No. 3, Spring, 1950, pp. 233–244.

Schulberg, Stuart, "The German Film: Comeback or Setback?" *The Quarterly of Film, Radio and Television*, Vol. 8, No. 4, Summer, 1954, pp. 400–404.

Verdone, Mario, "The Italian Cinema from Its Beginnings to Today," *Hollywood Quarterly*, Vol. 5, No. 3, Spring, 1951, pp. 270–281.

de Vergottini, Mario, "Gross Income of Films According to Some Social-Economic Characteristics," *Lo Spettacolo*, Vol. 10, No. 4, October–December, 1960, pp. iii–xv.

Willemetz, Lucy, "Projet d'Autofinancement pour la Production de Films dans le Cadre de la C. E. E.," *Revue du Marché Commun*, Vol. 6, No. 56, March, 1963, pp. 113–125.

D. OTHER PERIODIC PUBLICATIONS

Board of Trade Journal
E. E. C. Bulletin
The Film Daily
The Film Daily Year Book of Motion Pictures
The Journal of the Producers Guild of America
Variety

Index

Africa: market for American films, 98–101 *passim;* UNESCO and informational needs of, 100–01

Aldrich, Robert: 175

Allied High Commission: and film in West Germany, 103; trade restrictions policy, 103

Allied States Association of Motion Picture Exhibitors: 12

American Motion Picture Export Company (Africa): established, 100; relation to MPEA, 100; and Webb-Pomerene Export Trade Act, 100

And God Created Woman: 73, 86

Andreotti, Giulio: 26

Andreotti Act: and importation, 24–25, 39; and production loans, 150; and neorealism, 218n14

Antitrust: impact on American industry, 9–10; and competition, 10; and foreign films in American market, 70; and deconcentration program, 224n34

Arnall, Ellis: 81, 82

Asquith, Anthony: 178

Association Professionnelle des Cinéastes: 180, 228n1

Association Suisse des Distributeurs de Films: American membership in, 113

Associazione Nazionale Industrie Cinematografiche ed Affini: film agreement with MPEA, 13, 26, 39, 76–79, 106, 122, 175–176; relations with MPEA, 25–26; and unremittable American earnings, 122

Austria: film importation, 47–48; as market for American films, 47–48

— film industry: and coproduction, 190

Banca Nazionale del Lavoro: 24; loans to production, 150

Barabbas: 86, 230n27

Baremo: defined, 27; and American companies, 28–32

Bataille du Rail, La: 175

Behold a Pale Horse: 218n20

Belgium: film agreement with MPEA, 18; Chambre Syndicale Belge de la Cinématographie, 112–13; national film, defined, 152; production subsidy, 152–53; coproduction agreement, 195

— film industry: American investment in, 166

Benton, William: 124–25

Bicycle Thief: 178

Blum, Léon: 21

Born Free: 167

Boycott by MPEA: of Britain, 18–19, 44–45; of Spain, 28, 43–44, 93–94; of Denmark, 41–42, 58–59, 93–94, 115, 116; relation to American production decline, 116

Bridge on the River Kwai: 84

British Film Fund Agency: 153–54

British Film Producers Association: on foreign earnings of British films, 13–14; on French import quota, 22–23; on screen quota, 34; on allocation of production subsidy, 118–19; on American investment, 118–19, 171; on production subsidy, 153; on subsidy payments to American subsidiaries, 155; American membership in, 167–68

British Film Production Fund: operation, 154; rates of payment compared to other countries, 156; and American subsidiaries, 167–68, 170–71

British Monopolies Commission: 172

Buena Vista: 100

Byrnes, James: 21

Cabinet of Dr. Caligari, The: 8

Canadian Film Development Corporation: 227n34

Chambre Syndicale Belge de la Cinématographie: American membership in, 112–13

Clément, René: 175

Cleopatra: 10, 169, 216n5

Columbia Pictures: 12, 22, 26, 28, 31, 73, 84, 100, 167, 194, 218n20

Common Market: see European Economic Community
Content: of American films, changes in, 11–12; and culture, 15; and America's image, 127; and financing, 172, 178, 198–99, 223n4; and film nationality, 176, 178; of Euro-American films, 176, 178; of Italian films, 178; of British films, 178; internationalization of, 178, 198–99
Coproduction: Euro-American, impact on content, 12; defined, 181; and film nationality, 181; and production subsidies, 181; and quotas, 181; importance to European film industry, 181, 182; beginnings, 181–82; and production costs, 182, 184, 190–92; tripart films, 188, 190, 192; and EEC, 190, 196–97
— agreements: purpose of, 192–93; tripart, 193–94; details of, 193–95; quadpart, 194; overlapping nature of, 194–95; precedents for, 195–96; merging of, 196–97
— French: compared to national films, 182, 184–88; investment in, 186–87
— Italian: investment in, 190–92
— Spanish: compared to national films, 182

Davis, John: 76, 155
Denmark: MPEA boycott of, 41–42, 58–59, 93–94, 115, 116; as market for American films, 41–43, 58–59, 115–16; film importation, 41–43; box office receipts, 58–59; rental policy, 115–16; film prizes, 146
Department of State, 21, 33, 80–82; content of American films, 12; and West German film market, 104, 105, 134; and American films in Norway, 114
Devil's Disciple, The: 168
Distribution: economics of, 8; in United States, 87–89; in West Germany, 131; French subsidy to, 144–45
— American: in France, 60–61; in Norway, 61–62; in Britain, 62, 63
— international: and American companies, 14, 74, 171, 200–01; of European films, 179
Dr. Strangelove: 168
Dulles, John Foster: 81
Dutchman: 170
Duty, import: 18–19; in Italy, 24–25; in United Kingdom, 44–45

Earnings, unremittable American: 71, 72; in Britain, 19, 122; in France, 19, 122; in Italy, 26, 121–22; in Europe, 120–22; in West Germany, 131; and IMG Program in West Germany, 132–34; and American investment, 164–65; and American production in Italy, 175–76
El Cid: 174, 230n27
Entertainer, The: 73
Erhard, Ludwig: 140
Europe: as market for American films, 8–9, 23, 164; American film revenue in, 10–11, 66
— film industry: impact of World War I

Europe (continued)
on, 8–9; impact of American exportation on, 17; attitude toward American investment, 97, 201; characteristic of, 142; relation to governments, 144; EEC policy toward, 161–62; and coproduction, 181; craft aspect, 199
European Economic Community: and film industry, 95–96; American industry attitude toward, 96–98; and American investment, 97; members' production subsidies, 158, 159; harmonization of subsidies, 160, 161–62; policy on subsidies, 161–62; and European film production, 178–79, 180; coproduction among members, 190; coproduction agreements in, 194, 195; and coproduction, 196–97
— films of: and French distribution subsidy, 145; and Italian prizes, 146
Exhibition: divorced from production and distribution, 10; in West Germany, 129; Italian subsidy to, 145

Fair Bride, The: 230n27
Federal Trade Commission: 78–79, 220n15
Federation of British Film Makers: on foreign earnings of British films, 14; on American production in Britain, 119–20; American membership in, 120, 167–68; on subsidies to American subsidiaries, 168; on American investment, 172
Fédération Nationale des Distributeurs de Films: American membership in, 111–12
Film: as communication, 4, 95, 143, 149, 178, 180, 198–99, 202–03; as business, 7–8, 95, 142–43, 198, 200, 201, 203
Film bank: purposes, 146–47; National Film Finance Corporation, 147–49
Film nationality: 162–63; changes in, 52, 229n27; Belgian, defined, 152; British, defined, 155; British, relation to American investment, 167; French, defined, 157; French, relation to American investment, 173–74; Italian, defined, 158–59; Italian, relation to American investment, 174; and content, 176, 178; need for redefinition, 179; and coproduction, 181
Film production: financial aid to, in Europe, 144, 145; in West Germany, 102–3; in Britain, and NFFC, 147–49; in Belgium, and subsidy, 152–53; dependence on foreign markets, 198
Film Production Association of Great Britain: 149
Films, foreign: in American market, 68–74 passim, 83, 89; number of, in American market, 85; revenues in American market, 86–89
Finland: film importation, 48, 51; as market for American films, 48, 51
Foreman, Carl: 167, 227n35
France: as market for American films, 8, 19–22 passim, 54–55, 60–61, 64–66 passim; film agreement with United States, 19, 21–22, 175; film agreement with MPEA, 23–24, 80–81, 122; unremittable American

France *(continued)*
  earnings in, 19, 122; film production in,
  21, 22; screen quota, 21–22, 36; import
  quota, 21–24 *passim;* as market for British
  films, 22–23; liberal trade policy, 23–24;
  box office receipts, 54–55, 60–61; number
  of films circulating in, 64–66; Fédération
  Nationale des Distributeurs de Films, 111;
  distribution subsidy, 144–45; production
  subsidy, 156–58; production subsidy and
  American investment, 165–66; national
  film defined, 157; policy on subsidization,
  161; production costs, 184–88, 190–92;
  coproduction agreements, 193–95
  — film industry: American investment in,
  164–66, 173–74, 200; and coproduction,
  181, 182, 188; coproductions and national
  films compared, 182, 184–88; investment
  in coproduction, 186–87
  — films of: in American market, 13, 80–
  83; revenues in American market, 86
Freeman, Y. Frank: 128
From Russia With Love: 86
Fulbright, J. William: 121, 127

Gervaise: 73
Goldfinger: 89, 171
Griffis, Stanton: 222n3
Gross, H. R.: 134
Grupo Sindical de Distribucion Cinema-
  tografica: American membership in, 110
Guns of Navarone: 167, 171, 220n24

Hard Day's Night, A: 86
Hawk Films Ltd.: 167
Hecht-Hill-Lancaster Films Ltd.: 168
Hetzel, Ralph: 116
Horizon Pictures (G.B.) Ltd.: 167
Hyman, Edward L.: 71

Independent Motion Picture Distributors
  Association of America: 77–79, 81, 220n15
Informational Media Guaranty Program:
  established, 132; and propaganda, 132;
  and unremittable American earnings, 132–
  34
  — contracts: with MPEA, 133–34; with
  print media, 224n21
  — and West Germany: 132–34 *passim;*
  American film policy in, 134; film shortage in, 134
Investment, American: in British film industry, 14, 62, 86, 89, 148–49, 164–66, 169,
  171–73, 200, 201–02; in European film
  industry, 74, 175; in Italian film industry,
  86, 164–66, 173–76 *passim,* 200; and EEC,
  97; in French film industry, 164–66, 173–
  74, 200; relation to production subsidy,
  165–66; in Belgian film industry, 166; in
  Dutch film industry, 166; in Swedish film
  industry, 166; and British film nationality, 167; in Spanish film industry, 200
Ireland: film importation, 42–43; as market
  for American films, 42–43
Is Paris Burning?: 175, 185

Italian Film Export: 13, 77–80, 220n15
Italy: as market for American films, 8–9, 20,
  24–27, 38–40, 45–46, 52–54; film production in, 24, 46; import quota, 24, 26–27,
  39; screen quota, 24, 25, 36; unremittable
  American earnings in, 26, 121–22, 175–76;
  film agreement with MPEA, 26, 39, 76–79,
  106, 122, 175–76, 220n15; film importation, 38–40, 45–46; box office receipts, 52–
  54; exhibition subsidy, 145; film prizes,
  146; production loans, 150–51; national
  film, defined, 158–59; production subsidy,
  158–59; production subsidy, and American
  investment, 165–66; policy on subsidization, 161; attitude toward American investment, 175; coproduction agreements,
  193–95
  — film industry: American investment in,
  86, 164–66, 173–76 *passim,* 200; production costs, 190–92; and coproduction, 181,
  182, 188; investment in coproduction,
  190–92
  — films of: in American market, 12–13,
  76–80 *passim;* revenues from American
  market, 86; changes in content, 178

Johnston, Eric: 200, 222n15; on importance
  of foreign markets, 3, 108; on American
  market, 10; on American film content, 11;
  on American film exportation, 16; on
  trade liberalization, 36; on foreign films
  in American market, 74, 79, 82; on industry unity, 93; on EEC, 96; on developing
  new markets, 98–100; on unremittable
  earnings, 121; on propaganda, 126–27; on
  American films in West Germany, 128–29

Kaitlin Productions: 170
Key, The: 167
Kidnapped: 220n24
Kinematograph Renters Society: 102
Kingsley-International: 73
Knack, The: 73
Kracauer, Siegfried: 15, 178
Kubrick, Stanley: 167

Lady Killers, The: 73
Last Year at Marienbad: 221n27
Lawrence of Arabia: 167
Legion of Decency: 73
Loans: 227n34; to production, 146–51; to
  British films, 147–49; to Spanish films,
  149; to Dutch films, 149–50; to Norwegian
  films, 150; to West German films, 150; to
  Italian films, 150–51; compared to sub-
  sidies and prizes, 151
Longest Day, The: 10
Lopert Pictures: 73, 75

Malta United Film Company: 102
Mann, Anthony: 174
Mark, The: 73
Marshall Plan: 23
McClure, Robert A.: 131

Metro-Goldwyn-Mayer: 22, 26, 28, 30, 100, 167, 218n20

Military Government: in West Germany, 129–31 *passim;* American film companies' policy toward, 129–30; and American films in West Germany, 131; and West German film industry, 131; and unremittable American earnings, 131; confiscation of UFI properties, 136

Mon Oncle: 73

Monogram Pictures: 22

Motion Picture Export Association: on protection of European film industries, 21; relations with ANICA, 25–26; on British screen quota, 33; purpose of, 91–92; unity as policy, 93; trade policy, 94–95; attitude toward EEC, 96–97; and African market, 98–101; and American Motion Picture Export Company (Africa), 100; and Malta United Film Company, 102; and propaganda in American films, 104; policy in West Germany, 104–107 *passim,* 131; and trade restrictions in West Germany, 105–06, 117–18; and Spain, 110; and the Netherlands, 111; and Norway, 114; and Military Government, 131; contracts with IMG Program, 133–34; attitude toward UFI, 135

— film agreements with: Italy, 13, 26, 39, 76–79, 106, 122, 175–76; Belgium, 18; Britain, 19, 122; France, 23–24, 80–81, 122; Spain, 27–28; foreign countries, 220n15

— boycott of: Britain, 18–19, 44–45; Spain, 28, 43–44, 93–94; Denmark, 41–42, 58–59, 93–94, 115, 116

Mouse That Roared, The: 167

Mutiny on the Bounty: 10

National Catholic Office for Motion Pictures: 73

National Film Finance Corporation: financing of British films, 148–49; policy of Film Production Association of Great Britain toward, 149; on American investment, 169, 171; on production costs, 184, 231n5

Nationality of film: 162–63; changes of, 52, 229n27; relation to American investment, 167, 173–74; and content, 176, 178; need for redefinition, 179; and coproduction, 181

— defined: Belgian, 152; British, 155; French, 157; Italian, 158–59

Nederlandsche Bioscoop-Bond: American membership in, 110–11; production loans, 149–50

Netherlands, The: film importation, 40; as market for American films, 40, 59–60; box office receipts, 59–60; Nederlandsche Bioscoop-Bond, 110–11; production loans, 149–50; American investment in, 166

Never on Sunday: 73, 87

Night of the Generals, The: 194

Norway: film importation, 48, 50; as market for American films, 48, 50, 61–62, 113–14;

Norway *(continued)* film distribution in, 61–62; rental policy, 113–14; film prizes, 145–46; production loans, 150

Open Road Films Ltd.: 167

Paramount Pictures: 9–12 *passim,* 22, 26, 28, 31, 100, 127–28, 167, 175, 218n20, 222n3

Phaedra: 73

Prizes: 227n34; in Sweden, 145; in Norway, 145–46; aid to production, 145–46; in West Germany, 146; in Denmark, 146; in Italy, 146; as effective aid, 146; compared to subsidies and loans, 151

Production Code: 71

Production Code Administration: 11, 73

Production costs: and exportation, 8, 10–11; in United States, 10; and American investment, 166; and coproduction, 182, 184, 190–92; in Britain, 184, 231n5; in France, 184–88; and French coproductions, 190–92; and Italian coproductions, 190–92; and Spanish coproductions, 192; and coproduction agreements, 193; and internationalization, 198

Production subsidy: 227n35; and runaway production, 72; United Artists and, 94–95; rationale of, 144; compared to prizes and loans, 151; arguments against, 151–52, 226n16; integration under EEC, 162–63; as effective aid, 163; relation to American investment, 165–66; and coproduction, 181

— in Britain: 62, 118–19, 153–56, 169, 170; John Davis on, 155; and payments to American subsidiaries, 168, 170–71

— in Belgium: 152–53

— in France: 156–58

— in Italy: 158–59

— in West Germany: 159–60

Propaganda: and American films, 12, 23, 82, 104, 124–28 *passim,* 200; and African market, 100; and American government policy, 125; and West Germany, 128; and IMG Program, 132

Protection of film industries: need for in Europe, 15, 35; and American exportation, 16–20; rationale, 17–20 *passim;* need for in large markets, 20; and EEC, 96–97; in West Germany, 103

Pursuit of the Graf Spee: 76

Quota, import: 35, 179; and American films, 17; in small markets, 19–20; in France, 19–24 *passim;* in Europe, 20–21; in Italy, 24, 26–27, 39; in Spain, 27–32; contrary to free trade, 94; in West Germany, 104–05, 134; and coproduction, 181

— screen: 179; in Europe, 20–21, 36; in France, 21–22, 36; in Italy, 24, 25, 36; in Spain, 36; contrary to free trade, 94; and coproduction, 181

— screen, in Britain: 32–35, 173; MPEA attitude on, 33; impact on production, 34

Rank Film Distributors of America: 75–76
Rank Organisation: 75–76
Republic Pictures: 22, 26
Ritt, Martin: 168
RKO: 22, 26
Room at the Top: 73
Runaway production: 19, 72, 97, 165

Salem Films Ltd.: 168
Saturday Night and Sunday Morning: 73
Season of Passion: 168
Skouras, Spyros: 125
Society of Independent Motion Picture Producers: 81
Sodom and Gomorrah: 86, 174–75, 178, 229n27
Spain: film agreement with MPEA, 27–28; import quota on American films, 27–32; as market for American films, 27–32, 43–44, 222n3, 218n20; MPEA boycott of, 28, 43–44, 93–94; screen quota, 36; film importation, 43–44; Grupo Sindical de Distribucion Cinematografica, 110; production loans, 149; coproduction agreements, 193–94
— film industry: and coproduction, 182, 188, 190; coproductions and national films compared, 182; production costs, 192; American investment in, 200
Spiegel, Sam: 84, 167, 194
Spitzenorganisation der Filmwirtschaft: and trade restrictions, 103; and restrictions on American films, 105; purposes, 117; American membership in, 117–18
Spy Who Came In From the Cold, The: 168
Subsidy: see Distribution; Exhibition; Production Subsidy
Sweden: film importation, 48, 49; as market for American films, 48, 49; Swedish Film Institute, 145
— film industry: American investment in, 166
Swedish Film Institute: film prizes, 145
Swiss Family Robinson: 220n24
Switzerland: film importation, 40–41; as market for American films, 40–41; Association Suisse des Distributeurs de Films, 113; rental policy, 113

Taste of Honey, A: 73
Television: 9, 70–71, 198, 216n5
That Man From Rio: 73
Third Man on the Mountain: 220n24
Thunderball: 89
To Paris With Love: 73
Tom Jones: 86, 171
Trade, free: and quotas, 94; and MPEA policy, 94–95
Trade associations, European: American influence in, 109, 111–13, 117–20; American membership in, 108, 109, 119–20, 167–68
Trade liberalization: in Europe, 35, 36
Trade restrictions: in Africa and MPEA, 99–100; and American film industry, 101; need for in West Germany, 103

Train, The: 175
Twentieth Century-Fox: 22, 26, 28, 31, 100, 120, 167, 169, 218n20

UNESCO: on European film industries, 16–17, 25; and film production in Africa, 100–01
United Artists: 11, 22, 26, 73, 86, 89, 94–95, 100, 120, 167
United Kingdom: as market for American films, 8, 13, 20, 33–35, 44–45, 55–56, 62–63; import duty, 18–19, 44–45; MPEA boycott of, 18–19, 44–45; film agreement with MPEA, 19, 122; unremittable American earnings in, 19, 122; screen quota, 32–35; MPEA attitude on screen quota, 33; screen quota and production, 34; number of theatres, 34; film importation, 44–45; film production, 45; box office receipts, 55–56; production subsidy, 62, 118–19; production subsidy and American investment, 165–66; subsidy payments to American subsidiaries, 168; attitude toward American subsidiaries, 168–69; film distribution in, 62, 63; British Film Producers Association, 118–19; Federation of British Film Makers, 119–20; National Film Finance Corporation, 147–49; British Film Production Fund, 153–54; national film, defined, 155; American subsidiaries in, 167–68; coproduction, 194
— film industry: American investment in, 14, 62, 86, 89, 148–49, 156, 164–66, 169, 200, 201–02; attitude toward American industry, 14; impact of World War II on, 32; and screen quota, 34; as branch of Hollywood, 172–73; production costs, 184, 231n5
— films of: dependence upon foreign markets, 13–14; in United States, 13–14, 75–76, 86, 89; distributed by American companies, 14, 62, 63; in France, 22–23; success abroad, 172; content of, 178
United States: film agreement with France, 19, 21–22, 175; box office receipts for foreign films, 86–89
— as market for: American films, 10–11; Italian films, 12–13, 76–80 *passim,* 86; British films, 13–14, 75–76, 86; Spanish films, 27–28; foreign films, 68–70, 72–74 *passim,* 83–89; French films, 80–83, 86
— film companies and distribution: in France, 60–61; in Norway, 61–62; in Britain, 62–63; international, 74, 171, 200–01
— film companies' policy: in West Germany, 106, 129–31, 134; in Spain, 110; in Belgium, 112–13; in Norway, 113–14; in Denmark, 115–16; on propaganda, 125–28 *passim;* toward Military Government, 129–30
— film companies as members of: European trade associations, 108, 109; Nederlandsche Bioscoop-Bond, 110–11; Féd-

United States (continued)
ération Nationale des Distributeurs de
Films, 111–12; Chambre Syndicale Belge
de la Cinématographie, 112–13; Association Suisse des Distributeurs de Films,
113; Spitzenorganisation der Filmwirtschaft, 117–18; Federation of British
Film Makers, 120, 167–68; British Film
Producers Association, 167–68
— film companies' unremittable earnings:
in France, 19, 122; in Britain, 19, 122;
in Italy, 26, 121–22, 175–76; in Europe,
120–22; in West Germany, 130–31; policy
on, 164–65
— film industry: characteristics of early,
8–9; impact of World War I on, 8–9;
dependence on foreign markets, 10–11,
72, 108, 164; British attitude toward,
14; production decline, 24, 49–52, 70;
unity in, 92–93; attitude toward EEC,
96–98; attitude toward African market,
98–101 passim; relation to government,
124–28, 141, 143–44, 192–200; and German
re-education program, 128–29; attitude
toward monopoly in West Germany, 135,
139
— films of, in: France, 8, 19, 21–22, 23,
64–66; Britain, 8, 18–19, 44–45; Italy,
8–9, 24, 25–27, 38–40, 45–46; Europe,
16–20, 23, 35; Spain, 27–32, 43–44; the
Netherlands, 40; Switzerland, 40–41; Denmark, 41–43; Ireland, 42–43; West Germany, 46–47, 62, 64, 102–07 passim;
Austria, 47–48; Sweden, 48, 49; Norway,
48, 50; Finland, 48, 51
— films of, revenue from: Italy, 52–54;
France, 54–55, 61; Britain, 55–56; West
Germany, 56–57; Denmark, 58–59; the
Netherlands, 59–60; Europe, 66, 87
Universal Pictures: 22, 26
Universum Filmindustrie: as monopoly,
134–35; MPEA attitude toward, 135; and
Military Government, 136; and decon-

Universum Filmindustrie (continued)
centration, 136–40 passim; and German
economic miracle, 140–41

Valenti, Jack: 141, 200
Variety: on foreign film earnings in United
States, 83–88 passim
Viva Maria: 175

Walt Disney Productions Ltd.: 120, 167
Wanger, Walter: 169
Warner Brothers: 22, 28, 31, 62, 100, 120,
167, 218n20
Webb-Pomerene Export Trade Act: provisions, 91–92; and film industry, 94;
and American Motion Picture Export
Company (Africa), 100
West Germany: as market for American
films, 20, 46–47, 56–57, 102–07 passim,
130, 133; film importation 46–47; film
production, 47, 102–03; box office receipts,
56–57; age of films released in, 62, 64;
trade restrictions, need for, 103; import
quota, 104–05, 134; Spitzenorganisation
der Filmwirtschaft, 117–18; and American
propaganda, 124; re-education program
in, 128; and Military Government, 129–31;
unremittable American earnings in, 130,
131; film shortage, 130–31, 134; and IMG
Program, 132–34; Universum Filmindustrie, 134–35, 136; film prizes, 146;
production loans, 150; production subsidy, 159–60; policy on subsidization, 161;
coproduction agreements, 193–95
— film industry: economic condition of,
106–07; monopoly in, 134–35; American
attitude toward monopoly in, 135, 139;
deconcentration of, 136–40; opposition to
deconcentration of, 137–38; relation to
government, 160–61; coproduction, 182,
188, 190
Wilson, Harold: 14
World of Suzie Wong, The: 220n24